Japanese Frames of Mind

Cultural Perspectives on Human Development

Japanese Frames of Mind addresses two problems in the light of studies by Japanese and American researchers at Harvard University: Does evidence from Japan challenge basic premises of current psychological theories? Are the universals of human nature claimed by academic psychology more accurately seen as Western or Euroamerican patterns? The chapters provide a wealth of new data and perspectives related to aspects of Japanese parenting, child development, moral reasoning and narratives, school and family socialization, and adolescent experience. By examining Japanese findings against Western theoretical frameworks, the book calls for a new understanding of those frameworks as reflecting the ethnopsychology of Western countries. Written largely in nontechnical language, this book will appeal to developmental and cultural psychologists, anthropologists interested in psychological anthropology, educators, and anyone interested in Japan and Asian studies.

Hidetada Shimizu is Assistant Professor of Educational Psychology in the Department of Educational Psychology and Foundations at Northern Illinois University.

Robert A. LeVine is Roy E. Larsen Professor of Education Emeritus and Professor of Anthropology Emeritus at Harvard University. He is coauthor of *Childcare and Culture: Lessons from Africa* and coeditor (with Richard Shweder) of *Culture Theory: Essays on Mind, Self, and Emotion.*

Japanese Frames of Mind

Cultural Perspectives on Human Development

Edited by

Hidetada Shimizu
Northern Illinois University

Robert A. LeVine
Harvard University

CAMBRIDGE
UNIVERSITY PRESS

PUBLISHED BY THE PRESS SYNDICATE OF THE UNIVERSITY OF CAMBRIDGE
The Pitt Building, Trumpington Street, Cambridge, United Kingdom

CAMBRIDGE UNIVERSITY PRESS
The Edinburgh Building, Cambridge CB2 2RU, UK
40 West 20th Street, New York, NY 10011-4211, USA
10 Stamford Road, Oakleigh, VIC 3166, Australia
Ruiz de Alarcón 13, 28014 Madrid, Spain
Dock House, The Waterfront, Cape Town 8001, South Africa

http://www.cambridge.org

First published 2001

Printed in the United States of America

Typeface Palatino 9.75/13 pt.   *System* QuarkXPress 4.04 [AG]

A catalog record for this book is available from the British Library.

Library of Congress Cataloging in Publication Data
Japanese frames of mind : cultural perspectives on human development / edited by
Hidetada Shimizu, Robert A. LeVine
p. cm.
Includes bibliographical references and index.
ISBN 0-521-78159-0 (hb) – ISBN 0-521-78698-3 (pbk.)
1. Psychology – Japan. I. Shimizu, Hidetada, 1960– II. LeVine, Robert Alan, 1932–
BF108.J3J36 2001
155.8'952–dc21   2001025172

ISBN 0 521 78159 0 hardback
ISBN 0 521 78698 3 paperback

Contents

PART THREE. GROUP LIFE: THE YOUNG CHILD IN
PRESCHOOL AND SCHOOL

PART FOUR. ADOLESCENT EXPERIENCE

PART FIVE. REFLECTIONS

Notes on the Contributors

HIROSHI AZUMA is the President of the Japanese Psychological Association, Adjunct Professor of Psychology at Bunkyo Women's University, and Professor Emeritus at the University of Tokyo. He received his bachelor's degree in psychology at Tokyo University and his doctorate in educational psychology at the University of Illinois. Founder and President of the Japanese Society of Developmental Psychology, Dr. Azuma has been an active member of numerous international organizations and editorial boards. His research specializations include educational and developmental psychology. He recently has been working on cultural influences on psychological development.

NOBUMICHI IWASA is Professor of Education at Reitaku University and Researcher at the Institute of Moralogy in Japan. He received his master's degree in education from Keio University and doctoral degree in education from Harvard University. He currently is interested in moral development in a life-long perspective, especially the relationship between the development of interpersonal morality and social responsibility.

VICTORIA E. KELLY is a Japanese-English translator and marketing researcher in the Boston area. She received her bachelor's degree in anthropology at Oakland University and her doctorate in human development from Harvard University. She was a recipient of grants from the Fulbright-Hays Foundation and the Social Science Research Council and was Visiting Scholar at the Department of Psychological Research at Shizuoka University. Her research specializations include cross-cultural peer interactions and consumer psychology.

SHUSUKE KOBAYASHI is Assistant Professor of Child Studies at Notre Dame Seishin University, Okayama, Japan. He received his master's degree and doctorate in human development and psychology from Harvard University. His research interests include cultural and social aspects of child development and education in Japan. He edited a Japanese translation of Robert LeVine's papers, *Culture and Human Development* (1996), and papers by diverse hands, *Human Development and Education* (1999).

ROBERT A. LEVINE is Roy E. Larsen Professor of Education Emeritus and Professor of Anthropology Emeritus at Harvard University. He received his doctorate from Harvard University and master's and bachelor's degrees from the University of Chicago. His research concerns cultural aspects of parenthood, child development, and adult personality in African, Asian, North and Central American, and other societies. His most recent research is on the influence of schooling on maternal behavior in Nepal and Venezuela. He is the coauthor of *Childcare and Culture: Lessons from Africa* (1994) and the coeditor (with Richard Shweder) of *Culture Theory: Essays on Mind, Self, and Emotion* (1984).

MIYA OMORI is a consultant for several educational and mental health related corporations and organizations in Japan. She also is a counselor for children in Japan, which allows her first-hand contact with the many emotional challenges and academic dilemmas of youth in Japan today. She completed her master's degree in counseling and consulting psychology and received a doctorate in human development and psychology from Harvard University.

LOIS PEAK is a Senior Education Policy Analyst in the International Affairs Division of the Office of the Undersecretary, U.S. Department of Education. She served as the U.S. Department of Education project officer in charge of the 1995 Third International Mathematics and Science Study (TIMSS), and she authored the final TIMSS report, *Pursuing Excellence*. She received her doctorate in comparative human development from the Harvard Graduate School of Education, and her dissertation *Learning to Go to School in Japan* was published by the University of California Press. The research and analysis presented in this chapter were conducted in her private capacity. No official support by the U.S. Department of Education is intended or should be inferred.

YOSHIE NISHIOKA RICE is a freelance journalist in the Boston area. She received her doctorate in human development from Harvard University.

HIDETADA SHIMIZU is Assistant Professor of Educational Psychology in the Department of Educational Psychology and Foundations at Northern Illinois University. He received his master's degree in counseling and consulting psychology and doctorate in human development and psychology from Harvard University. He was a recipient of a Spencer Post-Doctoral Fellowship from the National Academy of Education and was Primary Researcher in the Case Study Project of the 1995 Third International Mathematics and Science Study (TIMSS). His research interests include acculturation of individuals, cultural influences on personality and behavioral development, cultural phenomenology, and minority experiences in Japan.

MERRY I. WHITE is Professor of Anthropology at Boston University and Associate in Research at the Harvard Edwin D. Reischauer Institute of Japanese Studies. She is a graduate of Harvard College and recipient of master's and doctoral degrees from Harvard University. She has been a consultant to a wide range of education and corporate institutions and to the U.S. congress. Her research has focused on Japanese education, family, and social issues. Recent publications include *The Material Child: Coming of Age in Japan and America* (1993) and *Home Truths: Families, Ideologies, and Common Sense in Japan* (in press).

Preface

Japan as Front Line in the Cultural Psychology Wars

Robert A. LeVine

The specter of Japan haunts Western psychology, posing the threat that presumed universals of human nature will be shrunk to local findings by disconfirming evidence from Asia. Margaret Lock's (1993) demonstration that Japanese women rarely experience the symptoms of menopause most often reported in North America is only the latest in a long series of indications over the last fifty years that something may be radically different about Japanese experience of the life cycle. Is Japan the mirror into which the titan of universal psychology looks and finds himself reduced to a dwarf – one local psychology among many in a world of unpredicted variations? This is the nightmare of cultural relativity from which European and American psychologists awaken to reassure themselves that their instruments have passed the tests of reliability and validity, and their findings have been replicated not only in Madison and Melbourne but even in Bogotá and Bombay (if only among university students). But psychology's "Japanese problem" – a particular case of the questions raised by all cultural variations in human behavior and development – is not so easily solved, and it needs to be confronted directly, as this volume does in provocative and illuminating detail.

Anthropologists waged intermittent guerrilla warfare against psychological universalism during much of the twentieth century. From the days of Malinowski (1927) and Mead (1928) onward, field data from non-Western societies have been used to attack and revise generalizations issued by Western psychologists and psychoanalysts. This empirical critique was given organized form in the middle of the century by John W. M. Whiting and Beatrice B. Whiting (Whiting, 1954; Whiting & Whiting, 1960; Whiting, Child, & Lambert, 1966), who provided systematic methods for marshalling field observations to address questions in developmental psychology. But American and European psychologists and psychoanalysts have rarely seen the need to take seriously these challenges from abroad, convinced as they are that their clinical or experimental methods give them access to the deepest levels of generically human biopsychology. In recent years, however, some developmental and social psychologists, under the banner of cultural psychology, have paid increasing attention to the possibility that the plasticity of human development and the varying environmental conditions under which it occurs, make knowledge of human diversity central to psychological understanding (Bruner, 1990, 1996; Cole, 1996; Greenfield & Cocking, 1994; Kitayama & Markus, 1994; Miller, 1997; Shweder et al., 1998; Stevenson & Stigler, 1992; Valsiner, 2000). For this new and vigorous attack – still resisted and ignored by mainstream psychologies – Japan must be the front line of the battle.

WHY JAPAN?

Why Japan? As an affluent urban society admired in the West for its achievements in technology, industrial production, education, and the arts, Japan commands the kind of respect that makes evidence of its distinctive psychological tendencies harder to ignore than if it were a "Third World" country. American psychologists seem able to discount evidence from non-Western peoples who are poor, isolated, and unschooled, however unjustifiable this may be from any scientific perspective. There may be a tacit assumption that such peoples – the rural majority of Africa, South Asia, Oceania, and South America – can differ from us psychologically without repealing the laws of psychological science. But the Japanese are not only among the winners in the contemporary world, they are also too familiar to Americans in their modernity, education, and wealth to ignore or discount. If it turns out that *their* psychological development diverges substantially from Euroamerican patterns presumed to be universal, the difference cannot be attributed to poverty, illiteracy, "backwardness," or marginality. Further, if they have reached some of *our* cherished goals in education, health, and other fields, but through radically different pathways from what we follow, then the Japanese evidence demands careful examination. The threat to psychological universalism is direct, palpable, and – it would seem – inescapable.

If Japan looms large as a promising battleground in the war of cultural psychology against universalism, it is also because Japanese conceptions of interpersonal relations, family life, education, and the life cycle – as described in a half-century of social science research by American and Japanese investigators – are as different from Western ones as those of any non-Western culture. In other words, there is no question as to whether Japan differs from Western societies in the ideologies, norms, moral concepts, and popular images that give meaning to social life and personal development. It differs substantially, often dramatically, sometimes inverting Western values entirely – as in Lebra's (1976) example of the contrast between Japanese social relativism – emphasizing the moral value of accommodating to the norms of differing situations – and the American moral virtue of integrity, defined in terms of maintaining personal consistency across varying situational norms. The question is how much difference such contrasts make to the psychological development and functioning of individuals.

Finally and most importantly, Japan has its own psychologists and psychiatrists, whose pioneering figures, Takeo Doi (1973, 1986, 1990) and Hiroshi Azuma (e.g., 1996; this volume), have provided a basis for reconceptualizing psychology in Japanese terms and contributed to the new cultural psychology. Both were trained in the United States after World War II – Doi in psychiatry and Freudian psychoanalysis, Azuma in academic developmental and educational psychology – and both discovered that the disciplines they studied were framed in terms of distinctively Euroamerican assumptions contrasting with those prevalent in Japan. They have argued forcefully that psychological studies operate not only with explicit theory and concepts but also with unexamined premises reflecting a naive or folk psychology derived from the culture of the investigator. Western psychological studies, despite their claims to universality, are no different in this respect from others, and Japanese concepts and models can help decenter psychological theory from its monocultural Euroamerican perspective.

Some psychologists in Japan have been pursuing research based on this line of argument. If their impact has been limited so far in American psychology, it may be due in part to their avoiding the combative tone of this Preface, which uses the very un-Japanese rhetorical device of a military metaphor – cultural psychology wars – to draw attention to evidence that contradicts theoretical expectation. Without a level of belligerency sufficient to generate serious debate in Anglo-American psychology and psychiatry, important findings can be overlooked. For example, when Mary D. S. Ainsworth introduced her famous Strange Situation (SS) to the child development field as a measure of infant attachment under conditions of moderate stress, she already knew that, for the Japanese infants studied by Keiko Takahashi (1986), who were rarely left with a person other than the mother (an average of 2.2 times in the month before being assessed) or even taken out of the home, the stress of being in an unfamiliar place with unfamiliar people was more than moderate (Ainsworth et al., 1978, xiv). In fact, a large proportion of the Japanese infants cried from the first episode of the SS onwards rather than only when separated from their mothers, indicating the high level of emotional stress of the unfamiliar situation for them (Takahashi, 1986). These findings indicate not only the culture-specificity of the SS as a context in which to assess attachment but also how customs of infant care can influence the behavior assessed by the SS – a point subsequently overlooked in universalist interpretations of the evidence on infant attachment. The Great Debate over the theoretical implications of early emotional development in Japan that might have been provoked by these findings in 1978 has not yet occurred. We hope this volume, particularly the chapters by Rice and Kobayashi, will provoke such a debate, jarring assumptions about what is normal and necessary in the early mother-child relationship that currently prevail in American child development research.

Japanese mothers operate with ideals of maternal commitment and strategies for teaching and control that would be regarded by childcare professionals in the West as unwisely fostering overdependence and unethically manipulating the emotions of young children (Azuma, 1996; Doi, 1973; Hess et al., 1980). As the studies of this volume show in detail, the standards by which Japanese childcare practices and early education would be classified as "developmentally inappropriate" (e.g., Bredekamp, 1987) are simply blind to the alternative pathways for normal childcare and development constituted by Japanese standards. By understanding in depth how the Japanese alternatives shape the contexts and experience of children from their preschool years to adolescence, we become capable of reconceptualizing *normal* human development in pluralist rather than universalist terms (Shweder et al., 1998).

In the remainder of this preface, I shall show how anthropological, linguistic, and sociological studies have contributed to a Japanese cultural psychology and in effect to the foundations of cultural psychology in general. Recent writings on cultural psychology have made use of ethnographic and other social science evidence, often in an ad hoc way, but they have not explained how cultural psychology is and should be related to social research. Here I propose two approaches from the toolkit of the social science subdiscipline of psychological anthropology: *ethnopsychology*, broadly defined as describing not only the vernacular categories of subjective experience in a culture and its models for personal and interpersonal behavior but also their uses in communicative practices; and *cultural psychodynamics*, the investigation of psychic equilibrium and disequilibrium in the various institutional settings that make up individual lives. Both approaches have been used in Japan, and together they form a background that gives broader and deeper meaning to the specific studies of this volume.

JAPANESE ETHNOPSYCHOLOGY AND COMMUNICATIVE PRACTICES

Ethnopsychology as an investigative approach describes the vocabulary for mental and behavioral phenomena and processes in a given language that bear directly on the experience of individuals. By translating the extended meanings of vernacular terms with their contextual specifications, the anthropologist is able to establish the categories and norms for the emotional and cognitive responses of individuals in a particular speech-community, as embedded in its communicative practices (Levy, 1973; White & Kirkpatrick, 1985). Ethnopsychology is limited, however, by the fact that some languages and cultures have a restricted vocabulary of mental states and processes, using bodily organs, social situations, or deities and spirits rather than personal thoughts and feelings in the cultural idioms that describe and explain individual behavior and its development (Lutz, 1988). Thus the cultures of the world are not equally amenable to ethnopsychological study, and this approach does not always lead to the kind of understanding sought in cultural psychology.

The contemporary Japanese, however, have an extensive repertoire of psychological concepts, and it has seemed to many observers that the translation of key terms from the Japanese language must be the first step toward psychological understanding (White & LeVine, 1986). Indeed, Doi (1973) organized an entire book around the one term *amae*, describing its referents and functions in adult social life, its developmental origins in the mother-child relationship, and its abnormal variants in psychopathology. In the studies that follow in this volume, terms – such as *amae, omoiyari, ikigai, kosodate, shudan seikatsu, uchi* versus *soto, honne* versus *tatamae* – are translated and play a major role in describing the relational contexts that make up the psychologically salient environments of Japanese individuals. These words are embedded in semantic fields that connect them, referentially and metaphorically, with social relationships, emotions, and ideological concepts that are salient in the popular culture of Japan and have been influenced by its philosophical, political, and literary traditions. But words, however rich their semantic connections, are just the beginning; an ethnopsychology is also comprised of narratives of person or self embedded in the conventional scripts for routine social interaction, public occasions, and biographical representation (LeVine, 1982). By examining the narrative content of these scripts in Japan, anthropologists and linguists have uncovered the wishes, fears, and ideals in terms of which Japanese men and women experience their lives and their relationships and toward which they organize the development of their children.

The classic book *Japanese Patterns of Behavior* (1976) by Takie Sugiyama Lebra is a case in point. Lebra, an anthropologist raised in Japan but trained in the United States, has lived in America and continued to conduct research in the country of her birth throughout her career. Her book synthesized a large body of diverse studies in several disciplines, using the extended translation of Japanese terms into English as a starting point for conveying to American and other Western readers distinctively Japanese views of psychologically salient topics ranging from everyday social interaction to parenthood and child development to psychopathology and therapy. She demonstrated how the difficult-to-translate words encompass a range of meanings embedded in Japanese scripts for appropriate interpersonal behavior, desirable parent-child relationships, and emotional disturbance and its treatment. One of the key terms is *omoiyari*, roughly translatable as empathy, but with the implications of sensitivity to the needs and feelings of others and anticipation of those needs and feeling in the planning of one's behavior. Lebra argued that parents take *omoiyari* as the goal for their children's development and shape their childrearing behavior accordingly; subsequent researchers (e.g., Hess et al., 1980; Clancy, 1986) showed how this model influences the mother-child relationship. *Omoiyari* is a major theme in the studies of the present volume; the chapters that follow demonstrate its influence in parental behavior (Rice and Kobayashi), group interaction and conformity (Peak and Kelly), adolescent anxiety (Shimizu), and intercultural experience (Omori). When parents and children alike have internalized the standards of interpersonal sensitivity represented by *omoiyari*, the social and psychological symptoms of such sensitivity are wide and deep.

One symptom is the cultural script for "apologizing" as described by Wierzbicka (1996). Apologies, or something roughly equivalent to the apology in Anglo-American discourse, abound in the normal communicative practices of Japanese, occurring in many contexts that contrast with those of Anglo-American speech: for example, the providing of hospitality to a visitor, talking about one's son to his hosts, the policy declarations of politicians. But these socially expected apologies and the behavior that accompanies them are intended – and interpreted – less as confessing a misdemeanor or even humbling oneself to the other than as demonstrating sincerity in one's concern for the feelings of others. Thus, the driver of a car should visit a minimally injured pedestrian in the hospital even when it is clear to all concerned that the driver was not responsible for the accident, and the prime minister whose personal affairs have diverted the attention of parliament from other matters should resign and apologize, even when his culpability has not been established. Culpability in these cases is beside the point; the focus is on the emotional upset an event has caused and the central actor's responsibility for restoring harmony by demonstrating sincere concern for the feelings of others. This principle reflects *omoiyari* and related concepts such as "*magokoro,* a sincere heart, or *sunao na kokoro,* a naive, receptive sensitive heart" (Kondo, 1990, p. 105). It suggests, in my opinion, that such concepts and the scripts related to them entail taking responsibility for the emotional states of others to a degree that exceeds the expectations embodied in the Anglo-American terms empathy or interpersonal sensitivity.

This "expanded" sense of responsibility for others (from an Anglo-American perspective) is a recurrent theme in descriptions of Japanese child-training goals and adult behavior. Mothers urge their young children to good behavior by calling attention to the impact it makes on their own (mothers') feelings and those of other children and even inanimate objects (Hess et al., 1980); children in preschools and schools are required to take responsibility for keeping the school clean and tidy (Lewis 1995; White, 1987). Japanese children are thus made to feel responsible for the care of their physical and social environment, including the feelings of those around them. A Japanese host is expected to anticipate the desires of a guest to such an extent that even asking the guest to express his preference (as in American norms) signals a failure of sensitivity (Doi, 1973; Wierzbicka, 1996). This intense sense of responsibility enhances trust and community participation in a way that an outsider can admire, but it depends on a willingness to diminish oneself vis-à-vis others that Anglo-Americans are likely to see as being at variance with their own standards of conduct. Japanese are often described as slow to criticize others directly but frequently engaging in self-criticism, as well as able to accept public criticism without the humiliation that Anglo-Americans experience. The cultural script for apologies also presents a diminished or inadequate self in normal contexts of social interaction. But public presentations of self may indicate only conformity with a code of public conduct. The question is how deeply the apologies, self-criticisms, and self-reproaches that are culturally scripted in Japanese communicative conventions represent the feelings of individuals. In other words, to what extent are they psychological phenomena as well as sociolinguistic codes?

The evidence that apologies, self-criticisms, and self-reproaches represent deep feelings rather than simply conformist behavior comes from observations of diverse Japanese individuals under varying degrees of social constraint. In Dorinne Kondo's (1990) account of her experience at an "ethical retreat center" for Japanese workers, for example, there are lessons in filial piety that include "[a]pologizing [to parents] for all the trouble we have caused and promising to improve in the future" (Kondo, 1990, p. 99). Kondo, an American anthropologist of Japanese parentage, expected the rehearsal of the confession to parents to elicit nothing more than embarrassment:

> But for most participants, the ethics teachings seemed to take on personal meaning at this point. To listen to the confessions, the room was full of selfish and egotistical people. Even the most rebellious young men who had been sent on company order seemed to take this exercise seriously. One of the foundry workers, labeled "insolent" by the teachers, tearfully poured out his emotions. He . . . remembered how tenderly his mother had cared for him during times of illness. Like others, he promised to appreciate all she had done for him and to be less selfish in the future. (Kondo, 1990, p. 99)

The performance of this man and the others described by Kondo could be interpreted as merely following a cultural script, but their emotional responsiveness to the script indicates at the least that they had acquired it as part of their experience of self. DeVos (1986) found similar themes of self-reproach in relation to parents in the responses by various Japanese subjects to the Thematic Apperception Test, suggesting that self-reproach, either in adaptive forms as constructive self-criticism or maladaptive forms as depression and withdrawal, is a recurrent psychological as well as cultural theme in Japan. It is important to realize that the Japanese population contains individuals who are alienated from its "sociocentric" cultural models of behavior and emotional expression, as documented by Mathews (1996), and that their numbers may be increasing, but the burden of evidence seems to suggest that the scripts for apologies, self-criticism, and self-reproach are psychologically salient for many Japanese. In the semantic field that connects *omoiyari* with self-reproach are high standards of interpersonal conduct that motivate altruistic behavior in Japanese social relationships but can also be experienced as burdensome sources of personal anxiety and anguish.

CULTURAL PSYCHODYNAMICS IN JAPAN

Cultural psychodynamics goes beyond the descriptive account of ethnopsychology to interpret culturally shaped individual experience in terms of psychic equilibrium, disequilibrium, and change. A Japanese example comes from William Caudill's ambitious investigation, left incomplete at his death in 1972. He documented that the average Japanese (in the early 1960s) slept and bathed with mother during the early years, continued sleeping with a family member until age fifteen, and then engaged in intergenerational co-sleeping again as a young parent (Caudill & Plath, 1966). He believed that this kind of physical closeness with another person became part of the ordinary person's intrapsychic equilibrium in the course of growing up. When that equilibrium was seriously disturbed by social stresses (as in the ongoing final industrialization that eliminated so many family businesses when he was there), sleep disorders would be one of the primary symptoms. He showed that sleep disorders were frequent among hospitalized Japanese mental patients (Caudill & Schooler, 1969) and that Japanese mental hospitals had institutionalized the culture-specific role of the *tsukisoi*, who would stay with patients and help them get to sleep (Caudill, 1961).

Caudill documented each of these assertions with quantitative data as well as ethnographic evidence. He described individual differences in the Japanese population, not only culturally homogeneous aspects of experience and practice. In interpreting the evidence, he argued that the closeness of child with mother and later with others was much more part of the inner regulation of the individual (interpersonal involvement in aspects of body management, like getting to sleep) than posited by orthodox psychoanalytic theory. He claimed that this closeness became a deep-seated emotional need, underlying normal family behavior in adulthood for most Japanese, reactions to extremely stressful conditions for some individuals, the manifest symptoms of hospitalized mental patients, and even the policies and practices of Japanese mental hospitals. Understood this way, the Japanese case represented a much greater penetration of cultural practices into the deepest parts of the psyche than Freudian or neo-Freudian formulations could accommodate. It thus called for a radical revision of psychoanalytic theory in cultural terms, which Caudill did not live to carry out. His unfinished work serves as an ideal, however, pointing the way to a cultural psychodynamics that refuses to take culture as window-dressing on a generically human psyche but insists on exploring the ways in which culturally organized experience sets the agenda for psychological patterns of normal development, adult functioning, and pathological breakdown.

It is no accident that the inspiration for Caudill's project of cultural psychodynamics came from Japan, which has, through its own cultural practices, challenged so many Western assumptions about the meanings of social life and human activities. This book continues that project's approach in its exploration of meanings in Japanese parenthood, childhood, and adolescence – meanings that shed new light on the experience of human development.

REFERENCES

Ainsworth, M. D. S., Blehar, M. C., Waters, E., & Wall., S. (1978). *Patterns of attachment: A psychological study of the strange situation.* Hillsdale, NJ: Erlbaum.

Azuma, H. (1996). Cross-national research on child development: The Hess-Azuma collaboration in retrospect. In D. W. Shwalb & B. J. Shwalb (Eds.), *Japanese childrearing: Two generations of scholarship* (pp. 220–40). New York: Guilford Press.

Bredekamp, S. (Ed.). (1987). *Developmentally appropriate practice in early childhood programs serving children from birth to age 8.* Washington, DC: National Association for the Education of Young Children.

Bruner, J. (1990). *Acts of meaning.* Cambridge, MA: Harvard University Press.

Bruner, J. (1996). *The culture of education.* Cambridge, MA: Harvard University Press.

Caudill, W. (1961). Around the clock patient care in Japanese mental hospitals: The role of the tsukisoi. *American Sociological Review, 26,* 204–14.

Caudill, W., & Plath. D. (1966). Who sleeps by whom? Parent-child involvement in urban Japanese families. *Psychiatry, 29,* 344–66.

Caudill, W., & Schooler, C. (1969). Symptom patterns and background characteristics of Japanese psychiatric patients. In W. Caudill & T. Y. Lin (Eds.), *Mental health research in Asia and the Pacific.* Honolulu: East-West Center Press.

Clancy, P. (1986). The acquisition of communicative style in Japanese. In B. Schieffelin & E. Ochs (Eds.), *Language socialization across culture* (pp. 213–49). New York: Cambridge University Press.

Cole, M. (1996). *Cultural psychology: A once and future discipline.* Cambridge, MA: Harvard University Press.

DeVos, G. (1986). *Socialization for achievement.* Berkeley: University of California Press.

Doi, T. (1973). *The anatomy of dependence.* Tokyo: Kodansha International.

Doi, T. (1986). *The anatomy of self: The individual versus society.* Tokyo: Kodansha.

Doi, T. (1990). The cultural assumptions of psychoanalysis. In J. W. Stigler, R. A. Shweder, & G. Herdt (Eds.), *Cultural psychology: Essays on comparative human development.* New York: Cambridge University Press.

Greenfield, P., & Cocking, R. (Eds.). (1994). *Cross-cultural roots of minority child development.* Hillsdale, NJ: Erlbaum.

Hess, R., Kashiwagi, K., Azuma, H., Price, G., & Dickson, W. (1980). Maternal expectations for mastery of developmental tasks in Japan and the United States. *International Journal of Psychology, 15,* 259–71.

Kitayama, S., & Markus, H. (Eds.) (1994). *Emotions and culture: Empirical studies of mutual influences.* Washington, DC: American Psychological Association.

Kondo, D. K. (1990). *Crafting selves: Power, gender and discourses of identity in a Japanese workplace.* Chicago: University of Chicago Press.

Lebra, T. S. (1976). *Japanese patterns of behavior.* Honolulu: University of Hawaii Press.

LeVine, R. (1982). *Culture, behavior and personality: An Introduction to the comparative study of psychosocial adaptation.* New York: Aldine de Gruyter.

Levy, R. I. (1973). *Tahitians: Mind and experience in the Society Islands.* Chicago: University of Chicago Press.

Lewis, C. C. (1995). *Educating hearts and mind: Reflections on Japanese preschool and elementary education.* New York: Cambridge University Press.

Lock, M. (1993). *Encounters with aging: Mythologies of menopause in Japan and North America.* Berkeley and Los Angeles: University of California Press.

Lutz, C. (1988). *Unnatural emotions: Everyday sentiments on a Micronesion atoll and their challenge to Western theory.* Chicago: The University of Chicago Press.

Malinowski, B. (1927). *Sex and repression in savage society.* New York: Harcourt Brace & Co.

Mathews, G. (1996). The stuff of dreams, fading: Ikigai and "the Japanese self." *Ethos, 24,* 718–47.

Mead, M. (1928). *Coming of age in Samoa.* New York: William Morrow.

Miller, J. G. (1997). Theoretical issues in cultural psychology and social constructionism. In J. W. Berry, Y. Poortinga, & J. Pandey (Eds.), *Handbook of cross-cultural psychology: Theoretical and methodological perspectives* (Vol. 1, pp. 85–128). Boston: Allyn & Bacon.

Shweder, R. A., Goodnow, J., Hatano, G., LeVine, R. A., Markus, H., & Miller, P. (1998). The cultural psychology of development: One mind, many mentalities. In R. M. Lerner (Ed.), W. Damon (Series Ed.), *Handbook of child psychology, Vol. 1: Theoretical models of human development* (5th ed., pp. 865–937). New York: John Wiley & Sons.

Stevenson, H., & Stigler, J. (1992). *The learning gap.* New York: Summit Books.

Takahashi, K. (1986). Examining the strange situation procedure with Japanese mothers and 12-month-old infants. *Developmental Psychology, 22,* 265–70.

Valsiner, J. (2000). *Culture and human development.* Thousand Oaks, CA: Sage Publications.

White, G., & Kirkpatrick, J. (Eds.). (1985*). Person, self and experience: Exploring Pacific ethnopsychologies.* Berkeley: University of California Press.

White, M. (1987). *The Japanese educational challenge.* New York: Free Press.

White, M. I., & LeVine, R. A. (1986). What is an *ii ko*? In H. Stevenson, H. Azuma, & K. Hakuta (Eds.), *Child development and education in Japan* (pp. 55–62). New York: Freeman.

Whiting, J. W. M. (1954). The cross-cultural method. In G. Lindzey (Ed.), *Handbook of social psychology* (Vol II, pp. 523–31). Cambridge, MA: Addison-Wesley.

Whiting, J. W. M., Child, I. L., & Lambert, W. W. (1966). *Field guide for a study of socialization.* New York: Wiley.

Whiting, J. W. M., & Whiting, B. B. (1960). Contributions of anthropology to the methods of studying child rearing. In P. H. Mussen (Ed.), *Handbook of research methods in child development* (pp. 918–44). New York: John Wiley & Sons.

Wierzbicka, A. (1996.) Japanese cultural scripts: Cultural psychology and "cultural grammar." *Ethos, 24,* 527–55.

Japanese Cultural Psychology and Empathic Understanding

Implications for Academic and Cultural Psychology

Hidetada Shimizu

Recent research in cultural psychology has given renewed attention to the problem of understanding Japanese behavior, experience, and development (Kitayama & Markus, 1994; Stigler, Shweder, Goodnow, Hatano, LeVine, Markus, & Miller, 1998; Shweder, & Herdt, 1990). In terms of the cultural psychology of the Japanese, the studies by Markus and Kitayama (1991) and Wierzbicka (1996) are at the forefront. Markus and Kitayama suggest, for example, that the Japanese, along with their East Asian cohorts, have a culturally distinct "construal of self," which "insists on the fundamental relatedness of individual to each other" (1991, p. 224). Wierzbicka (1996), by contrast, suggests that the "cultural scripts" guiding Japanese social behaviors, such as "apologies," are semantically distinct from their English counterparts. Therefore, to "apologize" has culturally distinct meanings in Japanese and in English.

In this Introduction, I shall argue that Markus and Kitayama's and Wierzbicka's approaches are steps in the right direction toward minimizing ethnocentrism in academic psychology. Both approaches, however, are too methodologically limited to capture the complexity of subjective experience in individual lives. Using hypothetical problems to elicit a restricted range of meanings of Japanese cultural norms for individuals, these three scholars do not consider the contradictory and multidimensional motives behind the interaction of culture and person. Without an empathic understanding

Reprinted by permission of the American Anthropological Association from *Ethos* 28(2): 224–47. Not for sale or further reproduction. The writing of this article was supported by National Academy of Education Spencer Post-Doctoral Fellowship. I am deeply indebted to Professor Robert LeVine for his encouragement, insights, and suggestions, which enabled me to write this Introduction.

of personal experience in the varied settings of individual lives, the evidence from formal assessment procedures is thin, and its validity questionable. Because investigators cannot know in advance the variability and complexity of indigenous experience, bypassing the individual experience, as Markus and Kitayama and Wierzbicka do, risks imposing the classification system of the investigators rather than that of the "natives."

First, I shall argue that the meaning of personal experience is often equivocal (i.e., open to two or more interpretations) and multidimensional (located in more than one level of experience). I shall use the concept of *omoiyari* (sensitivity to others) to illustrate that semantic and pragmatic definitions of the concept, such as those provided by Lebra (1976), alone cannot predict or fully capture the variety and depth of individual experience. The content of such personal experience cannot be captured by these static descriptors, because individual experiences are variable and multiplex and because they are influenced by motives that underlie observable behaviors.

Second, I shall argue that the empathic understanding of the lived experience of the Japanese (or any cultural or national group) cannot be achieved through the *experimental* approach (of Markus and Kitayama), which uses hypothetical situations to highlight intergroup (that is, Japanese versus American) differences; or the *cultural grammar* approach (of Wierzbicka), which attempts to translate culture-specific meaning into a "natural semantic metalanguage."

Finally, I shall consider the strengths and the limitations of Markus and Kitayama's and Wierzbicka's approaches in light of the psychologist Donald Campbell's (1988) previous attempt to combat naïve ethnocentrism (i.e., "phenomenal absolutism") of academic psychology.

EXPERIENTIAL APPROACH TO *OMOIYARI*

Before discussing the equivocal and multiplex natures of real-life experience concerning *omoiyari*, it is necessary to discuss first how this concept has been conceptualized in the anthropological literature on Japan. As Spiro (1993) points out, few anthropological studies have looked into the private experiences of people. Most of them attempted to translate cultural norms, particularly the meanings of culturally indigenous concepts and normative behaviors. Of these approaches, two types of analyses are most common: semantic and pragmatic definitions of the culture-specific concepts. The semantic translation gives formal, dictionary-like definitions of cultural concepts, whereas the pragmatic translation gives examples of normative contexts in which these concepts derive their culture-specific meanings.

Lebra's (1976) chapter on *omoiyari* in her book, *The Japanese Patterns of Behavior,* contains perhaps the most comprehensive and widely cited examples of semantic and pragmatic definitions of *omoiyari*. In terms of semantics, she defines *omoiyari* as "the ability and willingness to feel what others are feeling, to vicariously experience the pleasure and pain that they are undergoing, and to help them satisfy their wishes" (Lebra, 1976, p. 38).

In terms of pragmatics, she conceptualizes *omoiyari* as part of the larger cultural ethos of "social relativism." *Omoiyari* is an expression of "social preoccupation," the first element of social relativism, because the objects of Japanese individuals' primary concerns are not abstract ideas and principles but people inhabiting their social world. It is also part of what she calls "interactional relativism," the other component, in that individuals make personal decisions in conjunction with what they consider other people are thinking and feeling in a given situation. For example, if someone wants to go to a movie, but he or she also knows no one else wants to, he or she may decide not to go to honor other people's preference not to go. Another example Lebra uses is *ozendate*, where a Japanese host prepares things ahead of time in anticipation of what the guest may desire. According to the Japanese cultural script, it is improper to ask guests what they want to be served (for example, coffee or tea). Rather, it is appropriate to do a little research on the guest's taste ahead of time and serve them something based on an educated guess. Such intention, or *magokoro* – "sincere heart," as the Japanese put it – to serve others in the spirit of *omoiyari* is valued more highly than correctly guessing guests' preferences.

Many of Lebra's examples are culturally normative patterns of behaviors derived from her own knowledge as an expert interpreter of Japanese culture, a Japanese native, and a trained anthropologist. Few of them are descriptions of the lived experience of real-life individuals. Thus, the individual motives that exist behind these culturally normative scripts are left out. In other words, once a certain pattern of behavior is institutionalized as a cultural (i.e., shared) norm, individuals can always choose to act behind it, much the way a puppet master animates a scripted puppet play with his own emotions and interpretations. Such private motives are not revealed in the semantic and pragmatic definitions of the normative script alone, but through detailed descriptions of individual lives and circumstances from which the script derives more specific and deeper personal meaning. The variations and depths of such motives behind the *omoiyari* script will be discussed next.

The evidence is drawn from long-term, repeated interviews with adolescents in a Japanese high school – a private academic school. The interviewees

reflect on the issues of achievement, moral conflict, and interpersonal behavior (Shimizu, 1993a).[1] From these interviews, I wrote case studies of four
adolescents, three of whom will appear in this chapter: they are: Yasuhiko,
a fifteen-year-old boy with a history of being bullied; Yumi, a seventeen-
year-old girl who questions her own sincerity because she acts differently in
different social situations; and Takeshi, an eighteen-year-old boy who plays
soccer and volunteers his services fixing school bathroom switches broken
by delinquents. I also draw on data from an open-ended questionnaire administered to students in this school, personal experience as a native of
Japan and as an anthropological researcher there, and published works describing the real-life experiences and social behavior of Japanese people.

There are at least three heuristically distinguishable, if not exhaustive or
mutually exclusive, ways in which the *omoiyari* script can be experienced
and acted out by individual Japanese: to fulfill cultural common sense, to
sabotage, and to experience conflict and ambivalence.

Cultural Common Sense

When individuals think, feel, or behave in a certain way, and believe that
their actions are so perfectly "good" and "normal" that they are not aware
of or would not approve of any alternatives, they are conforming to scripts
that are part of "cultural common sense" (Geertz, 1983, pp. 73–93). *Omoiyari*,
as Lebra notes, is one such prevalent and idealized cultural common sense.
To be more precise, one can further divide the personal motives to fulfill the
omoiyari scripts as cultural common sense into subcategories: coerced and
willing conformity (see LeVine, 1982) and complacent conformity.

In coerced conformity, someone of a subordinate social position unilaterally adapts and performs the script for fear of punishment or concern for
survival (e.g., being fired from a job or ostracized from a community). People who succumb to coerced conformity are generally those in servant roles

---

[1]   The interview and questionnaire data were collected in a private Protestant junior and
senior high school outside of Tokyo. Two male and two female students were chosen haphazardly from each grade from the seventh to the twelfth. During our first interview session (one to one-and-one-half hours long), we talked about general aspects of their lives: the
past year, self-descriptions, school and home life, and so on. Some students agreed to more
interviews, and to these, I sent a letter asking them to remember experiences in which they
(a) worked very hard at something (achievement); and (b) had to make decision about right
versus wrong (morality). Follow-up interviews were conducted three, six, and nine months
later. During these interviews, the informants reflected on the meaning and implications of
their own experiences. I visited their homes to interview their parents. I also gave several
written, open-ended questionnaires to 198 high school students (118 girls and 80 boys).

and citizens under repressive dictatorships (LeVine, 1982). The notion, however, can be applied to people at large when they submit to normative pressures of given sociocultural roles that forbid or constrict expressions of private motives.

For example, Japanese society (and presumably many others, including the United States) offers many occupation- and social-status-related role behaviors that are so rigidly prescribed by linguistic scripts that individual speakers deviate little from them. One example is a merchant uttering a set phrase to attract customers, such as *"irrashai mase"* (come in and let us serve you). Also at a train station, people are reminded to step behind the white line (*"hakusen no ushiro made sagatte kudasai"*) to keep a safe distance from the incoming train. When passengers are about to get off the train, they are reminded again not to leave their belongings behind (*"owasure mono nai you otashi kame kudasai"*). One hears these set phrases over and over again in Japan as institutionalized expressions of *omoiyari*.

There are other variants of such fixed, occupation- and social-status-related *omoiyari* role behaviors. On the busy streets of larger cities, for example, pedestrians often encounter a person giving away pocket-sized tissues with a company's promotions printed on the back. The distributors will say something like, "How are you? Hot day, isn't it? How about a tissue to wipe off your sweat?" as if to say, "Here's my *omoiyari* for you. I am committed to maximizing your comfort." It is more than likely, however, that the tissue distributors are merely conforming to the sales tactics prescribed by their employers.

In willing conformity, by contrast, there is a high degree of congruence between culturally prescribed role behavior and the individual's desire to fulfill its requirements, so that enactment of the role behaviors creates personal satisfaction in the performer. The example of an eighteen-year-old boy named Takeshi (Shimizu, 1993a) below indicates that individuals not only conform willingly to *omoiyari* scripts, but go beyond them to generate their own, individualized *omoiyari* scripts. In Takeshi's school, there were a number of delinquents who routinely tampered with the light switches in a school bathroom. Takeshi volunteered to fix these switches with his teacher. Asked why, he explained that he was sympathetic to the delinquents. He learned from his mother, the school nurse, that these boys came from broken homes and knew no better way of expressing their individuality. So, he said, instead of punishing them, one needs to wait patiently for them to repent by modeling good behavior.

Cross-referencing this incident with other stories told by the same informant led me to believe that he wanted to fix these switches as a voluntary personal decision. For example, he decided not to tell a girl that he wanted to go out with because of his concern that, in doing so, he might bother her while she was preparing for all-important college entrance exams. He also quickly decided which college to attend in order to make his dying grandfather happy. These behaviors are all congruent with his self-professed (during the interview) personality of being kind and nice to others (*yasashii*). In his own words, there are so many starving people in the world, but he had all the food he could eat and parents to pay for his education. He said that he felt naturally obligated to repay the goodness he received from other people. Thus, it appears that he fixed the bathroom switches out of his genuine concern for the delinquents, not to submit to any external authorities (Shimizu, 1993a, p. 426).

Finally, the *omoiyari* script can be so standardized as a culturally prescribed role behavior that individuals perform the script without realizing its original meaning: attending and catering to other people's needs through empathy. Such rigid adherence to a specific script that appears empathic but permits no variation in the interests of an unanticipated call for empathic response is "complacent conformity." For example, my wife and I went to a discount store in a suburb of one of Japan's major cities to buy household items. We saw a little hut in which vendors were cooking and selling *takoyaki* (a grilled ball of flour mixed with a tiny piece of octopus, or *tako*, placed in the center), with the lively calling of, "*Irasshai mase irasshai mase*" ("Come in! Come in, please! We are ready to serve you!"). The person who was shouting this was a teenaged girl, who seemed to be hired to do this on a part-time basis. She seemed to epitomize her role as a *takoyaki* sales clerk: energetic, upbeat, and ready to serve. At this time, we found a crying child who obviously was lost and looking for her mother. Sensing that the child needed help, my wife asked the young women behind the *takoyaki* stand, "Excuse me, but this girl seems to be lost. Would there be a place where I can get help? Maybe someone can make an announcement." At this moment, the clerk looked as if she were caught totally off guard, and she suddenly looked away so that she did not have to respond to my wife. It was as if she refused to come out of her occupational role and help us personally. The point of the story is that individuals can become so deeply self-identified and entangled with their role that they become lost in it – almost to the point of being blinded by "role narcissism" (DeVos, 1973). Playing the role, they become complacently content and uncritical, making no effort to appreciate the original significance of the role.

Many teenagers appear to be particularly vulnerable to the complacent role narcissism. In a questionnaire I gave to teenagers in which they were asked to list three words to describe themselves, along with their strengths and weakness, ideal self and nonideal self (Shimizu, 1993a), I got the impression that some of the respondents were mechanically repeating words and phrases that are suited to idealized self-presentation. Examples of such words are *akarui* (lively and amicable), *yasashii* (kind and gentle), and the most frequently mentioned, *omoiyari* (empathy). My subsequent analysis, however, revealed aspects of their self-perception that are far from being so outgoing, gregarious, and nonintrospective. In response to questions regarding difficulties they face day to day in human relationships, they indicated their lack of kindness to others, and difficulty being truly empathetic to others. They also indicated a shortage of kindness and empathy among their peers. Thus, in the complacent form of *omoiyari*, individuals mechanically recite values or behaviors that are considered ideal in their culture without considering the personal ramifications of these values.

Sabotage

Sabotaging may be analogous to the psychiatric concept of sociopathy: the sociopaths manipulate other people and social institutions to satisfy selfish motive. Likewise, the saboteurs manipulate officially sanctioned meanings of *omoiyari* to justify their malevolence. For example, one of my informants, the "whipping boy" whom I call Yasuhiko, decided to use his karate skills to combat the bullies – he had been preparing to do this for years. Instead of fighting back, the bullies decided to use their streetwise intelligence. In front of spectators, they accused Yasuhiko as lacking *omoiyari*. They said that Yasuhiko was "bullying" them because he was using his "expert" karate skills to attack the "novices." The spectators could have known in their hearts that the bullies were the ones manipulating the norm of *omoiyari* to carry out their malevolent scheme. Feeling the need, however, to comply with the public ideal (*tatemae*) of *omoiyari* – that is, not taking advantage of the weak – they did not, publicly at least, point out the wrongness of the bullies' plot.

In other cases, individuals do not intend to deceive and do harm like the bullies. Rather, their private experience is such that it cannot be captured fully by the public semantic and pragmatic definitions of a cultural concept. Therefore, the individuals revise, or appropriate, the official meanings to give them more specific and personal meanings. I committed such sabotaging myself when I tried to explain the meaning of *omoiyari* to a class largely of Anglo-American students from my own point of view, as a

native of Japan. I decided to use one of the scenes described in Lafcadio
Hearn's essay, "At the Station" (1896). I read it some time ago, but this
episode struck me as an example that best depicted the Japanese sentiment
of *omoiyari*. The story goes as follows.

While fleeing a house he had just robbed, a man was accosted by a police officer, whom he killed. Later, the man was captured and returned by
train to Kumamoto, where he had committed the murder. A crowd of spectators (Hearn was among them) waited for him at the station. The prisoner
came out of the station escorted by a police detective. The detective called
for the mother and child of the murdered policeman to step forward. The
detective told the boy that his father was murdered by this man, and it was
his fault the boy had no father. The detective told the boy to take a really
good look at the man. Then the boy, frightened and sobbing, stared at the
prisoner for a long time, almost as if he wanted to pierce the man with his
stare. Then Hearn describes this sequence of events:

> The crowd seemed to have stopped breathing. I saw the prisoner's fea-
> tures distort; I saw him suddenly dash himself down upon his knees de-
> spite his fetters, and beat his face into the dust, crying out the while in a
> passion of hoarse remorse that made one's heart shake:
>
> "Pardon! Pardon! Pardon me, little one! That I did – not for hate was
> it done, but in mad fear only, in my desire to escape. Very, very wicked I
> have been; great unspeakable wrong have I done you! But now for my
> sin I go to die. I wish I die; I am glad to die! Therefore, O little one, be piti-
> ful! – forgive me!"
>
> The child still cried silently. The officer raised the shaking criminal; the
> dumb crowd parted left and right to let them by. Then, quite suddenly,
> the whole multitude began to sob. And as the bronzed guardian passed,
> I saw what I had never seen before – what few men ever see – what I shall
> probably never see again – the tears of a Japanese policeman.
>
> The crowd ebbed, and left me musing on the strange morality of the
> spectacle. Here was justice unswerving yet compassionate – forcing
> knowledge of a crime by the pathetic witness of its simplest result. Here
> was desperate remorse, praying only for pardon before death. And here
> was a populace – perhaps the most dangerous in the Empire when an-
> gered – comprehending all, touched by all, satisfied with the condition
> and the shame, and filled, not with wrath, but only with the great sorrow
> of the sin – through simple deep experience of the difficulties of life and
> the weakness of human nature. (Hearn, 1896, p. 11)

The problem with using this story to illustrate *omoiyari* is that it does not
seem to live up to *omoiyari*'s high ethical standards. As stated in Lebra's def-

initions of *omoiyari*, it – first and foremost – is an altruistic, prosocial behavior, so much so that it defines the standard of ethical behaviors for the
Japanese. But the example above depicts feelings of sympathy that the
spectators held for the criminal, and that the criminal begged from the spectators. How can this be *omoiyari*? As one student commented to me, "How
can empathy be empathy if it has to do with forgiving someone who killed
a man in front of his child?"

To me, and I suppose to many of my fellow Japanese, the personal meaning of *omoiyari* cannot always be articulated in terms of a single, explicit,
dictionary-like definition. Rather, its emotional meaning is embraced by a
family of interrelated concepts and contexts. In my mind, the meaning of
omoiyari falls among the notions of compassion (*ninjo*), indulgence (*amae*),
and sincerity (*makoto*).

Omoiyari is related to compassion (*ninjo*), because it has to do with forgiving others by mercy. In the creation myth of Kojiki and Nihongi, for example, the sun goddess Amaterasu repeatedly condones the cruel behaviors of her younger brother Susanoo (Pelzel, 1974, p. 7). Susanoo, as the
myth describes, "had from birth been a selfish, cruel, and unruly god,
whose very presence 'withered mountains and dried up rivers and seas.'"
As a result, his parents ordered him to "proceed to the nether world (or the
sea) to be its ruler where he could not harm the things of earth" (Pelzel,
1974, p. 7). But he ignored his parents' order and, instead, rose up to heaven
where his sister reigned as the ruler. There he continued to misbehave by
"breaking down the dikes around his sister's rice fields,. letting a piebald
colt loose in her fields at harvest time, defecating on the floor of her palace,
and so forth" (Pelzel, 1974, p. 7). But instead of punishing him, Amaterasu
kept on covering up for him:

> [She] did not protest these acts, however, in each case finding an excuse
> for them that was acceptable to her. For example, she decided that in tear-
> ing down the dikes among her fields he had been moved by a helpful in-
> tent, impractical as it was in actuality, merely to increase the area that
> could be planted to rice, and she imagined that what looked like excre-
> ment on her floor was really nothing but vomit that he had brought up
> during an otherwise forgivable bout of drunkenness. (Pelzel, 1974, p. 7)

To me, this story portrays *omoiyari* as *ninjo* (compassion and mercy).
Omoiyari is also related to *amae* – that is, "assum[ing] that [one] has another's good will, or take[ing an] . . . optimistic view of a particular situation order to gratify his need to feel at one with, or indulged by, his sur-
roundings" (Doi, 1981, p. 8). This interpretation has to do with indulging

someone who makes an unrealistic and often presumptuous demands for benevolence. For example, the term *tanomu* (to ask), usually used by a person asking for a favor, has a meaning "roughly midway between the English 'to ask' and 'to rely on,' implying that one is entrusting some matter concerning oneself personally to another person in the expectation that he will handle it in a manner favorable to oneself. . . . *Tanomu*, in other words, means nothing other than 'I hope you will permit my self-indulgence'" (Doi, 1981, p. 30). Again, it requires much *omoiyari* to permit such indulgence of others.

Finally, *omoiyari* can be understood in conjunction with the notion of sincerity that is designed to nullify the distinction between *tatemae* and *honne*. Normally, public morality is held as *tatemae*, the general consensus of a group to which one belongs, such as the law designed to punish those who break it. Individuals generally conform to *tatemae* willingly as long as they are able to conceal or contain their *honne*, that is, privately felt ideas and feelings, behind *tatemae*. But when individuals find it impossible to contain their *honne* behind *tatemae*, they can be momentarily excused for showing their *honne* by appealing to the sincerity of others. This, I believe, is functionally synonymous with the notion of *omoiyari*. Doi explains the principle as follows:

> [T]he Japanese notion of sincerity is intimately intertwined with the notion of *omote* (front) and *ura* (back). In everyday, normal circumstances, individuals display *tatemae* as "face" i.e., *omote*, and conceals *honne*, their real feelings, behind it. The cultural consensus is that individuals have their individualized and idiosyncratic *honne* behind *tatemae*. Respect for this general rule helps to maintain harmony among people. Should a conflict arise within an individual or group, however, the equilibrium between *tatemae* and *honne* is disrupted. It is such a time of trouble that the Japanese most often revert to the use of the concept of sincerity. In fact, there is one scholar who stated exactly this at the end of Tokugawa period; that to be "sincere" is to temporarily set aside the distinction between *tatemae* and *honne*, and to deal with the conflict on a "man-to-man" basis. To me, the latter signifies a temporary agreement, due to the emergent nature of the situation at hand, between the two (or more) parties that *amae* can be brought to the surface – i.e., to reveal one's naked heart, undisguised by *tatemae*. This, I believe, is at the heart of the Japanese notion of "sincerity." (Doi, 1986, pp. 107–08)

What the spectator did for the murderer indeed required *omoiyari*, just as Lebra defined it, "the ability and willingness to feel what others are feeling, to vicariously experience the pleasure and pain that they are undergoing, and to help them satisfy their wishes" (Lebra, 1976, p. 38). But to answer the student's question, why one would call the empathy of condoning a murder "empathy," I needed to consider three additional pragmatic contexts in which the personal meaning of *omoiyari* can be elaborated. In my view, all three, and possibly more, were necessary to justify the spectators' acts of *omoiyari* for the murderer. This is similar to a Shakespearean play with several subplots working together to generate a central theme.

Conflict and Ambivalence

Although the tendency for self-reproach among the Japanese has been widely reported by anthropologists and comparative educational researchers (see LeVine, Preface, this volume), relatively little attention has been paid to the individual experiences of conflict and ambivalence behind *omoiyari* as a cultural norm. During my study of adolescents in a Japanese high school, I found evidence that young Japanese look at the norm of *omoiyari* with a sense of conflict and ambivalence. They discover that it is too lofty an ideal to live up to and that everyone, peers and adults alike, is individualistic and self-centered one way or another. This experience gives adolescents feelings of conflict and ambivalence about the practical and moral value of *omoiyari*.

In an open-ended questionnaire given to adolescents aged twelve to eighteen, for example (Shimizu, 1993b), I found that *omoiyari* ranked highest consistently among words teenagers chose to describe their ideal self and social behaviors. When I compared responses across various sections of the questionnaire, however, a pattern emerged. Despite the overall affirmation of the value of *omoiyari*, most respondents considered that neither they nor other adolescent peers nor adults fully internalized or fulfilled this cultural ideal. Intrigued by this finding, I glanced at some responses across those given by the same individuals. There, I also found ambivalent attitudes toward *omoiyari*. Quite a few cases indicated that *omoiyari*, although a commendable trait, was unattainable by many and that people are too preoccupied with themselves to commit themselves fully to this cultural ideal. The following response (reproduced here in full) of a sixteen-year-old Japanese girl to the questionnaire demonstrates this dilemma:

Q: If I were to choose three words to describe myself:
A: They would be that I'm bashful (*tereya*), a crier (*nakimushi*), and lazy (*namakemono*).
Q: Three positive words that describe myself would be:

A: I don't express my opinions (*iken o iwanai*), follow others (*minna ni shitagau*), and persistent (*akippoku nai*).

Q: Three negative words would be:

A: I become arrogant at home (*ie de ibaru*), I am a crier ["crying bug"] (*nakimushi*), and I don't make myself clear.

Q: Ideally, I would like to be:

A: Charming (*kirei*), kind and gentle (*yasashii*), and be liked by everyone (*minna ni* sukareru).

Q: However, I don't want to be:

A: Vulgar (*busahoo*), egotistical (*wagamama*), and not be liked by anyone (*minna ni sukare nai*).

Q: What I consider important to accomplish in life:

A: Is to make the most out of my hobby/personal interests (*shumi o ikasu*).

Q: Because:

A: Right now, I don't feel that I'm free.

Q: I would like to accomplish this:

A: In my current life and by rebelling against my parents.

Q: What I consider the right thing to do:

A: Is to become someone who helps those who are in trouble.

Q: Because:

A: I am not such a person. How to become such a person? I'd just want to be one, that's all.

Q: What I consider the wrong thing to do:

A: Not to keep a promise.

Q: Because:

A: Everyone around me is that way [that is, they don't keep promises].

Q: How would I correct this:

A: I would talk with everyone.

Q: Most difficult things that I face with my relationships with others is to:

A: Express my opinions clearly.

Q: Why?:

A: Because I can't.

Q: What's the most important thing to do in interpersonal relationships?

A: To go along with others (*hito ni awaseru*).

Q: Why?:

A: Because I often had an experience like that.

Q: How to accomplish this?:

A: I wish someone could tell me (Shimizu, 1993b).

In these responses, I read few signs of unambivalent affirmation of *omoi-yari*. Rather, I sensed that the respondent was unsure, or even cynical, about the practice and moral value of *omoiyari*. She seems to think that being kind and gentle and helpful to others is a wonderful ideal. But in her real life, so much attention is paid to going along with others, that she is unable to express herself clearly. This could be why she feels "not free" and feels that she is behaving "arrogantly" at home. She says it is important to "keep a promise" because few people actually do so. Enmeshed in a world of personal relationships in which appearances are often in conflict with what is below the surface, she still believes it is important to "make the most out of her hobby and interests" and to "express her opinions clearly." At the same time, she wishes that "somebody could tell her" how she might accomplish this daunting task. Her responses reveal that her psychology is multiplex. In other words, she is communicating two or more contradictory messages simultaneously. Thus, despite the overall emphasis placed on the importance of *omoiyari*, her personal experience appears to be also filled with doubts, conflicts, and ambiguity.

My second piece of evidence comes from my experience of listening to real-life stories of Japanese teenagers. I have already talked about the whipping boy, Yasuhiko. In my conversation with his parents, I discovered that he had an unbending sense of justice, typical of that seen in Japanese samurai warrior melodramas, in which the "good guy" (*ii mono*) always prevails in the end. The real world in which this person lived his late elementary school and adolescent years was infested, however, by villains who sabotage such moral principles. He was lost there and described his circumstance this way:

> Whenever I'm feeling good, I'm also feeling confused. I feel like I'm being caught between joy and guilt, and I didn't know what to do. I asked myself, "Am I doing things all right? Am I doing something wrong by doing what I'm doing now?" (Shimizu, 1993a, p. 311)

His experience proved to be the opposite of what *omoiyari* scripts say about the world, and about what it ought to be. Such ambiguity in the meaning of the cultural script gives him a deep sense of disappointment. He noted, "Even if you try to help someone who is in trouble, others will think that you are being silly. There are some people who think that it's a waste of time to try to help someone." When I commended him for having such "a strong sense of justice," he countered me by saying, "Yes, but recently, my sense of justice is failing me" (Shimizu, 1993a, p. 350).

Yumi, the seventeen-year-old sophomore girl, is another informant who questioned the moral authority of *omoiyari*. First, she found a lack of sincerity in her motives to care for others. She felt compelled to take care of a little child in her relative's house. But she realized that her desire to seek approval from his and her own parents overrode her desire to do good for the child. She felt she was cunning (*zurui*). Next, she noticed that friendships among her females peers were fragile and maintained by empathy and agreeableness that was merely superficial. Few of them were willing to speak and act as they felt because doing so nearly always resulted in ostracism by their peers. In addition, she felt every one of her friends was also "cunning." To make her point, she gave me the following example:

> If you jokingly tell someone, "I don't like you very much, so leave me alone," with the slightest hint that you might actually mean that, then you see girls congregating after school and gossiping, "She says things too clearly," or "She's so immature to say things as she really feels." So I thought, "OK, so saying things clearly isn't 'adult-like.' Then maybe I should be just as cunning as everyone, and say one thing here and another thing there." (Shimizu, 1993a, p. 385)

Yumi's stories testify that the minds and friendships of female adolescents fall short of the idealized *omoiyari*. Hence, there is a paradox: In the society that idealizes *omoiyari*, young women are, at best, ambivalent about its standards.

HYPOTHETICAL AND CORRIGIBLE ANCHOR POINTS

The foregoing examples of the real-life experiences of real people show personal emotions and motives that are contradictory or even contrary to the normative scripts of empathy (*omoiyari*). Striving to generalize from the cultural norms to an individual subject, however, Markus and Kitayama and Wierzbicka exclude these contradictory and multidimensional motives that do not fit into the normative patterns.

Markus and Kitayama's Experimental Approach

Most of published studies by Markus and Kitayama on culture and self are based on written tests given to college students, in which the researchers have preidentified the range of culture-specific representations of self that they hope to bring into focus. These anchor points are fixed and inflexible, and lack multidimensionality to account for the equivocal and multiplex motives behind culturally constituted experience. Therefore, the phenomenological validity of Markus and Kitayama's evidence is limited because actual participation in real-life situations is left out.

Markus and Kitayama's key assertion is that the Japanese self is "interdependently construed" (contextually and socially constructed), whereas the American or Western self is, "independently construed" (individually and autonomously constructed). Their recent study (Kitayama, Markus, Matsumoto, & Norasakkunkit, 1997) exemplifies their position. Japanese and American college students were asked to read four hundred hypothetical situations – half of which were selected by college students in Japan and the United States to describe success situations (for example, when I make a great breakfast just for me), and the other, failure situation (when my favorite baseball team or actor/actress is overtly criticized). Subjects were then asked if their self-esteem (*jison-shin*) would be affected in each of these situations and if so, in which direction (increase or decrease) and to what extent (from 1 – slightly – to 4 – very much). The results indicate that American and Japanese students showed what the researchers called self-enhancing and self-critical tendencies, respectively. The U.S. students chose more success than failure situations as relevant to their self-esteem, such that they judged their self-esteem would increase more in the success situations than it would decrease in the failure situations (self-enhancing tendency). By contrast, the Japanese chose more failure than success situations as relevant to their self-esteem, such that they judged that their self-esteem would decrease more in the failure situations than it would increase in the success situations (self-critical tendencies).

The evidence supports their general theory that "American culture is organized around the view of the self as an independent and autonomous entity [that seeks] to find, confirm and express positively valenced internal attributes of the self" [i.e., self-enhancement] (Kitayama et al., 1997, p. 1260). Conversely:

> Japanese culture is organized around the view of the self as an interdependent and mutually connected entity [that seeks] to create and affirm a social relationship in which the self is seen as participating by fitting into and adjusting to such a relationships . . . [To] achieve the cultural task of fitting in it is important for one to identify consensual standards of excellence shared in a relationship . . . and to engage in the process of self-criticism by identifying those shortcomings, deficits, or problems that prevent one from meeting such standards. The result is a cultural force in the direction of self-criticism – namely, in the direction of attending, elaborating, and emphasizing negatively valenced aspects of the self. (Kitayama et al., 1997, p. 1260)

These arguments are valid concerning the conventional models of self-representations in the two cultures. As Lindholm (1997) points out, however, it is unclear as to what "agent" – "self," or "culture" – is doing the "construing" of the "independent" and "interdependent" selves. For example, Markus and Kitayama explain that:

> Experiencing interdependence entails seeing oneself as part of an encompassing social relationship and recognizing that one's behavior is determined, contingent on, and to a large extent organized by what the actor perceived to be the thoughts, feelings and actions of others in the relationship. (Markus & Kitayama, 1991, p. 227)

If the so-called interdependent self, however, can organize its experiences and actions according to the way it "[perceives] to be the thoughts, feelings, and actions of others in the relationship," is this self not, by its very own nature, an independent, rather than an interdependent, agent capable of determining its own destiny? Or, as Lindholm puts it, is it that "Markus and Kitayama are led by confusion in their model of agency to argue that the 'interdependent self' is socially constructed (construed), context-dependent, and includes others within its boundaries; yet it is also governed by a strong, calculating, self-regulating, and agentic inner monitor capable of systematically constructing (construing) a 'schemata' through which, in effect, it negates its own existence" (Lindholm, 1997, p. 409).

It cannot be denied that the "interdependent construal of self" is a culturally normative model of self-representation. Such a norm is most likely to be found in individual responses to experimental stimuli such as written tests. This normative tendency alone, however, should not exhaust or accurately replicate the subjective content of individual experience.

Conflict and ambivalence, which involve "culturally inadmissible . . . [and] socially unacceptable and morally questionable [individual motives]" (Lindholm, 1997, p. 409) are the case in point. Kitayama et al. (1997) explain, for example, that the self-effacement of Japanese subjects should not be taken as a sign of low self-esteem. Rather, it is a culturally shared response to viewing oneself in the context of social relationships and contexts where:

> [T]he primary life task involves fitting into and adjusting to social relationships. To achieve the task of fitting in, one may need to identify the ideal image of the self expected by others in a relationship, find what may be missing or lacking in the self in reference to this expected, ideal self, and then improve on these deficits and problems. (1997, p. 1254)

This explanation as a description of culturally normative pattern of self-presentations in Japan is convincing. (See, for example, DeVos [1973] for his idea of "role narcissism.") It seems, however, to leave out those aspects of personal experience that cannot be captured fully by the normative scripts alone for they are too idiosyncratic, personally shameful or painful, or socially and culturally inadmissible.

For example, Yasuhiko, the victim of bullying, invested much of his childhood trying to fit in with his peers. He tried karate because his father told him that he was too restless and precocious for his age to be accepted by his peers as a playmate. So hoping to be more normal and to gain peer acceptance, he tried to improve his concentration through karate lessons. Much of his effort, however, turned out to worsen rather than improve his situation (as we saw earlier, his principled moral stance against the bullies so angered them that they chose to bully him). In the end, he told me that all of his effort and his sense of justice were "failing" him. So, what was the most compelling reason he took karate lessons? It is one thing to explain, on the surface level, that the boy tried to be included by his peers, because, as with most of his Japanese cohorts, he was socialized to be "contextually interdependent." It is quite another to explain, on a deeper, more personal level, that most adolescents in Japan (and in the United States) long to be accepted by their peers. For Yasuhiko, however, the cultural ideal of contextual self betrayed him because of his tendency to be himself and choose his own moral stance. Hence, it was his sense of personal inadequacy (of not being part of the collective world of his peers) and determination (that is, individualized, therefore, contextually independent, not interdependent) to correct his "individualism" that directly motivated him to take the karate lessons.

In summary, Markus and Kitayama's primary data is a self-report about preferences and emotion in response to hypothetical situations. The data may reveal surface aspects of culturally normative behavior. It leaves out, however, much of the complex and deeper meaning that motivates individual social behavior and cultural experience.

Wierzbicka's Cultural Script Approach

The linguist Anna Wierzbicka's "universal metalanguage" (1992, 1993) allows systematic and culturally sensitive translation of interpersonal scripts from one language to another. By identifying in advance, however, the universal dimensions by which the cultural differences may be bridged, her metalanguage too lacks the flexibility to account for the variable and multidimensional motives that inform real-life interpersonal behaviors.

Specifically, Wierzbicka (1993) positions herself in between two opposing perspectives of cultural relativists (Kondo, 1990; Lutz, 1988), and universalists (Spiro, 1984). She disagrees with the relativists that psychological concepts (such as self) expressed in a given language are constrained by the normative assumptions of that language, so that psychologies expressed in different languages are mutually incommensurable ethnopsychologies. She thus agrees with the universalists that certain aspects of individual experience and behavior are recognizable as universally human. The problem inherent in the universalists' position, however, is whether or not it can articulate itself in a language free of biases of a particular culture, yet at the same time remain flexible enough to decode meanings embedded in the (presupposed) "psychic unity of mankind." To help solve this dilemma, Wierzbicka advocates use of her "natural metalanguage" based in lexical universals, that is, "simple sentences or short sequences of sentences that attempt to capture a society's tacit cultural norms 'from a native's point of view' and, at the same time, to express these norms in terms of universal human concepts" (1993, pp. 220–21).

In Wierzbicka (1996), the author attempts to apply her natural semantic metalanguage to reveal the "cultural grammar," which she defines as "a set of subconscious rules that shape a people's way of thinking, feeling, speaking, and interacting" that informs Japanese notions of "apology" and "self-effacement" (Wierzbicka, p. 521). From the relativist perspective, Wierzbicka argues that the Japanese concept of apology is qualitatively distinct from its English counterpart. First, the English concept of apology assumes that to apologize indicates an admission of guilt. The Japanese counterpart, by contrast, assumes that people need to apologize to show sincerity even if they are not at fault. She derives these examples primarily from a book written by Hiroko Kataoka (1991), entitled *Japanese Cultural Encounters and How to Handle Them*. This is essentially a travel guide for foreign visitors to Japan. It advises that if you are involved in a car accident in which someone is injured, even if you are not at fault, you must visit the victim and apologize to show how sincerely you feel sorry for him or her.

To account for the qualitative difference in the meaning of apology in English and Japanese, Wierzbicka proposes the use of her natural semantic metalanguage to reveal the "cultural grammar" of the Japanese apology scripts. One such script is:

When someone says to me something like this:
"You did something,
something bad happened (to someone/to me) because of this,"
it is good to say something like this to this person:
"I feel something bad because of this."

It is bad to say something like this to this person:
"I didn't do anything bad." (Wierzbicka, 1996, p. 533)

Wierzbicka argues that by the use of Natural Semantic Metalanguage, one can gain culture-specific understanding of psychological processes without undermining the "psychic unity of mankind." But the question remains: From the available pool of cultural scripts, how do individuals select one that best applies to their unique individual situations? Wierzbicka (1996) gives a partial answer to this question:

> The cultural scripts approach to social interaction does not assume that cultures are homogeneous, or that social practices and more can be described in the form of neat compulsory rules characterizing everybody's actual behavior. It acknowledges that cultures are heterogeneous, and that social behaviors in general, and speech behavior in particular, shows a great deal of variation. At the same time it assumes the reality of certain implicit cultural ideologies, which can shape not only people's actual behavior but, even more, their assumptions and expectations. *Cultural norms can be violated, ignored, or rebelled against, but this does not change the fact that both the norms that people (consciously or unconsciously) obey and those they (consciously or unconsciously) violate differ from one cultural system to another.* (1996, p. 528, emphasis added)

One factor that Wierzbicka has not addressed fully in her argument (indicated by the italics) is the role of individual psychology that interprets and gives personal meanings to the "cultural system." She admits that individuals "violate, ignore, and rebel against" cultural norms, but she does not explain how or why such personal interpretations of cultural norms widely vary across individuals or even within an individual. As I described earlier in this chapter, however, these personal interpretations and multiplex meanings of cultural norms influence individual behaviors as directly and deeply as their normative and collective counterparts.

Consider Wierzbicka's "apology script," for example. How does one know if, or to what extent, such a script corresponds with the true motive of the apologizer? To say that people apologize for things that are not their fault in order to show sincerity is one thing. To say (supposedly), however, that a politician makes a "sincere" public apology to save his political career in the long term, albeit risking the loss of his current office, is another story.

Consider also a story told by Yumi, whose friends talked about another girl who did not promptly return a book she had borrowed. In this case, it is more than likely that the following script described by Wierzbicka could have framed the motives of gossipers: When somebody (one of the gossipers) "did good" (loaned a book) for someone (the girl being gossiped about), "It is good (for the borrower) to say something like this to this person (lender): 'You did something good for me,' and therefore, you felt something bad because of this; I feel something bad because of this." In this case, the lender and her friends were upset about the borrower because the borrower did not acknowledge this cultural script. She took no personal action (for example, making a sincere apology) to appease the lender's (possible) "bad feelings" (being encumbered or inconvenienced as a result of lending the book).

For Yumi, however, the crux of problem was not so much her friend's violation of the normative scripts, but maintaining her and her friend's integrity by (Yumi's) not criticizing her (friend) behind her back. Yumi explained the context of her dilemma and conflict as follows:

> There was this girl who had the flu and was absent today. She's been unpopular among us girls, for quite sometime and getting bad remarks from us. . . . But personally, I had nothing against her. I didn't think she was a bad person, and I wasn't bothered by these trivial things for which they were criticizing her. But, you see, these girls were criticizing her only because she was absent today.

About her own conflicting and ambivalent feelings, she said:

> [My conflict was that] I didn't really dislike her in the first place, but when I heard what other people were saying, I began to dislike her, saying, "Yes, she did that to me, too." I mean, these are such trivial things. For example, when I was reading a comic book, she came to me and said, "I want to read it." Then, she snatched the book from me although I was only halfway through. So then I said to myself, "Well, I'll just have to read it later." But today I found out that she was doing that to everybody. They told me, "She always takes things away from you." So although what she did to me didn't disturb me in the first place, when I heard other people talk about it and asked me how I feel about it, I said, "I don't like it." But immediately after that, I found myself saying, "Is it O.K. for me to be saying such a thing?" (Shimizu, 1993a, p. 368)

Yumi told me that she "knew" that the "right thing" for her to do was "not to gossip," particularly because the girl's failure to return the book did not bother her personally. She eventually decided to gossip with her peers, however, because if she did not, they might have decided to ostracize her (for not "sharing" the guilty act). This seemingly petty incident points out two fundamental conditions of our actual (not hypothetical or ideal) consciousness: fallibility and paradox. No one follows the normative scripts of culture (apologizing when they forget to return something) or even personal scripts of moral behavior (not gossiping) with complete consistency. All people are fallible. The paradox is that everyone knows what they *should* do, but because of individual fallibility, no one follows the norms perfectly. Such equivocal, multiplex, and conflicting motives of individual behavior are simply out of focus in Wierzbicka's cultural grammar approach or Markus and Kitayama's experimental variance approach. Nevertheless, I argue, these deeper personal motives, these hopes, wishes, fears, anxiety, disappointment, or depressive episodes involved in "trying to become," rather than "already being," a normal (moral) member of a culture (as indicated by the collective representations of written tests, travel guide books, and normative cultural scripts) inform and motivate real-life behavior of individuals.

Markus and Kitayama's and Wierzbicka's approaches, although formulated with the intention of doing justice to both the particulars and universals of cultural experience, do not go directly and far enough into the psychological depths of cultural subjectivity. The problem that Markus and Kitayama and Wierzbicka tackle, however, is far from new in the field of cross-cultural psychology. Rather, they have nearly reinvented the old problems tackled, yet not fully solved, by the cultural psychologist, Donald Campbell. That is, Markus and Kitayama and Wierzbicka attempt to combat the ethnocentrism of academic psychology by pointing out the cultural specificity of Japanese psychology. Their insistence on directly comparable psychological data, however, has led them to a thin and superficial characterization of that culturally specific experience.

Combating Phenomenal Absolutism

The psychology of Japanese people (and other non-Westerners) is not quite what is conceived as universal by Western-trained academic psychologists. This is the point on which an increasing number of cultural psychologists and psychological anthropologists seem to agree. They are, in this sense, united against, to use Seagall et al.'s (1966) term, the "phenomenal absolutism" of Western academic psychology. In Campbell's view, phenomenal absolutism is the naive ethnocentrism of people who simply have not imagined that things could be other than the way to which they are accustomed (Campbell, 1988, p. 347). Provincial Japanese who think that food without rice is not a meal, or their American, Midwestern counterparts who think that food without meat and potatoes is not a meal, are examples. I am extending this metaphor to argue that Western-trained psychologists have, in the past, and currently continue to assume explicitly and implicitly that the psychology of all people conforms to the patterns, principles, and methodological paradigms formulated in their respective subdisciplines of formal psychology. Markus and Kitayama (1991) rightly criticize the phenomenal absolutism of academic psychology with respect to the notion of self:

> Despite the growing body of psychological and anthropological evidence that people hold divergent views about the self, most of what psychologists currently know about human nature is based on one particular view – the so-called Western view of the individual. . . . As a result of this mono-cultural approach to the self, psychologists' understanding of those phenomena that are linked in one way or another to the self may be unnecessarily restricted. (Markus & Kitayama, 1991, p. 224)

Thus, the phenomenal absolutism in psychology means ignoring concepts of human psychology unfamiliar to the investigators. Researchers may not be aware of, or informed about, other alternatives; or, even if they are, they may reject them or deny their relevance. This approach to psychology long ago became what Thomas Kuhn (1962) called "normal science." The social psychologists Hazel Markus and Shinobu Kitayama deserve respect for taking the courageous step of opposing the phenomenal absolutism of conventional academic psychology.

There is yet another, more subtle version of phenomenal absolutism, however, to which both Markus and Kitayama's and Wierzbicka's approaches seem to have succumbed: A form of tacit or secondary phenomenal absolutism based in the assumption of unwarranted omniscience by the hypothetical and fallible knower (or "knowing devices" such as written tests and universal metalanguage).

An analogy will illustrate my point. Suppose a mother has two children – a boy and a girl. The children have their own rooms, so neither knows what the other does in privacy. These children fight quite often, and they often give contradictory excuses for this behavior. Taking advantage of her authority as a parent, the mother installs surveillance cameras on the ceiling of each child's room. Still, neither child knows what the other does, but the mother knows what both children are doing, and, with the aid of the cameras, she hopes to gather evidence about why the children fight so much.

The mother's surveillance cameras are to the activities of the children in their rooms what the methodologies of Markus and Kitayama and

Wierzbicka are to the private or lived experience of Japanese (and that of other East Asian people) and Americans. Because they are localized, in their separate cultures, individual Japanese and Americans lack access to each other's lives. Cross-cultural psychologists, however, equipped with the objective device of a comparatively developed questionnaire or a metalanguage, possess vantage points that are unavailable to their informants. Cross-cultural psychologists transcend the boundaries of the two cultures and, godlike, look down on them from a contextually transcendent and epistemically superior position.

The problem with this approach is as follows: Whereas the naive phenomenal absolutists impose their own perspectives on all others, the tacit phenomenal absolutists claim to have established an epistemic priority of their conceptual or methodological position, allowing them to observe those aspects of phenomenon inaccessible to the naive phenomenal absolutists, or to their subjects. In this way, the researcher's perspective became prioritized over those of others. Such a claim, Campbell (1988) argues, is only hypothetical and corrigible. Yet the "tacit phenomenal absolutists" (as I call them) are often unaware of, or reluctant to admit, the danger of their corrigibility. Hence, the critiques of naive phenomenological absolutism have become the secondary, or tacit, phenomenal absolutists, for they have invested an unreasonably high degree of confidence (omniscience) in a highly corrigible and fallible viewpoint for the sake of comparative objectivity.

Specifically, Markus and Kitayama's and Wierzbicka's approaches identify *in advance* the universal dimensions over which the cultural differences they attempt to bring into focus may be bridged. Markus and Kitayama do this by sampling (experimentally elicited) situations to be included in their study and by limiting their studies to college students and written exams. Wierzbicka does so with her metalanguage. These methods, although bringing cultural differences into a single focus, are stationary and suffer from tunnel vision. They capture only selected aspects of subjective experience. In other words, Markus and Kitayama and Wierzbicka establish the conceptual equivalence of their categories prior to making any psychological comparison; in so doing, they have created a yardstick for measurement. In setting up a common standard of measurement, however, they reduce the dimensions to be described to those with which they are already familiar, rather than enabling discovery of new dimensions through their investigation. This approach sacrifices cultural and psychological depth for the sake of comparability, resulting in clear but superficial indicators of cultural differences.

Campbell's wisdom is that no single perspective from which we gain knowledge can be perfectly "anchored" – that is, omniscient, for each one of them is fallible (prone to biases as in phenomenal absolutism). E. Samuel Overman, editor of Donald Campbell's *Methodology and Epistemology for Social Sciences: Selected Papers,* and author of a brief introduction to the fourth section of the book, observes: "[Campbell] weaves a path between quantitative and qualitative knowing, between the goal of objectively and epistemological relativism, between behaviorist primacy and phenomenological absolutism" (Overman, 1988, p. 335).

Campbell's middle-of-the-road approach suggests a process of discovery unlike the fixed measurement procedures of Markus and Kitayama and Wierzbicka. The latter seek objective psychological knowledge, still believed in by most psychologists, yet given up long ago by philosophers of science (for example, Kuhn, 1962). The objective approach leaves no place for phenomenological exploration, for it limits itself to what can be measured by corrigible yet inflexible instruments. Campbell (1988), by contrast, came to believe that intersubjectivity is as good as anyone's objectivity can get. For example, in his introduction to Campbell's essay, "A Phenomenology of the Other One: Corrigible, Hypothetical, and Critical," Overman points out:

> Campbell affirms his belief that direct, nonpresumptive knowing is not to be our lot. Rather, indirect, inferential, mediate, and presumptive knowing are the best we can hope for. Phenomenological knowing of others is necessary but it too is corrigible, hypothetical, and critical – not direct. Campbell argues that we should not accept the epistemological primary of either behaviorism or phenomenology, but must combine the two into a phenomenology of the other one. (Overman, 1988, p. 335)

Campbell's call to the phenomenology of the other one seems the logical and natural extension of the study of cultural norms such as Markus and Kitayama's and Wierzbicka's. If the investigators' fallibility cannot be totally eliminated, we must learn to live with our fallibility by keeping us from the deceptively simple but imperfect approaches to overcome it. That is, being willing to accept our fallibility, we transcend it.

REFERENCES

Campbell, D. T. (1988). *Methodology and epistemology for social sciences: Selected papers.* Chicago: University of Chicago Press.

DeVos, G. A. (1973). *Socialization for achievement: Essay of the cultural psychology of the Japanese.* Berkeley: University of California Press.

Doi, T. (1981) *Anatomy of dependence.* Tokyo: Kodansha International.

Doi, T. (1986) *Amae no shuhen* [The context of amae]. Tokyo: Kobundo.

Geertz, C. (1983). *Local knowledge*. New York: Basic Books.

Hearn, L. (1896) *Kokoro: Hints and echoes of Japanese inner life*. Boston: Houghton Mifflin.

Kataoka, H. C. (1991). *Japanese cultural encounters and how to handle them*. Chicago: Passport Books INTC Publishing.

Kitayama, S., & Markus, H. R. (1994). *Emotion and culture: Empirical studies of mutual influence*. Washington, D.C.: American Psychological Association.

Kitayama, S., Markus, H. R., Matsumoto, H., & Norasakkunkit, V. (1997). Individual and collective processes in the construction of the self: Self-enhancement in the United States and self-criticism in Japan. *Journal of Personality and Social Psychology, 72*, 1245–67.

Kondo, D. (1990). *Crafting selves: Power, gender, and discourses of identity in a Japanese workplace*. Chicago: University of Chicago Press.

Kuhn, T. (1962). *The structure of scientific revolutions*. Chicago: University of Chicago Press.

Lebra, T. S. (1976). *Japanese pattern of behavior*. Honolulu: University of Hawaii Press.

LeVine, R. A. (1982). *Culture behavior and personality*. New York: Aldine.

Lindholm, C. (1997). Does the sociocentric self exist? Reflections on Markus and Kitayama's "culture and the self." *Journal of Anthropological Research, 53*, 405–22.

Lutz, C. (1988). *Unnatural emotions: Everyday sentiments on Micronesian Atoll and their challenge to Western theory*. Chicago: University of Chicago Press.

Markus, H. R., & Kitayama, S. (1991). Culture and the self: Implications for cognition, emotion, and motivation. *Psychological Review, 98*, 224–53.

Overman, S. E. (1988). Interpretive social science. In S. E. Overman (Ed.), *Methodology and epistemology for social sciences: Selected Papers* (pp. 335–6). Chicago: University of Chicago Press.

Pelzel, J. C. (1974). Human nature in the Japanese myths. In T. S. Lebra & W. P. Lebra (Eds.), In *Japanese culture and behavior* (pp. 7–28). Honolulu: University of Hawaii Press.

Seagal, M. H., Campbell, D. T., & Herskovits, M. J. (1966). *The influence of culture on visual perception*. New York: Bobbs-Merril.

Shimizu, H. (1993a). Adolescents in a Japanese school: *An ethnographic approach to achievement, morality, and behavioral inhibition*. Unpublished doctoral dissertation, Harvard University, Cambridge, MA.

Shimizu, H. (1993b). *Unpublished questionnaire data*. Harvard Graduate School of Education, Harvard University, Cambridge, MA.

Shweder, R. A., Goodnow, J., Hatano, G., LeVine, R. A., Markus, H., & Miller, P. (1998). The cultural psychology of development: One mind, many mentalities. In R. M. Lerner (Ed.), W. Damon (Series Ed.), *Handbook of Child Psychology, Vol. 1: Theoretical models of human development* (5th ed., pp. 865–937). New York: John Wiley & Sons.

Spiro, M. (1984). Some reflections on cultural determinism and relativism with special reference to emotion and reason. In R. A. & R. A. LeVine (Eds.), *Culture theory: Essays on mind, self and emotion* (pp. 323–46). Cambridge: Cambridge University Press.

Spiro, M. (1993). Is the Western conception of the self "peculiar" within the context of the world cultures? *Ethos, 21,* 107–53.

Stigler, J. W., Shweder, R. A., & Herdt, G. (1990). *Cultural psychology: Essays on comparative human development.* New York: Cambridge University Press.

Wierzbicka, A. (1992). *Semantics, culture and cognition: Universal human concepts in culture-specific configurations.* New York: Oxford University Press.

Wierzbicka, A. (1993). A conceptual basis for cultural psychology. *Ethos, 21,* 205–31.

Wierzbicka, A. (1996). Japanese cultural scripts: Cultural psychology, and "cultural grammar." *Ethos, 24,* 527–55.

PART I

MORAL SCRIPTS AND REASONING

ONE

Moral Scripts

A U.S.–Japan Comparison

Hiroshi Azuma[1]

INTRODUCTION

In the contemporary world, international tensions arising from conflicting practical interests are often moralized as oppositions between good and evil. The Japanese, for example (and possibly Asians more generally; see Miller, Bersoff, & Harwood, 1990), tend to place more importance on personal relationships than Americans and West Europeans, even in the transactions between large industrial firms and their subcontractors. A firm fosters close relationships with a few subcontractors, giving them priority. The subcontractors in turn will try to satisfy the requests of that firm, sometimes even sacrificing their own profits. During Japan's feudal period, which covered the seventeenth, eighteenth, and most of the nineteenth centuries, Japan was isolated from the outside world, and the social and geographical mobility of people was restricted. However one may judge the policies of the Shogun government, it must be acknowledged that there was no warfare during this period, Japan's literacy rate was among the highest in the world, and the threat of starvation and disease was lower than in most countries at the time. In that historical context, ingroup ties were strengthened and customary practices reinforced. Changing a longstanding partner for immediate profit was considered unethical and a threat to social stability. To deal only with loyal subcontractors was seen as a moral as well as

---

[1] Three major studies in this article were conducted in collaboration with: David Crystal (information-request study), Mayumi Karasawa (information-request interview and information generation interview), Christine Yeh (information generation interview), Mari Mashima (information generation interview and effort and time perspective interview), and Lauren Shapiro (effort and time perspective interview).

practical necessity. Of course such practices block the entry of new firms, including foreign subcontractors, to the market, and from the point of view of Anglo-American free-market ideology, they are unfair. By the later decades of the twentieth century, the globalization of trade brought Japanese and American concepts of fair trading practice into conflict with each other in both moral and material terms. In the moralization of economic conflict, one party stigmatizes the other as "bad," and hostility between nations can arise. Thus, the cross-cultural study of moral judgment is important, not only for academic theories but also for coping with social conflicts expectable in the coming century of further globalization.

I shall not attempt a philosophical analysis of morality, as philosophical positions on this subject tend to be derived from longstanding traditions (Judeo-Christian, Confucian, and so forth) that are themselves culturally biased. For the same reason I will not start with a comparison of moral codes. Murder, theft, betrayal, and adultery are considered immoral in most known culture of the world, but what is regarded as murder, theft, betrayal, or adultery varies from culture to culture. Moral judgment in this chapter, therefore, simply stands for any person's evaluation of any human act on the person's bipolar scale of good and bad. Perhaps morality in this sense can be traced to the biology of the human as a social animal, and so its deep bases might be universal. Explicit moral judgments, however, are culturally shaped, and the cross-cultural comparison of moral judgment reveals that different cultures foster different moralities.

When judged by moral standards prevalent in the United States, some Japanese moral concepts are questionable. Japanese feudalism was successful and stable for the more than 250 years of the Tokugawa Shogunate, which involved an elaborate role hierarchy. A person was expected to fit into the role assigned to him rather than choosing or creating his own role. Everyone was assigned to a social role, and his or her welfare depended on loyalty to the requirements of that role. There is a Japanese phrase, *"rashiku-suru,"* which means to behave in accordance with the pattern expected of a person in that role or position. For example, the "student *rashiku-suru*" was to behave, to talk, and to be dressed in the manner expected of a good student. When the student later became a bureaucrat, he was supposed to behave not like a student or a businessman but like a man with governmental responsibility. As long as one behaved in accordance with his or her role expectations, there was the assurance of a place in society.

The role perfectionism or receptive diligence of persons under these conditions fostered an aversion to standing out among others in a group that has often been observed among contemporary Japanese. A true story will illustrate this aversion. An American was appointed the new principal of a Catholic mission high school in northern Japan. She decided to honor "the best student of the month" based on good conduct, scholastic achievement, and popularity among friends, and to post the award winner's name on the bulletin board. This caused a panic among the good students because it meant they would have to stand out. When the practice began, one of the good conduct winners cried, repeating "It's unfair, we all did it together." Soon the practice was discontinued because the nominees were so unhappy. But another practice seemingly similar to this, the practice of nominating a head for each class, created no such problem. It was an assignment to a responsible leadership role with a stable position in the role structure of a class, not just the singling out a person from peers in the same role. Role-based security is at least as important for the Japanese as achieving an individual goal. This orientation significantly influences Japanese concepts of appropriate behavior and the work ethic. The United States has been a land of free mobility and open competition throughout the three centuries when Japan was under feudal isolation. Standing out and stepping out to attain achievement goals and accept public recognition had (and continues to have) positive meaning for Americans, but not always so in Japan (Weisz, Rothbaum, & Blackburn, 1984). Many other examples could be given. But our present concern is how social norms become personal moral judgments.

I propose the following theory: Culture influences moral judgment through stories and scripts that act as prototypes for the ways in which events would be morally relevant. Moral judgments is applicable to the conducts embedded in the stories composed around those scripts. Each culture is a reservoir of varied stories and scripts. Cross-cultural variations in moral judgment can at least partly be attributed to difference in the differences in the contents, structures, and accessibility of such scripts stored in the culture.

I shall deal primarily with the United States and Japan because I want to compare cultures that represent drastically different sociocultural traditions with minimal confounding of standard of living, education, and industry. The United States and Japan satisfy those requirements (Azuma, 1986). There are a few studies that have demonstrated differences between Americans and Japanese in their moral judgment using Kohlberg's moral dilemma story completions. Yamagishi has pointed out that Kohlberg's conventional stage starts earlier among Japanese than Americans, but the shift to the postconventional stage is later (A. Yamagishi, 1985). Iwasa (1989, 1992, this volume) has found that Japanese are not satisfied that the protagonist of Kohlberg's most prominent moral dilemma did everything possible before deciding to steal, and they suggested other measures that might have been tried first.

National characteristics, however, are omnibus surrogate variables. A cross-national comparison does not pinpoint the particular dimension of a culture that might explain observed differences in a behavioral domain (Cole, 1996). Several intervening concepts have been proposed to explain gross national differences in behavioral data between two countries. These are reviewed in the following section.

CONCEPTUAL ISSUES

In recent cross-cultural studies, the most frequent concept used to differentiate the East and the West, Asia and the West, the United States and Japan, has been the individualism–collectivism dichotomy (see Shimizu, Chapter 7, this volume). In discussing moral diversity, it is an easy temptation to explain the difference in terms of Japanese collectivism versus American individualism. Dating back to Ruth Benedict (Benedict, 1946), this dichotomy was prevalent in psychological comparison of the United States and Japan, perhaps because this distinction had a good deal of face validity. It seemed to fit observed differences in social behavior. Without further elaboration, however, the concept risks being a tautology: People behave collectivist-wise because their society is collective. Furthermore, there are various definitions given to collectivism. In a study comparing subjects from Hawaii, other parts of the United States, Australia, Japan, and Korea, Japan was high on collectivism, defined as the priority placed on group interest over personal interest, but was the lowest on the relatedness scale that is usually seen as another measure of collectivism (Kashima et al., 1995). The concept of collectivism tends to lump together virtually all cultures not characterized by Western individualism but that are heterogeneous in other respects. Individualism derives from ancient roots in the West, developing in a long and particular history that involved monotheistic religion, the Renaissance, capitalism, colonial development, and humanism. The "collectivist" societies of the world have a myriad of different histories. Thus, collectivism as a concept is negatively and poorly defined. Definitions in terms of bipolar scales did not show clear U.S.–Japan difference (Takano, 1999). Everyone has both the desire to be harmonious with others and to act as an individual (Rothbaum, Pott, Azuma, Miyake, & Weisz, 2000; Shimizu, Chapter 7, this volume). Easy dichotomization of the population is thus misleading. It seems more likely that collectivism and individualism as abstract concepts are dimensions of all cultures than that they are polar opposites. The distinction, nevertheless, has heuristic value in inspiring further thinking.

Markus and Kitayama's (1991, 1994) work uses the concept of self as an intervening variable between the individualism–collectivism dichotomy and various observed differences in behavioral variables. The concept of self that is likely to develop in an independent cultur is to think oneself to be a unique, self-sufficient entity that is clearly separated from others. The collectivist society, by contrast, would foster an interdependent construal of self that conceptualizes oneself to involve people who are close to the person. Assuming there is this basic difference in the concept of one's self, the authors have shown that it can account for a number of observed U.S.–Japan (or sometimes other Asian cultures) differences in behavior, including moral thoughts.

The advantage of this approach is that a psychological construct intervenes between culture and behavior. Instead of connecting cultural differences of behavior directly to differences in the whole culture and becoming trapped in a tautology, behavioral differences are interrelated with self-construals. Markus and Kitayama did not propose a dichotomous classification of cultures. No culture is limited to one kind of self-construal. And very few people will maintain one kind of self-construal throughout many different occasions. Two self-construals may be thought of as poles of a continuum along which people and cultures are plotted rather than as dichotomous categories. The problem of why and how different self-construals are formed in different cultures, however, still needs clarification. The construct validation of self-construals, also, will require a number of stepping stones that intervene between self-construals and behavior.

Another conceptual approach was taken by Yamagishi and Yamagishi (1994). Their dependent variable was general trust. It might be expected intuitively that collectivists would be more trusting than individualists, hence Japanese more than Americans. The result of a U.S.–Japan comparison made by the Yamagishis on general trust, however, showed just the opposite. They begin with the apparent paradox that the individualistic Americans are more trusting of other people in general than the collectivist Japanese. To explain it, they offer a socioeconomic theory of trust. They distinguish a "trust" society from an "assurance" society; the former is a society in which individuals are separate and can move freely, while the latter is one tied together by the mutual commitment of its members. This seems like a reformulation of individualism and collectivism, but the Yamagishis explain why the two dimensions are distinct. An ancient village or a closed fraternal guild exemplifies an assurance society. In such a society, there is no need to trust the individuals one is dealing with. Regardless of the personality and motivation of individuals, they will act appropriately in relation to another group member because of the ties of mutual commitment. One may be a thief outside of the village but never steal from fellow villagers. The world is full of risk and uncertainty, but one can be secure because of this confidence. The assurance society provides reduced uncertainty and anxiety. But it also means giving up the opportunity to profit from transactions with people outside of the circle of mutual commitment, where assurance does not prevail. In a trust society, where one deals with individuals without the guarantee of mutual commitment, it is necessary to believe that people in general are good, honest, and law-abiding within a framework of laws. General trust is required to engage in transactions in an individualistic society; it serves as the device for uncertainty reduction.

The Yamagishis argue that Japanese society is, relatively speaking, an assurance society compared with the United States. Americans have no communal assurance but rely upon their belief that people are not so bad and that laws will be observed by everyone; thus, transactions will be secure. In Japan, the feudalistic reign continued until the latter part of the nineteenth century, under which social and geographical mobility of the people was quite limited. In the United States, people have come from abroad to seek outside opportunities or freedom and did not form a feudal society. Thus, the Yamagishis account for the differential responses of Japanese and Americans to a trust scale by reference to social structural conditions. They avoid psychological intervening concepts. Yet, the question about the concept of assurance versus trust societies is what it predicts beside the trust score. We can make logical inferences but need empirical data.

In this chapter, I shall focus on socioculturally acquired scripts of how moral events take place and proceed, which hopefully is more tangible than deep-seated construals and broadly defined socioeconomical characteristics of the society. I propose a set of stepping stones, consisting of the scripts stored in a culture (cultural store of scripts), scripts stored in the mind of an individual (personal store of scripts), and the production of a story on which the moral judgment is based. A person will form within himself a large store of personal scripts acquired through the assimilation of his experiences and his exposure to cultural scripts. In making a moral judgment, he needs to have a story in which the moral act in question is embedded. Because a good story is not ready at hand on most occasions, he needs to produce a story. For this production, personal scripts will be scanned and the one that fits best to known circumstances and constraints will be activated. Thus, the distribution of scripts and the accessibility of each script in the personal store will influence the result of moral judgment.

Cultural scripts are differently distributed across human populations, but with a good deal of overlap. Different individuals sample and assimilate different subsets of their own cultural store, and in this modern world most people have assimilated samples from other cultural stores as well. We will look first into a few salient features of the Japanese cultural store of scripts.

STORIES REVEALING MORAL JUDGMENT

To compare the stories in which Japanese and American moral judgments are embedded, we need an elicitation procedure in which participants can seek and create the contexts of moral judgment rather than the heavily prestructured Kohlberg moral dilemmas. The process of moral judgment starts with receiving some kind of information about a morally relevant act or a moral event. The first step is to comprehend the information in temporal terms. What preceded and what followed the core event are as important as the core event itself. The antecedents to the event, the core event, and its consequences constitute a prototypical story. Comprehension of an event presupposes the availability or a construction of a plausible story (Bruner, 1990, p. 49).

The same event can be judged differently in differing contexts. In criminal courts, the prosecutor and the defense attorney try to convince the jury of different stories based on the same evidence. The story organizes the evidence and background in time and space. It is the story that provides a basis for a moral judgment. The frameworks for moral stories are the generalized knowledge as to how and in what context moral acts take place and what will follow after the moral event. This knowledge will usually be stored in person's mind in the form of prototypical stories, which we call moral scripts.

Certain features of moral scripts must be universal, or at least recurrent, all over the world, but other features vary across cultures and persons, reflecting differences in cultural meanings and personal experiences. The moral evaluation of a deviant act will depend on the story in which the act is embedded and hence on the moral script activated in an attempt to understand the act. A lie is bad in any culture. But it is possible to place the lying in the context of a sympathetic story or in an unsympathetic story. Cross-cultural differences in the repertory of moral scripts will lead to differences in how a deviant act is evaluated.

Every person has stored an enormous number of stories, synopses, and scripts that can be activated to comprehend events. Every culture is also a rich store of scripts and stories. Individuals learn them through peers, parents, instruction in school, reading material, other media, and daily observational learning. These sources of learning are parts of culture and provide the scripts specific to the given culture.

Television mysteries can illustrate this point. In them, the detective eventually catches the criminal. American programs almost usually end at that point, and the criminal is taken to jail or killed. In Japan, the program continues ten more minutes. The criminal starts talking, often in dialogue with the detective or a potential victim, telling of the frustrations in the hard life he has had, the depth of his painful resentment, or a trace of conscience that restrained him from committing further crimes, and he apologizes. The detective shakes hands with him and encourages him to start a new life when he finishes his prison term. The cultural difference reflects the differences in beliefs concerning what motivates crimes, who commits crimes, and what follows – in other words, the script of crime stories.

Findings from more structured assessments also suggest that the moral stories to which Japanese are exposed daily are different from American stories. As part of a cross-cultural research project codirected by Hess and Azuma (see Azuma, 1996), Japanese and American mothers of three-year-old and eight-month-old children were asked to imagine that their children were misbehaving, and asked to tell what they would say to control it (Conroy et al., 1980). Examples of bad behavior were: refusing to eat a vegetable dish served by the mother, painting on a wall, throwing a block at another child, and so on. The reasons mothers gave to get children to comply were coded into categories. Although 62% of American mothers appealed to status and rule, only 31% of Japanese mothers did so. Japanese mothers, by contrast, made attempts to suggest unwelcome consequences, most frequently psychological harm to self or others. They reported saying, "You will get ill if you don't eat the vegetables, and you will be lonesome if you cannot play with your friends"; "The farmers who raised the vegetables will be disappointed"; "The wall will hate to be painted and will cry"; and so on. Some 53% of the Japanese mothers appealed to feelings or consequences in this way, whereas only 30% of American mothers did (Table 1.1).

These findings suggest that Japanese and American children are socialized to evaluate morally problematic acts with reference to different story schemata. Other studies have found similar or consistent results. For example, Imai (1990) compared the contents of American and Japanese elementary school reading texts. In Japanese readers, the percentage of reference to warm interpersonal relationships was twice as large as the corresponding figure of the United States. Mention of social justice, self-assertion, and strong will was frequent in American readers and close to zero in Japanese readers. Tomo, Mashima, and Nomoto (1998) also compared British and Japanese elementary school language textbooks and found differences in moral priorities, behavior expected of people in different roles,

Table 1.1. *The bases of maternal appeals for the child's compliance*

	Authority	Rule	Feeling	Consequences
Japan	17.5	13.6	21.9	30.6
United States	45.6	16.9	7.9	22.3

and so on. The most striking difference was found in the attitude of the protagonist of the story toward an outside intervention such as a reprimand or critical comment. Its willing reception was found in 35% of British and 64% of Japanese stories. Moriya (1989) has also shown that the same story is differently contextualized and moralized by Japanese and Scandinavian children. Takahashi (1999) compared American and Japanese TV version of a Dutch story for children, "A Boy of Flanders." The American and Japanese versions deviate from the Dutch story in opposite directions. In the Japanese version, the boy is pictured as a nice, sweet, honest, and sympathetic person more than in the original. The American version also portrays him in positive terms, but he is sometimes cunning, and an episode in the original version that tells of the boy's honesty is dropped. The original theme of the story is the love and suffering of a triad consisting of the boy, an old man, and a dog, all of whom die by the end. The Japanese version follows this theme and concentrates more on empathy inducing scenes. The American version ends as a success story for the boy.

These findings indicate U.S.–Japan differences in the cultural stores of scripts. Cross-cultural variations in the repertory of moral scripts cause differences in the likelihood that one of them will be activated under given circumstances. This in turn will cause cross-cultural difference in the way a deviant act tends to be evaluated, even if two cultures share the same set of moral norms. Thus, the stories by which a moral act is comprehended differs characteristically between the two cultures in the theme, synopsis, and the logic that govern the flow of the events.

A number of studies have demonstrated cross-cultural differences in responses to a moral story (Miller, Bersoff, & Harwood, 1990; Yamagishi, 1985). The differences have been attributed to cultural variations in moral maturity, behavior norms, values, self-concepts (Markus & Kitayama, 1991), or to environments such as economic systems (Yamagishi & Yamagishi, 1994). Missing, however, were the stories that act as the proximal conditions generating differences in judgment. In this chapter, I will identify some culturally differentiated moral scripts that affect the production of stories on which judgments are based.

CONTENTS NEEDED FOR A MORAL STORY

In seeking the stories American and Japanese students generate in their
moral judgment, we avoided using structured stimuli like Kohlberg moral
dilemmas or moral development questionnaires, which restrict variability
in the stories.

Instead, we devised three methods. The first study was intended to find
out the materials participants need to construct a moral story, and used
what may be called the information-request method. Participants were presented with a number of skeletal description of deviant acts committed by
unidentified persons, which we will call core events. The second study was
to see how participants constructed a full story from partial information by
their imagination, using a story completion method in which, after the presentation of a core event, the participants were asked to make a complete
story creating descriptions of what preceded and what followed.

In each study, more than one hundred university students in the Tokyo
area and a comparable number of university students in the United States
participated. The number of male and female students was balanced, and
universities of various academic standing were represented. Interviewers
in both countries were graduate students in psychology or sociology.

The first study was designed and conducted during 1987–88. Each participant was interviewed individually, reading brief scenarios with skeletal
information about a morally dubious act (core event). An example is "Student D purposely injured teacher B." From a list of available information,
they were then asked to report what additional contextual information they
would need in order to make a moral judgment. Scenarios covered four areas: violence, lying, breaking laws and rules, and breaking promises. Here
we use data from the violence scenarios as examples. Data from other scenarios are similar in many important respects and the complete writeup is
under way.

After hearing a scenario, participants were asked to rate the protagonist's behavior on a six-point scale ranging from criminal (1) to absolutely
nothing wrong with it (6). They were then presented with a list of fourteen
questions related to various aspects of the scenario, such as the age, motivation, and feelings of the protagonist both during and after the action. As
an example, the list of questions used in the aggression scenario was as follows: Imagine you hear that student D purposely injured teacher E.

1. How old was D?
2. Has D ever done this kind of thing before?
3. What was the result of this action for D him/herself?

4. Generally, how was this action viewed by society?
5. How does D feel about the action now?
6. Why did D injure teacher E?
7. How long did D think about injuring teacher E before doing it?
8. What kind of home/family was D brought up in?
9. How badly was teacher E injured?
10. What were the social consequences of this action?
11. What kind of personality/social relationships does D have?
12. How did D feel at the time of the action?
13. Is D male or female?
14. What specific event led D to injure teacher E?

Participants were then asked to indicate which questions they needed to have answered in order to make a fair and accurate judgment in the situation. They were told they could choose as many questions as they wished. After making their choices, they were then asked to identify and rank-order five questions from among those chosen that they considered most important and give reasons for their first three choices. Finally, they were shown index cards one at a time on which were written the answers to the questions they had picked. After the presentation of each index card, students were asked how they would rate the protagonist's action, knowing this new piece of information. Changes in moral judgment were recorded. Each time the participant made a rating, the interviewer asked the reason for that rating.

Questions 5 (feeling at the time of the offense), 6 (motivation), and 7 (premeditation) were branched questions. For each of them, two different answers were prepared and assigned randomly to subjects who asked for this information. One of the two was an answer that would show the action in less objectionable light, whereas the other was the information that would show the action in more objectionable light. For example, in the cheating scenario, one answer to Question 7 (premeditation) was that the protagonist had no intention of cheating until he/she just happened to see another student's answer, whereas the other was that he/she prepared a crib sheet the night before. With the other eleven questions, the answers were identical for all subjects.

U.S.–JAPAN COMPARISON OF THE TYPE OF REQUESTED INFORMATION

The most visible finding from this information-request study was a cultural difference in the distribution of requested information. For each question,

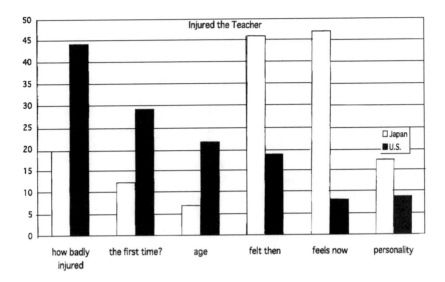

its percentage of being chosen as one of the first three choices was compared. Questions related to affective states, objective facts, and measurable consequences were the ones in which the two cultures clearly diverged. Figure 1.1 shows the frequency of choice for each information item among the most important top three in response to the aggression scenario. The responses for other scenarios paralleled to this one.

A higher percentage of Japanese than American students chose the questions related to emotional states as being among the three most important pieces of information in all three scenarios. An opposite tendency was found with respect to information related to objective facts and measurable consequences. More American than Japanese students ranked this type of information among their first three choices.

CHANGES IN MORAL JUDGMENT

Another notable cross-national difference was that Japanese tended to rate the objectionability of a given act more moderately than the Americans. This tendency was particularly marked with the ratings made during the earlier stage of question asking. As information accumulated through successive questions answered, the difference narrowed but did not disappear.

Perhaps the lack of information led the Americans to make the categorical judgment such as "violence is bad." But as more background was disclosed, the initial categorical judgment was moderated by taking in information that put the protagonist in a more favorable light. Japanese, by contrast, started with an assumption that there could have been a good reason for the action, and shifted the ratings down as some of the answers did not leave room for such a sympathetic assumption. The responses to branched questions provided a good support for this hypothesis. One of the two alternative answers would induce sympathy or understanding of the subjects (e.g., cheating on the spur of the moment), whereas the other would make them less sympathetic (e.g., cheating premeditatingly).

If our hypothesis was correct, the Japanese should change judgments more often when the answer was less sympathetic to the protagonist, because the possibility of the presence of a more acceptable reason had already been accounted for by the initial moderate judgment. Americans, by contrast, would respond more to sympathetic answers as their initial judgment of the core event under without further information tended to be categorical black or white.

The results confirmed our hypothesis. When the answer was an unsympathetic one, Japanese needed to change the judgment they had given to the core event. Their mean rating dropped significantly toward a more objectionable judgment. It remained almost unchanged when the answer gave a permissible context, as it had already been expected and exerted its influence on the initial decision. The American ratings, however, shifted toward the better end of the scale when the answer was sympathetic and stayed unchanged when the answer gave an unsympathetic context. The core event had been deemed morally questionable at best and, therefore, "bad" when categorically judged. Thus, the American participants started with a negative view that gave the force of novelty to ameliorating information about the protagonist.

Another direct test of the hypothesis was provided by reasons the subjects gave for their initial (uninformed) judgment. Nearly half of Japanese said that they moderated their judgment at least once, because they did not have information sufficient to condemn the protagonist. Americans also noted the insufficiency of information, but this knowledge seem to drive them toward a categorical decision. To condemn someone prematurely without sufficient justification is inappropriate everywhere, but it is especially so in a relationship-oriented culture in which interpersonal ties assume priority and being sympathetic to others is a moral imperative. One way to avoid this is to withhold definitive judgment until a detailed story is available and to fill the empty context with a vaguely sympathetic expectation.

In other words, the Japanese subjects tentatively thought there was a possibility that the protagonist had a good reason for the inappropriate act and adjusted their judgments for that possibility to avoid making false accusations. Americans generally assumed that an evil act was based on an evil mind, and the fact that the protagonist acted inappropriately made them less sympathetic to him. The story anticipated by the same information of the core event differed between the United States and Japan, and that resulted in a different interpretation of the event. With such cross-cultural variation in stories based on contrasting story environments, we may well assume that the Japanese stories and American stories had different scripts.

The prevalent response pattern among the American subjects may be characterized as fact-centered, categorical, and axiom-based. It resembles a courtroom decision process that is fact-centered, categorical, and axiom-based. We will call the knowledge about courtroom reasoning procedures the courtroom script. The pattern prevalent among Japanese was different. They are feeling-centered, tentatively generating information sympathetic to the protagonist, and much less axiomatic. This is the orientation we have when dealing with wrongdoing committed by a family member or close friend. The knowledge about how people reason about the objectionable act of a family member will be called the family script. Both courtroom and family scripts are shared across the two countries. Our results suggest, however, that the courtroom script is more accessible to the majority of Americans, and the family script is more accessible to most of the Japanese.

HOW CONTENTS ARE ARRANGED INTO A STORY

The information-request study has shown that respondents often use their imaginations to fill the empty slots of their script. Because their responses were constrained by prearranged questions, however, only the retrospective reports suggested this. In order to assess the moral script, it is necessary to look directly into the imagined stories that would have been constructed with a cultural moral script as a frame. In the next study, we asked our subjects to create an imagined story around the core event.

This study employed a story completion method designed during 1993–94. Participants were asked to create contexts for a given core event, examples being "Susan lies to her mother about a recent grade on an important final exam," "Jeff makes a fist and hits his friend Don in the jaw," "Some of Julie's friends are talking about her behind her back," and so on.

After the presentation of a core event, participants were asked to make up a full story by generating the action that preceded the core event and that which followed it. Subjects were again college level students in the California Bay area and the Tokyo area. Sixty American and sixty Japanese, divided equally by males and females, participated and were individually interviewed. Following a demographic interview, the participant was shown a sentence as a "core event" and was instructed to "Please write 1–3 lines before and after each sentence to create a more complete story. Write what you believe most likely happened in each situation." The same process was repeated for the other core events. After writing all the stories, participants were asked to rate how bad each core event was.

The difference between American and Japanese subjects in this rating was statistically significant only with betrayal and aggression scenarios. Americans rated aggression to be more objectionable and Japanese rated betrayal to be more so. With other scenarios, too, there was a tendency among the Americans to judge offenses against general norms to be more objectionable and among Japanese to judge offenses against interpersonal friendship to be more serious.

The theme and contents of completed stories were coded by a coding system jointly developed by the cross-cultural group. When there was any disagreement between coders in category placement, categories were reconsidered and revised until a perfect consensus was attained. Table 1.2 shows some of the coding categories we have used.

As might be expected from the results of the information request study, Japanese stories were relationship-oriented and mentioned feelings more often than the American stories. With Susan's lie as the core, 45% of Japanese stories were coded as relationship-oriented. Only 17% of American stories also fell in this category. Seventy-five percent of Japanese and 45% of Americans mentioned Susan's feelings, and 40% of Japanese and 17% of American stories mentioned the feelings of the mother. Forty-five percent of the Japanese and 30% of the American stories ended with the relationship between Susan and mother improved. The same tendency was highly consistent through different scenarios. Even with the violence scenario of Jeff hitting Don, 24% of Japanese and only 5% of Americans concluded their story with an improved relationship between Jeff and Don. For example, a number of Japanese stories assumed that Jeff intended to correct Don's bad habit and that the friendship between the two became closer afterwards, as Don was thankful for this friendly concern. Thus, Japanese were more likely to end the story by reconciliation or restored interpersonal harmony.

Table 1.2. *Coding Categories.*

1. Relation orientedness.	Each story was rated if it was fairly concerned with the relationship between the protagonist and the other party.
2. Sympathetic presentation.	Whether the protagonist was described sympathetically or not.
3. Feelings 1.	If the feeling or emotion of the protagonist is described.
4. Feelings 2.	If the feeling or emotion of the other party is described.
6. Relationship at the beginning of the story.	Whether two actors of the story were in good relationship before the core event happened.
7. Relationship at the end.	Whether the restoration of a good relationship between two actors was suggested.
8. Cause.	Whether there was a description of the event, emotion, or act as the cause for the situation that led to the moral act. For example, having not studied as the cause for a bad grade or a long-standing resentment as the cause of a fight.

The Japanese also tended to give more sympathetic descriptions of the protagonist. With Susan's lie scenario, for instance, Susan was very often described to be well intended, hardworking, or filial. For example, one of the Japanese stories assumed that Susan's mother had heart disease and she wanted to protect her mother from a sudden shock. Another said that Susan got good grades but lied about that because of her modesty.

ANALYSIS OF STORY STRUCTURES

The percentage differences discussed above are consistent with the results of the information-request study and other related studies: The Japanese, in comparison with Americans, pay more attention to relationships and feelings, avoid confrontation, and suspend categorical judgment. An important aspect of produced stories that eludes this comparison is how the stories are structured or sequenced. A few illustrative stories produced around the core of Susan's lie by American and Japanese subjects are quoted below.

American

"Susan disobeyed her mother when she went to a concert on a school night instead of studying for her final exam. She was completely prepared for it, but since she was hung over she ended up flunking her test. So she lied to her mother because she could not admit that her mother was right. But because Susan was such a good student the grade on the final exam was overlooked and her grade for the class was unaffected. So she had a great time at a concert with no retribution. Looks like her mother was wrong."

"Susan has been doing poorly in school and is told that if she doesn't do better she won't be able to go to a certain concert. Susan fails her algebra final, thereby earning a D in the class. She lies to her mother about the grade. She goes to the concert happily, but when her mother receives the report card she realizes what happened and Susan is grounded for the entire summer."

"Susan, if you don't do well in that psychology class, then you are not allowed to go to Hawaii. Of course, Susan did not pay attention to her mother's words and, of course, she failed the exam since she stayed up the night before packing for the trip she had planned for four months now. Who needs psychology when there's Sam and well-tanned men waiting for her."

Japanese

"The result of the final examination was important for Akiko (Susan) as it will affect the selection of the college where she would be accepted. Akiko did reasonably well so far, and this made her mother's expectations expand. But a conflict in her sports club prevented her from studying and she ended up with a poor grade. Since her mother was against the club activity that could interfere with her study, she might forbid further participation in the sports club. So she lied, and her mother's expectation expanded more. At that point, she felt very guilty and confessed the truth, while telling her mother how important the club life was for her. Mother said that she would accept it this time, and Akiko promised to work hard both on club and college entrance."

"Akiko (Susan) wanted a telephone in her apartment. She discussed the matter with her mother and mother told her that she could have one if she earned a good grade in the examination. She worked hard for the exam but the questions were unexpected ones and she did very poorly. So, Akiko lied about the grade. Mother was very pleased and hooked a telephone up in her apartment. But Akiko felt guilty and finally told her mother the truth about the telephone. It was the first and the last of Akiko's use of that telephone."

"Akiko worked hard for the final examination, but earned a poorer grade than she had expected. So she lied, as she did not want to disappoint her mother who was so supportive. But in the bottom of her heart, she felt sorry for having lied."

The American stories are motivation-driven histories of why the protagonist did what he/she did and what happened to satisfy or frustrate his/her need. In American stories, the protagonist often does not feel regret or guilt. Japanese stories, in comparison, are feeling-based histories of relationships until at the end reconciliation or benevolence restores the relationship. Only a few even suggest that the protagonist is punished. These differences in moral stories seem to reflect the moral scripts underlying the stories.

Scripts prescribe how information is interrelated and how the stories are sequentially organized. They reflect a shared belief of how things happen, proceed, and end in a moral story. In order to catch this, we identified five parts of a story. In temporal sequence they are, the initial state, the event that caused the core event happen, the core event, the event that followed the core event, and the consequential state. The content of each part was identified for each story created by our subjects. With Susan's lie story, two patterns were found to account for more than half of the responses in each country. Pattern A characterizes confrontation-oriented stories, and pattern B characterizes good relationship orientation.

An example of confrontation-oriented pattern A runs as follows:

1.	Initial state	Parent's pressure to achieve
2.	Cause of the core	In rebellion, Susan did not prepare
3.	Core event	Poor achievement and Susan lies
4.	After the core event	a) Mother finds out the truth
		b) Mother does not find out the truth
5.	Consequential state	a) Mother angry and Susan rebellious
		b) No problem and Susan has no remorse

An example of a relationship-oriented pattern B runs as follows:

1.	Initial state	Harmonious mother-daughter relations or nothing to tell
2.	Cause of the core event	No mention, poor performance just happened
3.	Core event	Poor achievement and Susan lies
4.	After the core event	a) Mother finds out but forgives
		b) Mother does not find out the truth

5. Consequential state a) Mother understands or consoles Susan
b) Susan confesses in remorse and mother accepts

Out of 60 American respondents, 33 gave the Pattern A stories but only seven gave Pattern B. Pattern A was clearly the mode. By contrast, 22 out of 60 Japanese respondents produced Pattern B stories and 9 produced Pattern A. Pattern B was modal among the Japanese. Note that Pattern A is basically a confrontation approach and Pattern B is a relationship-oriented approach.

EFFORT AND TIME PERSPECTIVE INTERVIEW

One of the impressive differences between the stories by Americans and those by Japanese was that the American protagonists were willful and persistent in pursuing their own needs, whereas the Japanese protagonists were less insistent and more accommodating to situational demands. This difference may be linked to an attitude toward life that affects the quality of a person's basic morality. In order to study this possibility, our third study was conducted.

Participants were given ten minutes to write an answer to each of the following questions: "Recall two or three occasions during the last few months when you worked hard purposefully"; "Assuming that everything goes pretty well, please describe a typical weekday in October twenty years from now. Please describe your whole day. What do you do, what do you think, and what do you feel?"; and "What about seven years from now?"

The answers were coded and analyzed. Among the many significant findings, only those closely related to the present topic will be given. In the answer to the question of purposeful effort, 70% of American answers described success or failure in achieving the purpose. The corresponding figure for the Japanese student was only 28.6%. By contrast, the process of applying effort, that is, how hard the person worked, was described in 81.3% of Japanese stories, while the corresponding figure for American stories was 42.3%.

We call this tendency to be concerned with how the instrumental activity is performed rather than with the achievement of the goal as a process orientation. It contrasts with the American achievement orientation. The process orientation results in vagueness of the image of the future or the goal. This was evident in writing about twenty years from now as well as in seven years from now. Japanese descriptions of a day in the future were vague, abstract, and essentially applicable to a day in the present. For example, "Twenty years from now, I will still be in the job I have, will start to enjoy it, and will live every day with a feeeling of fruitfulness." The Americans had a strong tendency to be concrete and to write about what they would have achieved. In the descriptions of a day twenty years from now, the job the person was engaged was clear in 71.1% of the American responses, while it was clear in only 44.6% of the Japanese responses.

Why are the Japanese more process oriented? One possibility is that a process orientation is the psychosocial residue of a traditional feudal social system. A feudal system is based on the stability of roles a person is expected to take. Rather than seeking to achieve an ambitious goal, one should stick to one's role as a small part of the machine known as society. This set of social expectations favors individual adaptation through role-perfectionism, the tendency to find satisfaction in performing a role perfectly and flawlessly. There was a stable and successful feudal system in Japan until 150 years ago, whereas the United States, as a nation, has never experienced a feudal system. There also is probably a difference between the United States and Japanese students in the story grammar, the normative framework that makes the reader feel that a story is a good story.

CONCLUSIONS

Three studies described above revealed that the process of moral judgment involves active story construction. There are U.S.–Japanese differences in the information people require for making moral judgments and the ways people arrange information into a story. The finding suggests that some features of stories constructed by people of different cultures are related to their difference in actual moral judgments.

In addition to moral judgment, the cultural store of scripts and hence the personal store of scripts affect many other behavior patterns, expectations, judgments, and emotional responses. This approach is different from an explanation in terms of countries or cultures in general, because both cultural and personal scripts are distributed across human populations with a good deal of overlap. The approach used here enables us to see cultural differences as individual variations in the aggregate rather than as a simple, sharp categorical distinction. It also could be used to predict how personal judgments change with the changes in and diffusions of cultural stores of scripts. By appropriately sampling responses, we can observe and infer the cultural store of scripts that generates them. The personal store of scripts may be somewhat harder to assess, but it is accessible to this kind of empirical investigation.

Beyond the post hoc explanations offered here lies the future of moral scripts in a changing world. Rapid progress in international communication is integrating the world into one social unit or network. People share stories and other artifacts the world over, and people interact face to face or by electronic means. Cultural differences in moral judgment may well gradually decrease. Future society will not, should not, and cannot be a closed society like feudalistic Japan. Naive individualism and belief in fair competition will also become obsolete as we have to live on a small planet sharing space and resources. We need moral scripts that integrate confrontation and interdependence. To achieve such a goal requires the study of moral beliefs and moral stories of different cultures and different persons together with actual moral decision-making processes. Cross-cultural comparisons have been criticized on methodological grounds (Cole, 1996). It is true that they have inherent methodological difficulties such as the ambiguities of culture as an independent variable, because each culture may be seen as a unique configuration of many factors. But a clean decisive study is not the only kind of good research. The accumulation of comparative evidence from various social sciences will, with a concerted effort to integrate knowledge, reveal better pathways to the understanding of our own and other cultures.

REFERENCES

Azuma, H. (1986), Why study child development in Japan? In H. Stevenson, H. Azuma, & K. Hakuta (Eds.), *Child development and education in Japan* (pp. 3–12). New York: Freeman.

Azuma, H. (1994). *Nihonjinn no shitsuke to kyouiku* [Socialization and education to become a Japanese]. Tokyo: University of Tokyo Press.

Azuma, H. (1996). Cross-national research on child development: The Hess-Azuma collaboration in retrospect. In D. W. Shwalb & B. J. Shwalb (Eds.), *Japanese child-rearing: Two generations of scholarship* (pp. 220–40). New York: Guilford Press.

Benedict, R. F. (1946). *The chrysanthemum and the sword.* Boston: Houghton Mifflin.

Bruner, J. S. (1990). *Acts of meaning.* Cambridge, MA: Harvard University Press.

Cole, M. (1996). *Cultural psychology: A once and future discipline.* Cambridge, MA: Belknap Press of Harvard University Press.

Conroy, M., Hess, R. D., Azuma, H., & Kashiwagi, K. (1980). Maternal strategies for regulating children's behavior: Japanese and American families. *Journal of Cross-Cultural Psychology, 11*(2), 153–72.

Imai, Y. (1990). *Amerika jin to nihon jin: Kyokasho ga kataru tsuyoi kojin to yasashii ichiin* [Americans and Japanese: Strong individual and tender-minded member told in school textbooks]. Tokyo: Souryu Shuppan.

Iwasa, N. (1989). *Situational considerations in moral judgment: A Japan-United States comparison.* Unpublished doctoral dissertation. Harvard University, Cambridge, MA.

Iwasa, N. (1992). Postconventional reasoning and moral education in Japan. *Journal of Moral Education, 21*, 3–16.

Kashima, Y., Kim, U., Gelfand, M. J., Yamaguchi, S., Choi, S. C., & Yuki, M. (1995). Culture, gender and self: A perspective from individualism-collectivism research. *Journal of Personality and Social Psychology, 69*, 925–37.

Markus, H., & Kitayama, S. (1991). Culture and the self: Implications for cognition, emotion and motivation. *Psychological Review, 98*, 224–53.

Markus, H., & Kitayama, S. (1994). The cultural construction of self and emotion: Implications for social behavior. In S. Kitayama & H. Markus (Eds.), *Emotion and Culture: Empirical studies of mutual influence* (pp. 89–130). Washington, D.C.: American Psychological Association.

Miller, J. G., Bersoff, D. M., & Harwood, R. L. (1990) Perceptions of social responsibilities in India and the United States: Moral imperatives or personal decisions? *Journal of Personality and Social Psychology, 58*, 33–47.

Moriya, K. (1989). A developmental and cross-cultural study of the interpersonal cognition of the English and Japanese children. *Japanese Psychological Research, 31*(3), 108–15.

Rothbaum, F., Pott, M., Azuma, H., Miyake, K., & Weisz, J. (2000). The development of close relationships in Japan and the United States: Paths of symbiotic harmony and generative tension. *Child Development, 71*, 1121–42.

Takano, Y., & Osaka, E. (1999). An unsupported common view: Comparing Japan and the U.S. on individualism-collectivism. *Asian Journal of Psychology, 2*(3), 311–41.

Tomo, R., Mashima, M., & Nomoto, T. (1998). A content analysis of interpersonal coping behavior in Japanese and British primary school textbooks. *Japanese Journal of Educational Psychology, 46*, 95–104.

Takahashi, A. (1999). *Eiga furanda-su no inu no nichibei hikaku: Shudai henyou no bunkateki youin* [U.S.–Japan comparison of the filmed version of "A Boy of Flanders": Cultural factors in the change of theme]. *Research Bulletin of Musashino Women's University, 34*, 117–26.

Weisz, J. R., Rothbaum, F. M., & Blackburn, T. C. (1984). Standing out and standing in: The psychology of control in America and Japan. *American Psychologist, 39*, 955–69.

Yamagishi, A. (1985) *Nihon ni okeru doutoku handan no hattatsu* (The development of moral judgment in Japan). In S. Nagano (Ed.), *Doutokusei no hattatsu to kyouiku* (Education and the development of morality). Tokyo: University of Tokyo Press.

Yamagishi, T., & Yamagishi, M. (1994). Trust and commitment in the United States and Japan. *Motivation and Emotion, 18*, 129–66.

TWO

Moral Reasoning among Adults

Japan–U.S. Comparison[1]

Nobumichi Iwasa

The purpose of the study reported here is to compare development of moral reasonings of Japanese and American adults using the Moral Judgment Interviews techniques. Hypothetical moral dilemmas used in the interview are constructed so as to make the theme of conflicting moral values as clear as possible, and the interviewee presented with such a dilemma is expected to reveal his or her sociomoral perspective and understanding of justice structure in trying to solve it.

Kohlberg, based on his analysis of people's responses, identified six stages of moral development suggesting that these stages are culturally universal and in an invariant sequence (Kohlberg, 1958, 1969, 1976, 1981). He described each stage as follows:

Stage 1	Heteronomous morality
Stage 2	Individualism, instrumental purpose, and exchange
Stage 3	Mutual interpersonal expectations, relationships, and interpersonal conformity
Stage 4	Social system and conscience
Stage 5	Social contract or utility and individual rights
Stage 6	Universal ethical principles

The first two stages are called preconventional level, Stages 3 and 4, conventional level, and Stages 5 and 6 postconventional or principled level. In the new Standard Issue Scoring system, however, Stage 6 was dropped from the scoring manual because of nonexistence of cases in the collected data,

[1] This chapter is based on the author's doctoral dissertation submitted to Harvard University Graduate School of Education in 1989 (Iwasa, 1989).

and transitional Stage 4/5 and Stage 5 are called postconventional level (Colby & Kohlberg, 1987).

Regarding the cultural universality of the stages, Snarey (1982, 1985) made extensive reviews of cross-cultural research literature on moral development by that time, and concluded that the results of all available studies generally supported Kohlberg's hypothesis that moral development occurs through an invariant, upward sequence of hierarchical stages. Some researchers raised questions, however, about the universality of the stages. In addition to the scarcity of higher-stage reasoning, in some cultural areas the ideology underlying the definition of the higher stages became the focus of discussion. Vasudev argues that "the question of what constitutes principled moral thinking remains open and debatable" (Vasudev, 1984, p. 166), and suggests two Indian concepts of nonviolence and of unity of all life as candidates for principles other than justice. Dien (1982) states that Kohlberg's six-stage hierarchy reflects "the idea which derives from Western traditions that man is an autonomous being, free to make his own choices and to determine his own destiny" (p. 333). In China, by contrast, the Confucian conception of morality has been the cultural ideal, of which the nucleus is *Jen*. She explains, "It has been variously translated as 'love,' 'benevolence,' 'human-heartedness,' 'man-to-manness,' 'sympathy,' and 'perfect virtue.' It is basically the deep affection for kin rooted in filial piety and extended through the family circle to all men" (p. 334).

Thus, in a context of cross-cultural research, the conception of postconventional stages become crucial. Kohlberg characterized postconventional stages as adult stages not reached until the late twenties or later, by its "prior-to-society perspective" and more prescriptive and universalizable judgments in comparison with conventional stages, which take a "member-of-society perspective" and try to conform to social rules and expectations. The following quotations, however, show that he was well aware of the cultural diversity of moral development and a necessity of the scoring manual to be more open to reasoning in other cultures:

> It is possible that in other cultures, principles are held which are distinct from ours, and moral reasoning is used that does not fit the structures described by Kohlberg. (Nisan & Kohlberg, 1982, p. 874)

> The scoring manual needs to be fleshed out with culturally indigenous examples of reasoning at the higher stages if it is to avoid missing or misunderstanding the reasoning of subjects from a different cultural background than that of the subjects on which the manual was based. (Kohlberg, 1984, p. 620)

CHARACTERISTICS OF AMERICAN AND JAPANESE CULTURES

When American and Japanese cultures and societies are compared, the former is often characterized by its people's tendency to consider themselves separate and independent from each other, and the latter by its people's tendency to regard themselves as related members of a group.

How ought we to live? How do we think about how to live? Who are we, as Americans? What is our character? These were the questions Bellah and his colleagues asked their fellow Americans when they conducted a penetrating study, "Habits of the Heart," of the American people. In their report of the study, they consider that the most important single characteristic of the American people is individualism. They say: "American cultural traditions define personality, achievement, and the purpose of human life in ways that leave the individual suspended in glorious, but terrifying, isolation" (Bellah, Madsen, Sullivan, Swidler, & Tipton, 1985, p. 6). According to them, such a sense of isolation in American people cannot be overcome even by bonds of marriage and parenthood. To the question of whether she was responsible for her husband, Margaret, one of their interviewees, replied, "I'm not. He makes his own decisions." Asked about children, she said, "I . . . I would say I have a legal responsibilities for them, but in a sense I think they in turn are responsible for their acts" (p.16). Bellah and others' observation is that "everybody likes to get their own way," and, therefore, "the only way to run a relationship is to strive for 'fairness'" (p. 16).

Caudill and Weinstein (1969) summarized different emphasis in the two cultures by saying that "Japanese are more 'group' oriented and interdependent in their relations with others, while Americans are more 'individual' oriented and independent" (p. 14). They found that such different views of individuals and human relationship in the United States and Japan have effects on three- to four-month-old babies (Caudill & Weinstein, 1969). Their cross-cultural study of childrearing patterns in the two countries is considered one of the best evidences that the environments of infancy and early childhood are shaped by cultural values (LeVine, 1977). Caudill (1973), after reanalyzing the above data, states:

> In America, the mother views her baby as a potentially separate and autonomous being who should learn to do and think for himself. For her, the baby is from birth a distinct personality with his own needs and desires which she must learn to recognize and care for. She helps him to learn to express these needs and desires through her emphasis on vocal communication so that he can "tell" her what he wants and she can respond appropriately. . . . In the same way that she thinks of her infant as

> a separate individual, she thinks of herself as a separate person with
> needs and desires which include time apart from her baby so that she may
> pursue her own interests and act as a wife to her husband as well as a
> mother to her baby. (p. 43)

In contrast,

> In Japan the mother views her baby much more as an extension of her-
> self, and psychologically the boundaries between the two of them are
> blurred. The mother feels that she knows what is best for the baby, and
> there is no particular need for him to tell her what he wants because af-
> ter all, they are virtually one. Thus, in Japan, there is a greater emphasis
> on interdependence, rather than independence, of mother and child, and
> this emphasis extends into adulthood. (p. 43)

The emphasis on interdependence, rather than independence, of mother
and child is not limited to that particular relationship in Japan. It not only
extends into adulthood, as Caudill observed, but also into other human relationships. Scholars in various disciplines uniformly stress interpersonal
harmony, collectivism, and so on as characteristic of the Japanese and
Japanese society. For example, Nakamura (1961–62, Eng. tr. 1964) points out
the tendency to emphasize human relationships as characteristic of Japanese thinking. He says, "Due to the stress on social proprieties in Japan another characteristic of its culture appears – the tendency of social relationships to supersede or take precedence over the individual" (p. 409). In this
context, he refers to the elaboration of honorifics in the Japanese language.
From a psychiatric point of view, Doi (1962: 1971, Eng. tr. 1973) explained
Japanese mentality in terms of *amae*, a mentality "to depend and presume
upon another's benevolence" (1962, p. 132). It is not surprising, therefore,
that Japanese people, growing in such a cultural climate, have learned
habits of the heart quite different from those of Americans.

METHODS

The purpose of the present study is to answer the following three research
questions: (a) How do American and Japanese people differ in their response to the Moral Judgment Interview?; (b) How do postconventional
reasoners in the respective countries differ from conventional counterparts?; and (c) How do they differ in their action choice as a response to the
manipulation of situational factors?

All subjects involved in this study were adults over twenty-three years
old, most of them with experience of graduate education at the time of

Table 2.1. *Number of Subjects in the Two Countries*

	Male	Female	Total
United States	31	32	63
Japan	26	26	52

interview or in the past. Most of them were recruited at graduate schools in several universities both in the United States and in Japan. The number of subjects who participated in this study is shown in Table 2.1.

Moral Judgment Interview Form B Dilemmas Used for Stage Scoring

In order to score people's moral judgment stages, Kohlberg's Moral Judgment Interview (MJI) Form B dilemmas were used. They are Dilemma IV (Dr. Jefferson on mercy killing), Dilemma IV' (a judge on Dr. Jefferson's crime), and Dilemma II (Louise on sister's lie to her mother). Their actual stories are given in the Appendix.

The Heinz Dilemma (MJI Form A Dilemma) and Its Situationally Modified Versions

Following the interview with the above Form B dilemmas to identify people's moral stages, the main interview was conducted using Dilemma III (Heinz on stealing a drug for his wife) shown in the Appendix. After presenting the original dilemma and hearing the subject's action choice and his or her reasoning, a series of situationally modified versions were presented in order to see how he or she would respond to the changes of situational factors. There were four modified versions, each version being a combination of two levels in the severity or favorability of the consequence of an action both on the actor and on the other person involved. Key features of the four modified versions, which were labeled Situations 1, 2, 3, and 4, are shown in Table 2.2.

The order of presentation of the first two modified situations was different, depending on people's initial action choice in response to the original dilemma. The modified version presented first was the one most likely to replicate the subject's action choice in the original dilemma, and the next one was the one most likely to change the subject's original action choice. For instance, when a subject's response to the original Heinz dilemma was

Table 2.2. *Combinations of Foreseeable Consequences for the Actor and the Other in the Four Modified Situations*

	If Heinz steals the drug	
modified Situations	**Heinz's wife will live**	**Heinz will be**
Situation 1	for 5 to 10 more years.	free without being discovered.
Situation 2	only for several months.	caught and put in jail for one year.
Situation 3	for 5 to 10 more years.	caught and put in jail for one year.
Situation 4	only for several months.	free without being discovered.

"Heinz should steal the drug," the version first presented was Situation 1, in which predicted consequence was "Heinz's wife will live for five to ten more years, and Heinz himself will be free without being discovered." The next version was Situation 2, in which predicted consequence was "Heinz's wife will live only for several months, and Heinz himself will be caught and put in jail for one year." By contrast, if the subject's original response was "Heinz shouldn't steal," the order of presentation of the above two versions were reversed. That is, Situation 2 first, then Situation 1.

If the subject changed his or her action choice after being exposed to the second version, only then were the third and fourth versions, that is Situations 3 and 4, presented to determine which factor, either the consequence on the actor or the consequence on the other, was decisive in the subject's decision change. Situations 3 and 4 are mixtures of positive and negative consequences on the actor and the other. When the subject didn't change his or her action choice at the second situation, Situations 3 and 4 were not presented.

All interviews were done by the present author in subjects' mother tongue, and were tape-recorded and transcribed.

Stage Scoring

Concerning the American data, the first half, which were obtained two years earlier than the second half, were scored by the author using the Standard Issue Scoring Manual. The second half were scored by an American scorer from the Center for Moral Development and Education of Harvard University. All Japanese interviews were scored by the author partly because of the possibility of losing some important nuances during the translation process as well as the immensity of the translation work, and partly because of the nonavailability of a Japanese scorer experienced with Standard Issue Scoring system.

Interrater reliability between the above-mentioned American scorer and the present author was relatively high. A correlation coefficient between the two scorers for the weighted average scores for ten American interviews was $r = .86$. Although nine-point-scale global scores by the two scorers differed in four cases out of ten, three out of the four different cases were within the same level. That is, only one subject was scored to be conventional by one scorer and postconventional by the other. That subject was scored highest among conventional subjects by one scorer, however, and lowest among postconventional subjects by the other. Because one of the developmentally important distinctions in this study is between conventional and postconventional levels, the difference of this size can be acceptable.

RESULTS

Distribution of Subjects in Terms of Stages

When scored with Standard Issue Scoring Manual using Moral Judgment Interview Form B dilemmas, the number of subjects scored in each stage were as shown in Table 2.3.

Responses to The Heinz (MJI Form A) Dilemma

1. **Action Choices in the Original Dilemma.** The action choices made by subjects are shown in Table 2.4.

Table 2.3. *Number of Subjects in Each Developmental Category*

		United States		Japan	
Level	Stage	Male	Female	Male	Female
	3	1	2	1	1
Conventional	3/4	6	12	5	4
	4	14	12	12	14
Postconventional	4/5	6	4	6	7
	5	4	2	2	0
Total		31	32	26	26

Table 2.4. *Action Choices in the Original Heinz Dilemma*

Action Choice	United States		Japan	
	Conventional	Postconventional	Conventional	Postconventional
Heinz should steal	30	14	21	4
Heinz shouldn't steal	16	2	15	10
Ambiguous	1	0	1	1
Total	47	16	37	15

As can be seen in Table 2.4, there is a marked difference in action choices between the United States and Japan at the postconventional level in the Heinz dilemma (fourteen autonomous and two heteronomous choices in the United States versus four autonomous and ten heteronomous choices in Japan[2]). While American postconventional reasoners had a strong tendency to say, "Heinz should steal the drug," Japanese counterparts tended to choose "Heinz shouldn't steal the drug" alternative. The difference was statistically significant (The Fisher exact probability test, $p = .003$).

2. Consistency and Change of Action Choices as a Response to Changes of Situational Factors in the Dilemma. When subjects were presented with second situations with prospects of consequences totally different from the first situations, some of them changed their action choices and some of them didn't. The number of subjects who did and did not change their action choices in the second situation of the Heinz dilemma are given in Table 2.5.

[2] In Kohlberg's theory, the concept of autonomy as "an independent and self-legislative stance taken in making moral judgments" (Colby and Kohlberg, 1987, p. 315) is important. His distinction between the heteronomous type and autonomous type in moral judgments is derived from the Piagetian distinction between heteronomous morality and autonomous morality in connection with the theories of Baldwin and Kant. Kohlberg and his colleagues have developed a coding scheme for these moral types using the same interview materials as the Standard Issue Scoring for moral stages. There are nine coding criteria on which the heteronomy-autonomy distinction is based, and "choice" is one of them. For example, in the Heinz dilemma, for someone's response to be judged autonomous, its action choice has to be "Heinz should *steal* the drug," because the choice of stealing supports the woman's right to life as opposed to obeying the law. If it chooses "not to steal," the response to the Heinz dilemma is regarded to be of heteronomous type. Thus, the distinction between autonomous and heteronomous types is closely connected with the content aspect of moral judgments.

Table 2.5. *Action Choices in the 1st and 2nd Situations*

Action Choices		United States		Japan	
1st Situation	2nd Situation	Conventional	Postconventional	Conventional	Postconventional
should steal	should steal	10	12	15	3
should steal	shouldn't steal	8	1	6	1
should steal	ambiguous	12	1	0	0
shouldn't steal	shouldn't steal	4	2	13	9
shouldn't steal	should steal	7	0	1	1
should not steal	ambiguous	5	0	1	0
ambiguous	various	1	0	1	1
Total		47	16	37	15

From this table it is clear that most American postconventional reasoners supported Heinz's stealing as morally obligated conduct and kept that choice even in Situation 2, while the overwhelming majority of Japanese post-conventional reasoners were against Heinz' stealing and didn't change that attitude even in the second situation, that is, Situation 1 in this case. This cultural difference of direction of stable action choice was statistically significant (The Fisher exact probability test, $p = .003$). This can pose an important issue in Kohlberg's theory of moral development, and shall be discussed in more detail later. Furthermore, two-thirds of American conventional subjects changed their action choices, but a great majority of Japanese conventional reasoners didn't change their action choices. Again, this result is a little perplexing, and shall be discussed in more detail later. Qualitative analysis of individual moral reasoning is discussed next.

Postconventional Reasoning and Decision Changes by American Subjects

Twelve out of sixteen postconventional reasoners chose autonomous action, or the act of Heinz's stealing, in the original dilemma and their choice remained unchanged in Situation 1 (positive-positive)[3] and Situation 2 (negative-negative). All of them were quick to discern the structure of the dilemma as a conflict between one's right to life and one's right to property. A#55 (F),[4] for example, saw the problem in this situation as "the decision whether or not to steal the drug to save his wife's life as opposed to respecting the property rights of the druggist." A#13 (F) commented, "We've got conflicting rules or issues. One is the sanctity of life, the other is the sanctity of property."

Defining the dilemma as a problem requiring a dichotomous decision between the right to life versus right to property, they uniformly said, "Heinz should steal." Their reasons were clear-cut, like "To protect the life of his wife. Her life supersedes the rights of the druggist. Because the right to life supersedes the right to property" by A#55 (F). Here is another example:

---

3 As shown in Table 2.4, this signifies desirability of foreseeable consequences of the action in question (Heinz's stealing in this case) on the other (his wife) and the actor (Heinz). "Positive-positive" means positive consequences are expected for both, and, therefore, Heinz's stealing is easy to support. In Situation 2 (negative-negative), however, it is more difficult to keep the choice of Heinz's stealing.

4 This means American female interviewee, case #55. Japanese interview cases are identified by a "J" at the beginning.

A#80 (M): Original Situation

WHAT SHOULD HEINZ DO IN THIS SITUATION?
If he's really exhausted every other possible alternatives, then I think he should steal the drug.

WHY SHOULD HE?
Because I think it's a higher moral requirement to save life than to respect the sanctity of property. The sanctity of human life is a higher value than the sanctity of property, although certainly in general property should be respected.

Thus, ten postconventional reasoners further extended Heinz's duty to save life not only to intimate persons but to any human being. To the question, "If Heinz doesn't love his wife, should he steal the drug?," A#13 (F) replied, "I don't think the considerations of the relationship should determine whether or not. . . ." A#9 (M), a Stage 5 reasoner, spelled out the obligation in the following way: "Even if he doesn't love his wife, it's important for him to steal the drug because she is an individual human being, and he has a certain obligation, I think, in terms of generic human type of obligation to prolong. I mean, if it's within his power to prolong her life and there is no other means to obtain it, Yes."

Such a sense of obligation of one human being toward another human being was extended even toward strangers. Asked if Heinz should steal for a dying stranger, A#9 (M) continued to say, "I don't think it really makes that much difference whether it's his wife or (if) he is in love, or just (a stranger). . . . Why? Again, it's a humanitarian moral code type of thing. If it is a situation where you can help someone else live, then you have an obligation, whether it's enemy or friend or whatever, to help them in a way you can."

Because their reasoning was so fundamental, abstract, and universalizable, being based on justice-oriented balancing considerations, their positions in Situation 2 remained unchanged. What follows are several examples of reasons given by postconventional subjects. A#86 (M) said, "I am assuming that this woman is not in pain for those six months or ten years and not requesting to die. I don't think the time is an issue." A#73 (F) said, "Because even if he can prolong his wife's life for six months, he has the need to do that. Because it is possible that in the six months a more powerful drug could be found that would save her life. So, as long as she is alive and conscious, and making decisions for herself, I believe he should steal the drug."

The value of six months of life, much less positive than the five to ten years' prolongation given in Situation 1, was still precious from their point of view. A#13 (F) and A#18 (F) explained this in the following ways.

A#13 (F): Situation 2 (negative-negative)

SHOULD HEINZ STEAL THE DRUG?
Assuming that her life would be prolonged in a good quality of life, then I would say Yes.

WHY?
A year in jail isn't very long compared to six months of life for someone. We value time so much as human beings. We are so aware of when we will die and there is so much joy in every moment of life that those six months could be magnificent treasures.

A#18 (F): Situation 2 (negative-negative)

SHOULD HEINZ STEAL THE DRUG?
I think he should steal the drug. Six months is still six months. And there is always a possibility even though the doctors said six months. . . . Life becomes very precious when it is about to go. And that means that life is only precious when one realizes how important it is for the person to live, even a few days in many cases.

Even six months of life was so precious that A#18 (F) extended Heinz's obligation to steal to strangers, saying, "Yes. The person is not a stranger the minute when you begin to be involved, you begin to care (about) that person."

Thus, postconventional reasoners grasped the problem, on the most fundamental level, as a conflict between one's right to life and a right to property. For them, human life was the source of every human value, and, therefore, the overwhelming priority of right to life was obvious. Once an obligation to save a human life is worked out based on a dichotomous framework, such a formula could be generally applicable to a wide variety of situations. Compared with the precious value of human life, the risk of one year in jail was no problem, and six-month prolongation of life was still of great value. These are the reasons that the postconventional reasoners were not susceptible to change, in spite of the manipulation of utilitarian consequences.

Conventional Reasoning and Decision Changes by American Subjects

Some conventional subjects showed an action choice pattern similar to most postconventional subjects. Ten conventional subjects made autonomous action choices of Heinz's stealing without change, while four made consistent heteronomous choice opposing Heinz's stealing. The former subjects' reasoning had a lot in common with postconventional reasoners, considering the dilemma basically as a conflict between the value of life versus value of law or property, and, therefore, rendering an overwhelming weight on the obligation to save life.

The overwhelming majority of conventional subjects changed their action choices, however, depending on the difference in the favorability or severity of predicted consequences. Thirty-two people changed their action choices either from autonomous choices or from heteronomous choices to other categories of response as opposed to fourteen who didn't.

Following excerpts from A#12 (M)'s response to the Heinz dilemma are an example of a change from autonomous choice to heteronomous choice.

A#12 (M): Original Dilemma

SHOULD HEINZ STEAL THE DRUG?
Yes, he should. Because the druggist is acting like a thief, like a criminal. He's overcharging. He's being unfair. And in this particular case his greed is creating difficulties for someone else.

DOES HEINZ HAVE A RESPONSIBILITY TO STEAL THE DRUG?
Yes, he does.

WHY?
Because his wife is suffering and she might live if the drug is administered. So it's his responsibility to help her sustain her life. And the biggest responsibility we all have is to contribute to the sustenance of life.

IF YOU WERE IN HEINZ'S POSITION, WOULD YOU STEAL?
Yes.

The subject, rather than defining the problem on a fundamental level as a conflict between one's right to life and right to property, as postconventional subjects did, emphasized the druggist's greed and unacceptable behavior for a person in his role and used this as a justification for Heinz's stealing. Although he stressed that it's Heinz's responsibility to steal, the obligation to save a human life was applicable only within the limited range of intimate relationships. The interview continued:

A#12 (M): Original Dilemma

IF HEINZ DOESN'T LOVE HIS WIFE, SHOULD HE STEAL THE DRUG?
If he doesn't love his wife, I don't think he's going to, it's a question of should. I think it's a difficult situation . . . should or shouldn't. Even if he doesn't love her, the fact that they've been married, the fact that he's known her, the

fact that he's spent a significant amount of time and his life with her, it's a question of should, meaning should he risk his freedom, going to jail, in order to prolong the life of someone he doesn't love. Um, I guess if I did not love her, would I do it? Maybe not. I guess not. It would be hard. It would be very hard.

The subject experienced a certain conflict as to whether or not he should follow the role of a husband at the risk of going to jail. His major concern here was conformity to interpersonal roles and expectations. The obligation to save human life, based on such conventional level considerations, was extended to a strangers in Situation 1 because, A#12 (M) said, the woman was "going to live five to ten more years and (the husband is) not going to get caught. No problem." Such utilitarian calculation of positive and negative consequences led the subject to change the autonomous position to a heteronomous one when the predicted consequences were negative for both parties in Situation 2.

A#12 (M): Situation 2 (negative-negative)

SHOULD HEINZ STEAL THE DRUG?
No, because (it is a) trade-off . . . this is a negative balance. You are buying three to six months of her life with one year of yours. And that's not a very equal trade-off.

A#16 (M) is another example of decision changes from an autonomous choice to a heteronomous one. The subject extended Heinz's obligation to steal the drug to include even a stranger. He pointed out the irrelevance of selfish considerations in Situation 1 by saying, "I'm not sure the consequences about whether he gets caught or doesn't get caught are the most important things or are the things that should weigh (in) his decision. But primarily the fact that it will enable his wife to keep living." In Situation 2, the above autonomous choice was reversed to "Heinz shouldn't steal." The reason was that "the benefits of his stealing the drug at that point are pretty negligible. It's not going to make much of a difference if he does it or not."

Such a skeptical evaluation of several months' prolongation of the patient's life was most clearly expressed by A#10 (F). In Situation 2 where the woman's life was predicted to be prolonged only for several months, the subject responded, "No. She's in terminal cancer. That's very painful. I don't. It's more like the first question (the Dr. Jefferson Dilemma or Dilemma IV concerning mercy killing, used for stage scoring). I would not prolong the life in pain." In such cases, the change of action choices was not a response to the consequences for the acting self, but rather, a response to the consequences for the other.

For A#79 (M), the prediction of less favorable consequences on both Heinz and his wife changed the implication of the stealing on their relationship. He said:

A#79 (M): Situation 2 (negative-negative)

SHOULD HEINZ STEAL IN THIS SITUATION?
I think if that is the probable path of events, it seems to me that it would be more important to be with his wife, than to be locked up in jail during that period. And if he was sure that the drug would not permit his wife to live more than six months and he would be in jail for all that, plus more, it would not be in his interests or his wife's interests, to steal the drug.

Next, seven subjects changed from a heteronomous action choice to an autonomous one. They assumed certain negative consequences for Heinz when they said that he should not steal in the original dilemma. In the absence of such negative consequences and also due to the positive consequence on the patient in Situation 1, however, they changed their positions to "Heinz should steal." A#90 (M) is an example of this category:

A#90 (M): Original Dilemma

SHOULD HEINZ STEAL THE DRUG?
No.

WHY NOT?
Because stealing the drug is not only illegal but it's unfair to the druggist.

WHY IS IT UNFAIR TO THE DRUGGIST?
Because the druggist owns it, he made it, and the druggist has the right to dispense it and control it.

A#90: Situation 1 (positive-positive)

SHOULD HEINZ STEAL THE DRUG IN THIS CASE?
If he is not only sure but correct that the druggist will never notice it is gone, . . . then he should steal it .

WHY?
Because the druggist will never miss it, then it will never hurt the druggist.

In all cases, the orientation of conventional reasoners toward conformity to interpersonal roles and social rules made their decisions more susceptible to change. This was due to the fact that these moral criteria were more concrete and narrow in their application and, therefore, allowed more exceptions.

Overall, American subjects, both conventional and postconventional, were quite consistent with Kohlberg's theory and its research framework.

The most outstanding finding from American data is that postconventional subjects were much more stable in their autonomous action choice in spite of the changes in situational factors, while conventional subjects changed their autonomous and heteronomous action choices more frequently as a response to the situational factors.

Kohlberg's research framework requires each to make a dichotomous choice between autonomous values and heteronomous values[5] and to come up with prescriptive judgments.[6] Within this framework, a distinction between postconventional and conventional reasoning is made; the former is a more abstract, fundamental, and universalizable judgment based on the universal value of human life, equal respect for basic human rights, liberty, and autonomy of individuals and so on; the latter, from "a member of society perspective" (as opposed to "prior to society perspective" by the former), makes judgments bound by interpersonal expectations and concrete social rules.

Most of the American subjects, easily accepting the dichotomous framework of the dilemma, balanced the priority of the two values in conflict. Postconventional subjects were quick to grasp the dilemma as, in essence, a conflict between the two abstract values, and in their weighing or balancing process they appealed to universal values such as human life as a central aspect of respect for human worth. Such prescriptive and universalizable judgments were not susceptible to change when exposed to various situational arrangements. By contrast, reasoning by conventional subjects, based on conventional rules and expectations without any abstract universalizable principles, were more susceptible to change.

Indigenous to American society as well as Western liberal tradition, Kohlberg's theory appears to be quite congruent with reasoning by conventional and postconventional subjects as well as their action choice pattern.

Postconventional Reasoning and Decision Changes by Japanese Subjects

As Table 2.5 shows, the stability of action choices by Japanese postconventional subjects to the Heinz dilemma was manifest. The actual content of

---

5 The first MJI question in the Heinz dilemma, for example, asks, "Should Heinz steal the drug for his wife?" expecting a subject to answer Yes or No first, and then to give his or her reason for the choice, instead of asking "What should Heinz do?" The scoring manual also corresponds to the dichotomous structure of the MJI question by arranging Criterion Judgments under two categories: one supporting autonomous value, the other supporting heteronomous value.

6 In the scoring manual, one of the "scorable criteria" for scoring people's interviews is that an interview judgment contains a prescriptive judgment using, for example, "should."

their action choices, however, was opposite in direction to those of American postconventional reasoners. Ten out of fifteen postconventional subjects said, "Heinz shouldn't steal," and nine of them repeated the same response throughout the different versions of the dilemma. Because Kohlberg regarded the "Heinz shouldn't steal" type of choice as "heteronomous" choice, how can this be explained? Are many of Japanese postconventional reasoners heteronomous, or are they reasoning at a conventional level as far as the Heinz dilemma is concerned? Or else, does this suggest a necessity of some reconsideration on the part of Kohlberg's theory?

One outstanding feature in many Japanese postconventional reasoners was that they did not define the dilemma as a problem demanding a dichotomous choice between life and law as most of their American counterparts did. Rather, their decisions were expressions of their understanding that the crux of the moral problem in the Heinz dilemma was how to pursue the way to achieve both values rather than giving up one for the sake of the other. Six postconventional subjects didn't easily accept the assumption that "Heinz tried every legal means, and got desperate" in the original story, and stressed a necessity to take other avenues than stealing. One of them, J#17 (F), being asked what should Heinz do in this dilemma, said, "Since he has tried every measure, he might have nothing other than this (stealing), but I believe that there are still other means he can take, . . . it's too early to take recourse to stealing. I would not steal because I would definitely behave in some other way." They, for example, preferred to use the news media, an appeal to public opinions, fund raising, and so on. Thus, they resisted fitting into the research framework in which respondents are expected to make an "either life or law" choice.

For them, to assume that Heinz exhausted "every legal means" meant, it seems, detachment from the reality of the dilemma, relegating the dilemma situation to a mere arrangement to lead subjects to be engaged in intellectual arguments about the relative importance of life and property or law. Japanese postconventional reasoners, rather, stuck to the realities Heinz was in, and recommended that Heinz seek other positive ways, thus seeking solutions to actualize both alternatives. J#46 (F), even when she was reminded that Heinz thought he had already exhausted every legal means, rejected the option of Heinz's stealing, saying, "Even if he considers that he has tried all available means, other people might be able to suggest other possible measures, and so, he should ask others' opinions, and try, for example, by posters, writing to the media or whatever. . . . Stealing is not right by any means."

Is this sticking to the actual possibilities of other measures just avoidance of confrontation and hard decisions on the part of Japanese postconventional subjects? Again, is this a failure or inflexibility on their part to think within a framework set by the researchers, putting aside for a while their own perspectives? Answers to these questions appear to be "No." For them, endorsing Heinz's efforts to seek other means, rather than just stealing, does not appear to be an evasion of tough decisions but a positive choice based on moral grounds.

For them, the most important thing was not just to let her survive by all means, but to live gracefully, with human dignity. J#41 (M) said, "to do so (stealing) means that we put values on prolonging our lives. Matter of justice is (not). . . . living by doing wrong things. If I were his wife, I couldn't endure that he has to steal for me." Even in the second situation (Situation 1) he continued to say, "I wouldn't steal because, as I said before, it is not good to prolong one's life even by doing wrong things." J#36 (M) echoed the same tone saying, "Although human life has to be saved, . . . respect for human life should be made, and best effort should be made, but it should be made by morally allowable measures." Even to the most tempting arrangement in the Second Situation he said, "I wouldn't steal since I have tried all possible means legally and morally allowable."

Thus, they were not intellectually weighing the relative importance of the right to life versus the right to property based on the assumption that Heinz had exhausted every legal means as American postconventional reasoners did, but they were tying to prescribe the most practical moral avenue within the given situation.

Especially, three postconventional subjects seriously questioned if the wife, under those circumstances, really wants to live longer with the fact that the drug was stolen relegating her husband to becoming a criminal. J#29 (M), a Stage 5 reasoner, who considered it Heinz's responsibility not to steal, assumed that his wife would be sad if he stole. These subjects seem to be primarily concerned about the quality or dignity of the wife's life rather than outward violation of conventional rules. They valued an honorable and blameless life, even if not prolonged, rather than a life prolonged with a stolen drug. This makes an interesting contrast with American postconventional reasoners who supported Heinz's stealing even for six-month prolongation with the drug. A#18 (F), as already quoted, said in Situation 2:

A#18 (F): Situation 2 (negative-negative)

I think he should steal the drug. . . . Life becomes very precious when it is about to go. And that means that life is only precious when one realizes how important it is for the person to live, even a few days in many cases.

Both A#18 (F) and J#29 (M) are well aware of the preciousness and importance of the last minute of human life, but the ways to secure that preciousness differ: the former struggling to make it longer, the latter trying to make it purer and cleaner.

Furthermore, some of the Japanese postconventional reasoners questioned the practical universalizability of the choice of Heinz's stealing. J#17 (F) said, "It is not a wise way to break into the store and grab it. If people were behaving on that level, the problem (would not be solved), everybody would start breaking into the store. The problem is not only Heinz's personal problem. Rather, with all those facts, with information about what the druggist is saying, other methods such as appealing, if not legal confrontation, to the newspaper, would be much more powerful. That would be, in the end, much better than just breaking into the store and stealing it." J#41 (M) also stressed the necessity to make this a social problem rather than an isolated personal problem.

Moreover, Japanese postconventional reasoners universalized moral obligation to save a human life in a different direction from American postconventional reasoners, who said Heinz should steal not only for his wife but for strangers. In response to the question, "Does Heinz have a responsibility to steal in this case?," J#46 (F) said, "No. The doctors have responsibility. It is her doctors who have responsibility to manage to obtain the drug, if you mention responsibility at all. Heinz has no responsibility to steal."

Thus, the attitude of many of Japanese postconventional subjects to the Heinz dilemma was so fundamental, though in a different way from their American counterparts, that their action choices were very stable when they responded to the situationally modified versions of the dilemma. When presented with the second situation, which is the hardest situation to keep the original action choice, J#17 (F) was firm in her action choice.

J#17 (F): Second Situation (positive-positive)

SHOULD HEINZ STEAL THE DRUG IN THIS CASE?
Even in that case I think he shouldn't.

WHY?
The problem here is not that it's likely to be found out by the druggist, or it's easy to steal or the length of her life being prolonged with the drug. The most important problem is that the druggist is withholding such an effective drug in order to make money himself. The very fact that he is charging ten times more than he spent for the drug is wrong. Other conditions are, I think, peripheral. However favorable the situation may be, you should not consider

this issue on the level of stealing. The crux of the problem is the fact that such a druggist is allowed to do anything he likes. If you don't solve this problem in some way, you are just scratching the surface of the problem.

Thus, it is clear that postconventional people both in the United States and Japan, though found in substantial numbers, do not necessarily have the same basic attitudes toward moral problems in the dilemmas that are the key device for the stage scoring procedure.

Conventional Reasoning and Decision Changes by Japanese Subjects

In a striking contrast with postconventional subjects, who showed strong consistency in their action choices against Heinz's stealing throughout the different versions of the dilemma, Japanese conventional people had a greater preference for Heinz's stealing. As already mentioned, ten out of fifteen postconventional subjects said, "Heinz shouldn't steal" in the original dilemma. Approximately three-fifths (twenty-one out of thirty-seven) of the conventional subjects, however, chose "Heinz should steal." There was a tendency of level difference of action choice though it did not reach a significant level (χ^2 = 2.48, df =1, p.20). Moreover, more than two-thirds of the subjects who chose autonomous action (fifteen out of twenty-one) continued to choose the same action even in the second situation in which situational arrangements appear to be the hardest to keep that choice. Such a distribution pattern of conventional subjects resembled that of American and Japanese postconventional reasoners rather than their American conventional counterparts. What does this mean, and how can this be explained?

Many of the Japanese conventional subjects, unlike the postconventional ones, accepted the dichotomous framework of the dilemma rather easily, and balanced the relative importance of the value of human life versus property. Once the dichotomous framework was accepted, the value of life appeared to them much greater than the obligation to obey the law. They applied this rule "to respect human life more than anything else" to the various versions of the dilemma. Even though the consistency of their action choices resembled those of American postconventional subjects, the structures of their reasoning was, naturally, different from those of the American higher stage reasoners.

First, reasoning by the conventional subjects in support of Heinz's stealing often stressed the importance of human life over any other considerations. That reasoning was not elaborated beyond just the statement of the great importance of human life. For example, J#13 (F), without questioning the assumption that Heinz had tried every legal means, said, "It's all right to steal the drug in this case. SHOULD HE STEAL? Yes, he should steal. WHY? Because there are no other legal means, and his wife's life could be saved by the use of the drug. Even if he has to go to jail for that, he should steal. WHY? Because life is more important."

Second, in spite of their insistence on the importance of human life, they didn't say that it was Heinz's responsibility to steal in most cases. J#6 (F) was a typical example. After replying "It's permissible for Heinz to steal," she said, "When you ask me to answer dichotomously in either should or shouldn't, I think, 'he should steal' would be my answer, though I am basically of the opinion that stealing should be avoided by all means. . . . DOES HEINZ HAVE A RESPONSIBILITY TO STEAL? No." Such less prescriptive definition of Heinz's stealing was expressed more clearly by the discrepancy between what subjects think Heinz should do and what they would do in Heinz's position. J#19 (M), when asked if Heinz should steal the drug, responded, "I don't know if Heinz should steal or not, but I would steal. . . . Because I want to save my wife."

Third, conventional subjects' reasoning didn't show universality. Many of them stopped saying "Heinz should steal" when they were asked if "Heinz should steal the drug if he doesn't love his wife."

J#34 (M): Original Dilemma

Again, I am not comfortable with the word "should." If he doesn't love his wife, he wouldn't have any emotional urge to save her at the cost of violating the law. If he doesn't feel like saving his wife, he shouldn't do that.

Thus, reasoning by conventional subjects, although it consistently supported Heinz's stealing in both Situations 1 and 2, had the structure similar to those of conventional reasoning shown by American conventional reasoners. Why, then, were their action choices much more consistent than those of their American counterparts?

One possible explanation would be that they accepted the dichotomous framework of the story rather easily, on the one hand, and their rather rigid application of the rule or formula that human life should have priority over and above anything else, on the other. The dilemma framework that required subjects to make a dichotomous choice between life and law may have led them to think rather theoretically, or to be engaged in a kind of intellectual play, instead of thinking practically and contextually, although the latter way of thinking is often regarded as characteristic of Japanese people as shown in their postconventional counterparts.

Consistency of action choices by conventional subjects was seen among those who were against Heinz's stealing, as well. Thirteen out of fifteen who opposed Heinz's stealing in the original dilemma didn't change their position in the second situation. This pattern of distribution of action choices coincided with those of postconventional reasoners who were against Heinz's stealing. Why were the action choices against Heinz's stealing so stable at the conventional level? A part of the explanation may come from the rather less flexible application of the conventional rule not to steal in the face of dichotomous choice. For example, J#22 (M) said,

> *If asked whether or not Heinz should steal, I think Heinz shouldn't steal.*
>
> WHY NOT?
> *Because it is against the law. It's not a right thing to do legally as well as morally.*
>
> WHAT WOULD YOU DO IN HEINZ'S POSITION?
> *I would continue to raise money.*
>
> WHAT WOULD YOU DO IF YOU COULDN'T GET ENOUGH MONEY FROM YOUR EFFORT AFTER TRYING EVERY LEGAL MEANS?
> *If I exhausted such measures, I might steal.*

J#23 (M), being asked what Heinz should do, said,

> *If I were in his position, I would steal.*
>
> HOW ABOUT HEINZ?
> *I think Heinz shouldn't steal.*
>
> WHY WOULD YOU STEAL?
> *If my wife's life would be saved with the drug, I could put my wife's life first, since I would be freed even after I become a criminal, and my life wouldn't be in danger.*
>
> WHY NOT FOR HEINZ?
> *Because I assume that he is a law-abiding person.*

The above J#22 (M), to the second situation where situational arrangements were most favorable, said, "I would steal." Thus, these two subjects under this category showed inner fluctuation or discrepancy between "I would" responses and "he should" responses in spite of outward consistency in their action choices, just like the conventional subjects who consistently supported Heinz's stealing.

Many of the conventional subjects whose heteronomous action choices were stable, however, showed certain characteristics common to their post-conventional counterparts. That is, they didn't easily accept the dichoto-mous choice of the dilemma, and they considered it more moral to try to live gracefully than to prolong one's life by all means. Like postconven-tional reasoners, some of them also stressed the importance of treating the problem as a social issue instead of treating it as his isolated problem.

Thus, the consistency of action choices by conventional subjects in this category may be explained either by their rigid application of a rule against stealing or committing a crime or by their commonality with the charac-teristics of postconventional reasoners. In sum, Japanese subjects, both con-ventional and postconventional, showed different attitudes to the dilemma as well as different action choice patterns from American counterparts.

DISCUSSION

Universality of Postconventional Stages and Their Distinction from Conventional Stages

In Kohlberg's stage theory of moral development, the most controversial part has been the postconventional stages, and one of the most fundamen-tal sources of the criticisms of these stages lies in the fact that cases of such higher stage reasoning are rarely found in empirical data except in a few studies. Under such circumstances, the present study was intended to pro-vide substantial material for discussion on principled or postconventional stages. By choosing well-educated adults as our subjects, we could identify a substantial number of postconventional subjects – 16 in the United States and 15 in Japan – although Stage 5 cases were 4 and 2, respectively.

From the size of cases of postconventional subjects found in both coun-tries, we will be able to make a certain generalization about postconven-tional stages. A fully principled stage or Stage 5 as an adult stage as well as Stage 4/5 could be identified both in the United States and in Japan us-ing the Standard Issue Scoring system. Furthermore, the fact that conven-tional and postconventional reasoners in both countries responded differ-ently to the various situational factors with structurally different reasoning provides a fairly solid basis for considering postconventional stages as separate stages beyond conventional stages. Thus, these results can be considered to support the validity and universality of postconven-tional stages in Kohlberg's stage theory of justice reasoning as a domain of moral development.

Cultural Differences in Moral Judgment

In spite of the existence and qualitative distinction from conventional reasoning, however, postconventional reasoning in the two countries revealed
rather different attitudes to the moral problems in the dilemmas. For example, American postconventional subjects showed consistent autonomous action choice based on universalizable justice reasoning with
emphasis on the overwhelming priority of the right to life over the right to
property. This is congenial to Kohlberg's conception of Stage 5 as a fully
principled stage as well as his autonomous-heteronomous distinction in
moral judgments. At the conventional level, the initial autonomous choice
by most of the subjects fluctuated according to the changes of situational
arrangement because of the relative lack of abstract, universalizable prin-
ciple-oriented thinking.

Japanese postconventional subjects, however, showed heteronomous
choice in the Heinz dilemma. They didn't fit in Kohlberg's scheme of dichotomous choice. Instead of balancing the values of life versus law or
property detached from the actual situation, they stuck to the circumstances projected from the story and worked out a heteronomous choice.
They were not choosing "law" as opposed to "life," but they were choosing "life with honor and dignity," while trying to maintain social order and
harmony. They were not just conformists in the conventional sense.

The fact that Japanese postconventional reasoners were not mere conformists can be confirmed by their responses to Dilemma IV, the dilemma
of Dr. Jefferson who is requested to perform euthanasia by a terminal cancer patient agonizing with great pain (Appendix). The fact that six postconventional reasoners out of nine clearly chose mercy killing shows that
they were not necessarily conventional law-abiding people. A part of the
transcript of J#29 (M) is as follows:

J#29 (M): Dilemma IV (Dr. Jefferson's dilemma of mercy killing)

WHAT SHOULD DR. JEFFERSON DO IN THIS SITUATION?
*Well, I think he should honor her request. . . . in a situation where it is obvi-
ous that her life is ending very soon, I think it is her right to decide how she
would end it. A human being has a right to make that decision. Since she has
made a decision about her life, Dr. Jefferson should honor her decision.*

SHOULD HE MAKE THE DECISION ALONE OR SHOULD HE TALK WITH
SOMEONE ELSE?
*Well, as for the decision itself, he can make it by himself in his relations with
the patient, but when he executes it, he should talk with the group of doctors
and reach a consensus.*

WHY?
Because it is against the law, and the legal problem cannot be solved quickly, but prior to the legal problem it is important for the group of doctors to have a consensus concerning this issue. . . . This is a problem which may need a change of the law. This is not a problem to be dealt with just in terms of personal or empathetic relationship between the doctor and patient.

IS IT ACTUALLY RIGHT OR WRONG FOR HIM TO GIVE THE WOMAN
THE DRUG THAT WOULD MAKE HER DIE?
I think it is right, . . . I mean morally right . . . in the sense that he respects his patient's will. Legal problem remain, though.

In this way, it is clear that Japanese postconventional subjects did not always choose the issue of "law" as opposed to the issue of "life" (or quality of life). Rather, most of them were genuine postconventional reasoners.

The consistent heteronomous action choices in the Heinz dilemma presented by Japanese postconventional subjects raise a serious problem in the stage scoring system. It appears that the scoring manual cannot properly score the kind of reasoning presented by Japanese postconventional reasoners. The scoring system may be a little biased by Kohlberg's conception of autonomous judgment based on the dichotomous choice, which often leads subjects' reasoning to be detached from projected realities of the situation. At the postconventional level, for example, Criterion Judgments that are against Heinz's stealing are scarce – and nonexistent at Stage 5 – and, therefore, there are virtually no Criterion Judgments to which a certain type of reasoning by Japanese postconventional subjects could properly be matched. In this sense, responses by Japanese postconventional subjects call for serious examination of the composition of Criterion Judgments at postconventional stages.[7]

---

7 The scoring manual contains many Criterion Judgments for each stage, and the essence of the process of stage scoring lies in finding a "match" between interview judgments as actual responses from people and Criterion Judgments in the manual. Kohlberg and his colleagues considered people's moral judgments in response to the Moral Judgment Interview to have three dimensions: (a) action choice or value choice that subjects make in the face of the dilemma; (b) the moral value or object of concern that subjects use to justify the choice in the dilemma; and (c) the ways in which the significance of a value is construed. They called these three dimensions "issue," "norm," and "element," respectively (Colby and Kohlberg, 1987). Thus, Criterion Judgments are predetermined units of moral judgment, each comprised of various combinations of issue, norm, and element. These Criterion Judgments are devices to score people's moral judgments, but at the same time they define each stage (Kohlberg, Levine, & Hewer, 1983). In this sense, the composition of Criterion Judgments at each stage acquires crucial importance for the whole theory.

Japanese conventional subjects, on the contrary, showed, in their action choices, a tendency similar to American postconventional subjects rather than their conventional counterparts, although their reasoning was, naturally, less sophisticated than those of American postconventional reasoners. It appears that Japanese conventional reasoners, in contrast with their postconventional counterparts, easily adapted to the dichotomous research scheme and, as a result, showed more consistent action choices than their American counterparts. In other words, it seems that Japanese postconventional reasoners, having their own perspectives about the dilemmas, stuck to their own understanding of the dilemma, but conventional subjects were overwhelmed by the apparent priority of one value over the other in the dilemma. Because of the weight placed on the autonomous value, as opposed to the heteronomous value, they felt the dilemma to be beyond practical negotiation. It is not clear, however, how morally relevant the dilemma questions appeared to be to them, except as an intellectual game.

Apart from the action choices and their supporting reasoning in the dilemma mentioned above, Japanese subjects came up with responses which were hard to match with Criterion Judgments in the manual. As Snarey (1985) suggested, those difficult-to-score materials must reveal ways of thinking not reflected in the scoring manual. Besides judgments against Heinz's stealing, most of the difficult-to-score material by Japanese subjects was oriented to maintaining and improving relationships.

The Louise Dilemma used for stage scoring (Appendix), for example, requires interviewees to make a dichotomous choice about whether or not Louise should tell her mother what her sister, Judy, had told Louise about Judy's lie, which was caused by the mother's breaking the promise to Judy. A Stage 5 reasoner didn't consider that that was the crux of the problem and didn't make a dichotomous choice, but proposed seemingly the best solution to the moral problem in the dilemma as follows:

J#28 (M): Dilemma II or The Louise Dilemma

WHAT SHOULD LOUISE DO IN THIS SITUATION?
Louise should talk with Judy and try to make Judy tell her mother on her own.

WHY SHOULD SHE DO THAT?
Because I think that's the way for Louise to achieve two things fairly well. One, for Judy to reestablish her relationship with her mother which seems to be in conflict now; two, for Louise to keep Judy's trust.

Clearly, the composition of postconventional Criterion Judgments are out of balance in the sense that individual autonomy and freedom are over-stressed, ignoring the fact that every human being cannot exist outside of human relationships and forgetting the fact that too much emphasis on in-dividual freedom and autonomy can lead to the breakdown of stable hu-man relationships.

Another set of reasons that are difficult-to-score are related to a sense of connectedness with the much wider world. As already mentioned, a ma-jority of Japanese postconventional reasoners made autonomous action choice in Dilemma IV or Dr. Jefferson's dilemma. There were, however, three postconventional subjects who were against Dr. Jefferson's adminis-tering the drug. They uniformly showed a basic understanding of human life in terms of connectedness to the much wider world. This sense of con-nectedness to the outer world is not necessarily a variety of Stage 4 rea-soning, which often reflects just a member-of-society perspective of certain religious dogmas. For example, a male postconventional subject expressed his sense of connectedness of human life in the following way:

J#41 (M): Dilemma IV

IS THERE ANY WAY A PERSON HAS A DUTY OR OBLIGATION TO LIVE WHEN HE OR SHE DOES NOT WANT TO, WHEN THE PERSON WANTS TO COMMIT SUICIDE?
We should not try to kill ourselves. We can say that our lives are not our own property nor our belongings. Life of each individual is, so to speak, sustained and made possible by and within the larger life as a whole. If we consider in this way, we cannot end our life based on our emotional considerations. . . .
WHAT DO YOU MEAN WHEN YOU SAY OUR LIFE IS SUSTAINED AND MADE POSSIBLE?
It means that human life can exist only in mutual interdependence within the larger life as a whole.

A female postconventional subject also expressed her similar understand-ing of human life:

J#25 (F): Dilemma IV

WHAT SHOULD DR. JEFFERSON DO IN THIS SITUATION?
It is very difficult to answer, but since I believe in destiny-type of thing, she should try to live as far as she is alive. It is very hard to see the patient suf-fering, but I think the dignity of human life should be respected.
WHY SHOULD HE RESPECT LIFE?
This is my personal opinion, but . . . as far as we are alive, we should accept

and follow our destiny which is beyond our control. We human beings are a part of the whole existence.

SHOULD DR. JEFFERSON GIVE HER THE DRUG THAT WOULD MAKE HER DIE?
No. I don't have any religious guilt feeling about killing oneself because of suffering, but I think it is the way of human being to try to live our mortal life. Even if the person requests to be killed because of severe pain, I don't think he or she ultimately knows what he or she is doing. So, I think it would be better to entrust the final decision to nature. Those kind of things are beyond human judgments.

IS IT ACTUALLY RIGHT OR WRONG FOR HIM TO GIVE THE WOMAN THE DRUG THAT WOULD MAKE HER DIE?
Again, it is not right. . . . Can I explain my personal experience?

YES, PLEASE DO.
I lost my father and brother in a very short period of time, and facing their deaths I thought death is a harsh thing. I also thought that human beings, at the bottom of their hearts, want to live no matter how much they suffer. It is a humane thing. However, Nature, which is beyond human control, eventually gives you death without fail. Until that time human beings should try to live, and that is a humane thing. . . . I came to think in this way not because of special belief in a religion but spontaneously from my own experience. . . . I came to think that there is the truth or providence in this universe.

SHOULD THE WOMAN HAVE THE RIGHT TO MAKE THE FINAL DECISION?
Certainly, it is her own life, and I think she has the right. However, I, myself, put the providence of nature above each individual human being, and, therefore, I don't think she should.

Such a sense of connectedness of the human being to the universe or a sense of cosmic modesty could not be found in the samples of American postconventional reasoners and is in contrast with the image of man in Stage 5. Existence of such reasoning as well as reasoning by postconventional subjects oriented toward better human relationship and better connection with society may raise a serious question about the definition of postconventional stages and, therefore, construction of Criterion Judgments in the scoring manual.

In this connection, it is suggestive that Chikuro Hiroike (1928), the pioneer of the historical study of Oriental system of law, clarified the conception of *ortholinon*[8] as the central principle of a morality beyond the conventional

---

[8] Hiroike coined this term to denote the connected existence of human beings.

level. It is based on the awareness of the fact that the life of each individual is nurtured, sustained, and developed by various benefactors at present as well as in the past, physically (or bodily), socially (or nationally), and mentally (or spiritually). Hiroike argues that only when each human individual truly becomes aware of such connectedness and indebtedness to those benefactors at large can he or she attain true freedom and autonomy. In this sense, individuation and autonomy, which find full expression in Kohlberg's model of man at postconventional stages, need to be supplemented, it seems, by a postconventional expression of the connected aspect of human existence, interpersonally, socially, and naturally or universally.

References

Bellah, R. N., Madsen, R., Sullivan, W. M., Swidler, A., & Tipton, S. M. (1985). *Habits of the heart: Individualism and commitment in American life.* Berkeley: University of California Press.

Caudill, W., & Weinstein, H. (1969). Maternal care and infant behavior in Japan and America. *Psychiatry, 32,* 12–43.

Caudill, W. (1973). Tiny Dramas: Vocal communication between mother and infant in Japanese and American families. In W. P. Lebra (Ed.), *Mental health research in Asia and Pacific: Vol. 2, Transcultural research in mental health* (pp. 25–48). Honolulu: University Press of Hawaii.

Colby, A., & Kohlberg, L. (1987). *The measurement of moral judgment: Vol. I, Theoretical foundation and research validation; Vol. II, Standard issue scoring manual.* New York: Cambridge University Press.

Dien, D. S. (1982). A Chinese perspective on Kohlberg's theory of moral development. *Developmental Review, 2,* 331–41.

Doi, T. (1962). "Amae": A key concept for understanding Japanese personality structure. In R. J. Smith & R. K. Beardsley (Eds.), *Japanese culture: Its development and characteristics* (pp. 132–9). Chicago: Aldine Publishing Company.

Doi, T. (1973). *The anatomy of dependence.* Tokyo: Kodansha International. [originally in Japanese, 1971].

Hiroike, C. A. (1928). *Treatise on moral science: A first attempt to establish moralogy as a new science.* Kashiwa, Japan: The Institute of Moralogy.

Iwasa, N. (1989). *Situational considerations in moral judgment: A Japan-United States comparison.* Unpublished doctoral dissertation, Harvard University, Cambridge.

Kohlberg, L. (1958). *The development of modes of moral thinking and choice in the years ten to sixteen.* Unpublished doctoral dissertation, University of Chicago, Chicago.

Kohlberg, L. (1969). Stage and sequence: The cognitive-developmental approach to socialization. In D. A. Goslin (Ed.), *Handbook of socialization theory and research* (pp. 347–480). New York: Rand McNally.

Kohlberg, L. (1971). From is to ought: How to commit the naturalistic fallacy and get away with it in the study of moral development. In T. Mischel (Ed.), *Cognitive development and epistemology.* New York: Academic Press.

Kohlberg, L. (1976). Moral stages and moralization: The cognitive-developmental approach. In T. Lickona (Ed.), *Moral development and behavior* (pp. 31–53). New York: Holt.

Kohlberg, L. (1981). *Essays in moral development: Vol. 1, The philosophy of moral development.* San Francisco: Harper & Row.

Kohlberg, L. (1984). *Essays on Moral Development: Vol. 2, The psychology of moral development.* San Francisco: Harper & Row.

Kohlberg, L., Levine, C., & Hewer, A. (1983). *Moral stages: A current formulation and a response to critics.* New York: Karger.

LeVine, R. A. (1977). Child rearing as cultural adaptation. In P. H. Leiderman, S. R. Tulkin, & A. Rosenfeld (Eds.), *Culture and infancy: Variations in the human experience* (pp. 15–27). New York: Academic Press.

Nakamura, H. (1964). *Ways of thinking of Eastern people: India, China, Tibet and Japan.* Honolulu: University Press of Hawaii. [originally in Japanese, 1961–62].

Nisan, M., & Kohlberg, L. (1982). Universality and variation in moral judgment: A longitudinal and cross-sectional study in Turkey. *Child Development, 53,* 865–76.

Snarey, J. R. (1982). *The social and moral development of kibbutz founders and sabras: A cross-cultural and longitudinal study.* Unpublished doctoral dissertation, Harvard University, Cambridge.

Snarey, J. R. (1985). Cross-cultural universality of social-moral development: A critical review of Kohlbergian research. *Psychological Bulletin, 97,* 202–32.

Vasudev, J. (1984). *A study of moral reasoning at different life stages in India.* Unpublished doctoral dissertation, University of Pittsburgh, Pittsburgh.

APPENDIX

Moral Judgment Interview Form B Dilemmas

Dilemma IV. There was a woman who had a very bad cancer, and there was no treatment known to medicine that would save her. Her doctor, Dr. Jefferson, knew that she had about six months to live. She was in terrible pain, but she was so weak that a good dose of a painkiller like ether or morphine would make her die sooner. She was delirious and almost crazy with pain, and in her calm periods she would ask Dr. Jefferson to give her enough ether to kill her. She said she couldn't stand the pain and she was going to die in a few months anyway. Although he knows that mercy killing is against the law, the doctor thinks about granting her request.

Dilemma IV'. Dr. Jefferson did perform the mercy killing, by giving the woman the drug. Another doctor saw Dr. Jefferson give the woman the drug, however, and reported him. Dr. Jefferson is brought to court and a jury is selected. The jury's job is to find whether a person is innocent or guilty of committing a crime. The jury finds Dr. Jefferson guilty. It is up to the judge to determine the sentence.

Dilemma II. Judy is a twelve-year-year old girl. Her mother promised her that she could go to a special rock concert coming to their town, if she saved up babysitting and lunch money so that she would have enough money to buy a ticket to the concert. She managed to save the $15 it cost plus another $5. But then her mother changed her mind and told Judy that she had to spend the money on new clothes for school. Judy was disappointed and decided to tell her mother that she had only been able to save $5. That Saturday she went to the performance and told her mother that she was spending the day with a friend. A week passed without her mother finding out. Judy then told her older sister, Louise, that she had gone to the performance and had lied to her mother about it. Louise wonders whether to tell their mother what Judy did.

Moral Judgment Interview Form A Dilemma

Dilemma III. In Europe, a woman was near death from a special kind of cancer. There was one drug that the doctors thought might save her. It was a form of radium that the druggist in the same town had recently discovered. The drug was expensive to make, but the druggist charged ten times what the drug cost him to make – he paid $400 for the radium and charged $4,000 for a small dose of the drug. The sick woman's husband, Heinz, went to everyone but he could only get together about $2,000, half the cost. He told the druggist that his wife was dying and asked him to sell it cheaper or let him pay later. But the druggist said, "No, I discovered the drug and I'm going to make money from it." So having tried every legal means, Heinz got desperate and considered breaking into the man's store to steal the drug for his wife.

PART II

MOTHER AND CHILD AT HOME

THREE

The Maternal Role in Japan

Cultural Values and Socioeconomic Conditions

Yoshie Nishioka Rice

The intense involvement of Japanese mothers in their children has been considered as one of the critical ingredients of the nation's educational success. This chapter aims to illustrate the Japanese mothers' steadfast involvement in their children as a manifestation of cultural values, which are not exclusive to but strongly associated with the maternal role, within the current socioeconomic conditions. The first part of the chapter will be devoted to theoretical discussions of the above view. The second part will provide empirical data drawn from a questionnaire survey and individual interviews with mothers to substantiate it. Closing thoughts will be given in the third part.

1

New Notion of Japanese Mothers

To conceptualize the centrality of their children to Japanese mothers, I have proposed calling the Japanese mother's role that of *kosodate mama* (childrearing mother). Because *kosodate* literally translates into English as childrearing, the term *kosodate mama* may appear to be redundant. The wording, however, serves well for the purpose of highlighting Japanese mothers' commitment, not exclusively to examination-geared education as manifested in the *kyoiku mama*, but to the whole welfare of the child, and the recent breed of mothers who can afford and are expected to concentrate their energy and time on childrearing.

In daily conversation, the word *kosodate* may be used as follows:

kosodate no kuro: hardship in childrearing
kosodate no yorokobi: pleasure in childrearing

kosodate ni sennen suru: concentrate on childrearing (often used when a mother abandons or postpones her other pursuits)
kosodate ni muchuu: to be absorbed in childrearing
kosodate ga ichidanraku suru: the most intense phase of childrearing is finished
kosodate kara kaiho sareru: to be freed from childrearing

Judging from the way the word is ingrained in the everyday vocabulary, Japanese seem to believe that there is a period in childrearing that requires the intense and undiverted attention of caretakers, during which both pleasure and hardship can be experienced. Nonetheless, such a description is hardly a monopoly of Japanese childrearing. What is remarkable is the singularity and exclusiveness of their childrearing responsibility. The emergence of *kosodate mama* was precipitated by the Japanese culture and the current socioeconomic conditions.

Cultural Values

Many anthropologists of Japan have observed a general tendency of commitment to and perfection of one's assigned role as a way of actualizing the self (role commitment; Lebra, 1976, role perfectionism; Befu, 1986, role narcissism; DeVos, 1973). The role of mother is still the primary role for many Japanese women who have children. This commitment to the maternal role claims the utmost priority among women's other pursuits. Observes Befu (1986), "Neglect of one's responsibility as a mother is inexcusable under any circumstances" (p. 25). Neglect of the mother's role is inexcusable not only in the eyes of society but also in the mind of the mother herself, because the role of mother defines her. S. Vogel (1978) explains:

> For the Japanese housewife, it is this mothering that provides her purpose in life, her *ikigai,* as Japanese describe it, and even her self definition. Since her whole identification is with her role as mother of a family, she puts herself into her tasks and her family relationships with a professionalism that calls forth not only total devotion but also continued efforts to learn and improve. Her feelings of satisfaction, even her feelings of success as a person, are directly tied to her feelings of success in her profession of caring for her family. (pp. 17–18)

Along with this cultural value of role commitment (hereafter I shall employ Lebra's terminology), *amae* (Doi, 1973) can be observed to be significant in the manifestation of the role of the mother, although possibly with different intensity and realization. *Amae* is argued to originate in the infant's dependence on its mother and later on to be extended to other relationships. Kumagai (1981) concedes that *amae* is accepted as "an a priori definition of parental love itself" (p. 258) and "a critical ingredient in the successful nurturing of a child" (p. 258). Furthermore, Azuma (1986) notes that there has been "the scheme of indulgence-dependence-identification-controllability" in Japanese pedagogy. "The feeling of interdependence helps the child assimilate the hopes and values of the parents, thus enhancing the child's educability" (p. 8).

These two cultural values are crystallized in the *kosodate mama* under the current socioeconomic conditions of Japan.

The Socioeconomic Conditions

Japan was a largely rural, agricultural society before World War II. The heavy domestic workload (without the convenience of running water, gas, or electric machines) and substance production, which was incorporated within the role of mother, left little time for a mother to be directly involved with her children. A childhood memory of Kunio Wakai (1990) provides the flavor of what the mother and child interaction might have been in the prewar era. Wakai grew up as the youngest child in a farming house in the Tohoku area.

> I cannot ever recall having been read picture books by my mother. Picture books were not a common household item then, and moreover, my mother, born in the Meiji period (1868–1912), had hardly attended elementary school and therefore could barely read *hiragana*.[1] However, I remember well that she regularly told me stories at bedtime. Though she had to work till late at night, as soon as she was done, without even taking a break, she would come to my side. . . . Then, I could get full attention of my mother, who had been too busy to play with me during the day. More than anything, the happiness and comfort of falling asleep while feeling her warmth close to my body made this night time story telling so much more memorable.

Note the *amae* feeling through the physical proximity between the child and his mother, which was a treat after a long and hard day of work. Also notice that teaching her child academic matters as basic as *hiragana*, was not the requirement of the mother; physical labor was. This certainly echoes the observation made in *The Women of Suye Mura* (Smith & Wiswell, 1982) that

---

[1] One of the three Japanese writing systems, considered to be the most basic.

"one of the criteria for a good wife" in a poor agricultural Suye village in the 1920s was that "she be a good worker" (p. 178). The quote of a man from Kumamoto is further telling: "A wife need not be educated; she is to be a mother" (p. 180). The massive industrialization and urbanization after World War II, however, brought about various social and economic changes, which affected the role of the mother and the intensity of the *amae* relationship. Because the bulk of the population migrated to cities, the three-generational household system, that is, where cohabiting members shared (though not equally) subsistence production, household chores, childcare, and so on, broke down. In the cities, husband-fathers have become paid workers and assumed the role of the breadwinner, and wife-mothers assumed the role of housewife. A much reduced domestic workload, thanks to modern technology, and the diminished, if not absent, responsibility in substance production, afford mothers more time and energy to spend on their children. As the fertility declines (for example, around 5 in the 1920s to 1.46 in 1993), a mother is not likely to have an older child to delegate the care of a younger child but tends to focus more on fewer children. Because fostering *amae* interdependence is seen to work positively to enhance the child's educability (it is part of Japanese childrearing theory), mothers are likely to create and sustain a more intense relationship with the children in order to improve their children's academic performance, which has become the key in the children's future occupational success. Isolation of the mother-child dyad in the contemporary nuclear family in urban areas strengthens the inseparability of the two. *Kosodate* (childrearing) in present Japan denotes more personal, direct, and intense involvement of the mother in raising children.

With the cultural value supporting a commitment to one's assigned role and in order to keep fostering a strong mother-child bond, the intensity of the maternal involvement in children has been amplified. Thus, a theoretical model of viewing the maternal role as a product of the relationship between cultural values (role commitment and *amae*) and socioeconomic conditions can be formed. With this conceptual model of the Japanese maternal role in mind, the focus will turn in the following section to a discussion of my questionnaire and interview surveys with Japanese mothers who had kindergartners.

2

I had the opportunity to live in Nagoya, Japan from December 1991 to February 1992. Mothers – totaling 195 – who had their children enrolled at either of two kindergartens[2] in that city participated in my questionnaire survey. The questions ranged from those concerning background information to those pertaining to childcare share, assessment of mothering, definition of the maternal role, future plans, and job situations. Several among those mothers took part in individual interviews. Findings from these two projects and the mothers' informal comments will be examined in this segment.

Mother as the Sole Caretaker

We will start out with some demographic data. The great majority of the mothers in this survey lived in nuclear families. The number of children per family ranged from one to five, with more than 60% of the families having two children.[3] Those families who had children age twelve or older amount to nineteen. These numbers suggest that most families do not have grandparents, other kin, or older children within the immediate household and there are few hands available for or capable of childcare.

How do mothers and fathers, who often are the only two capable members of the family, share childcare? Almost all the mothers (182) thought "both parents" should decide on the principles of educating and rearing children rather than the mother or father alone, or another person. Nevertheless, 70% of the mothers (137) admit that it was they who actually take care of the children.

This admission is further supported by the length of the fathers' interaction time with their children. On a workday, 75% of the fathers spend with their children equal to or less than sixty minutes. Twenty-five percent of the fathers spend thirty minutes each workday with their children. Another quarter spends less than that, including 11.5% of fathers spending no time. Subtract the mothers from this scene, and the interaction time between the fathers and their children on a workday shrinks even smaller. With the mothers absent from the immediate scene, about four-fifths of the fathers spend equal to or less than thirty minutes with their children, including 43.2% of fathers having no interactions with their children alone. This is hardly a case where one may say childcare is shared by the fathers.

---

[2] Kindergartens in Japan are not incorporated within a compulsory elementary school system, athough, nonetheless, almost all children have some sort of preschool experience. At any rate, Japanese kindergartens more closely resemble large American childcare centers or preschools, in terms of its status in preschool education.

[3] There was only one family with five children. In this particular case, four children are stepchildren who are older than the biological child of the mother.

The absent father is so much a reality of the Japanese family that the majority of the mothers surveyed have made it a custom to eat early dinner with their children and prepare another meal for their husbands who come home well after the children have gone to bed.

Other data are available regarding the childcare share between the parents. The mothers were asked to chose an appropriate answer after reading the following hypothetical story.

> You have been looking forward to going out with your friend on a Saturday afternoon, but your child got sick. It's not very serious; he seems to have caught a little cold. If you go out with your friend, you cannot take care of the child. But if you cancel the date, you don't know when you can go out with your friend next time. What would you do?
> a. leave the child with my husband and go out as planned
> b. leave the child with my husband and go out but come back early
> c. cancel the outing
> d. other (describe)

Close to half of the mothers chose to compromise and selected b. The compromise may have been made between the mothers' desire to appear neither unconcerned with the sick child (besides their genuine feeling that they may become too worried about the child to enjoy the outing if it were carried out as planned) nor preoccupied with the child when his/her sickness is not serious and the husband is watching the child. About the same portion of the mothers answered that they would cancel the outing. One mother commented, "In reality, I try to avoid outings to which children are not permitted." The answers for those who chose "d. other" vary. Some mothers felt strongly the need to emphasize more care for and attention to the child's sickness and feelings. One mother wrote, "After giving the child medicine, if (he) says it is OK for me to go out, then I'd go. But if not, then I wouldn't. Even after going out, I'd call home to make sure everything is OK." Another mother wrote, "If my husband is going to watch the child and if the child says it's OK (to stay with the father)." Six mothers said they would ask their female relatives who live close by instead of the husbands. These answers suggest uneasiness of the mothers to leave their children with their husbands and/or preference to leave the children with a female relative.

An interesting point is found in the comparison of two groups of the mothers (i.e., the mothers who previously answered that mainly they take care of their children and the mothers who stated that they and their husbands share the childcare). Among the former group, 48% said they would go out but come back early and 44% said they would cancel the outing. The percentages for the latter group: go out but come back early – 37%, cancel – 46%. This result suggests that the mothers who said they share childcare with their spouses are no more at ease in leaving their children when they are sick with the husband-fathers than the mothers who are the main child-care givers, a point that raises a question of how much or whether child-care sharing is really taking place.

By contrast, it is possible that, though ordinarily the husbands help out with the childcare, when it comes to the child's sickness – a weakened state of the child may induce more interdependence – the mothers become more unwilling to be separated from the child and/or attuned to the child's condition. A mother whose daughter has a severe case of asthma, said,

> I can sense when we have to rush her to the hospital. I am like a sensor. Even when she seems to be having a mild attack and my husband thinks that it is going away soon, I can just tell it is very serious and take her to the doctor's. The doctor would say, "Oh, you made it just in the nick of time." Or when she coughs and struggles to breathe, and he thinks we have to take her in, I say, "No, give her a minute," and she becomes fine. There have been many episodes like that. I can just tell, but not my husband, though, of course, he cares about our daughter. I don't know what it is – gut feeling only a mother has, I guess.

At any rate, contrary to what the mothers think should be the case, often they are the ones left to take up the childcare responsibility. The mothers do not, however, blame their husbands – at least overtly – for causing the discrepancy. Instead, the mothers are seen shielding their husbands from potential criticism with remarks such as "It's not his fault (that he can't take care of the children)," or "It's not that he doesn't, but he can't (because of his work schedule)." This tendency is in accordance with the observation that the most important responsibility of a Japanese husband-father is that he be a good provider (Lebra, 1984; Imamura, 1987). Because support-ing his family financially is a husband-father's obligation, if his commit-ment to the job and socialization with his colleagues and business associ-ates is seen as contributing to his success at work and results in little time spent with the family, it is received with great tolerance by the wife.

If a husband's very limited contribution to actual childcare is regarded as a result of the constraints of his work schedule, which wives understand as a part of a mass phenomenon – husbands everywhere in Japan come home too late and tired to do anything around the house – then it becomes a norm. Because it is a norm, the husband's late homecoming should be accepted and not be blamed on the individual. This acceptance, in turn, dictates or reinforces what a wife-mother should do, because there are just as many husbands who come home late from work as there are wives who stay home and take care of children. In other words, in this normalized, and polarized or complementary role-assignment system, mothers take up the sole responsibility of childrearing. Such an idea is accepted by the mothers. For instance, the questionnaire results show that the husbands criticize their wives for their mothering, often despite the lack of their own involvement in childrearing. A father told his wife to read books more often to their children, in spite of the fact that he "seldom" does so. Some of these criticized mothers report that they felt it is easier said than done and felt rebellious toward their husbands. But most of the mothers (in fact, including even those who felt rebellious) thought that their husbands were right to point out these issues. Comments such as, "He (the husband) can see things better because he is the third party," reveal that mothers' behavior toward their children should be understood as part of a mother-child dyad, which does not include the fathers.

Thus, the fathers' physical absence from home not only puts limitations on their participation in childcare but also reinforces the idea that childrearing is the mothers' responsibility.

Accepting the Maternal Role

Concrete examples of the prevalent full-time motherhood can be found in the occupational status and history of the mothers. The majority of the mothers surveyed are full-time housewife-mothers. As many as twenty-two mothers, out of the 164 mothers who have claimed that status, rather than stating that they are part-time workers, turned out to have part-time jobs or *naishoku*. This itself is an indication of the full-time housewife-mother position as a norm to which to aspire. Those who had no jobs at the time of the survey were asked if they previously held a job, if so when, and why they quit. Twelve mothers (8.1%) said they never had had a job; 137 (91.9%) held a job in the past. More than half who answered affirmatively were involved in clerical work. Former teachers (elementary school, kindergarten, nursery school, etc.) comprised 11.3%. The duration of employment ranged from less than a year to nineteen years; however, more than one-third quit their job after working three years or less. One-fifth quit during the next two years. Their reasons for quitting were predominantly marriage-/childbirth-related (62.7% listed marriage, 23.9% listed childbirth, and 4.5% listed the two factors as their reasons for terminating work).

The idea of accepting full-time housewife-motherhood seems undeniably strong.

In light of the work life led by most men, marriage or starting a family means for women to complement the man's role, which is to take care of the home and children full-time. Collectively, these women seem to have chosen to become full-time housewife-mothers, having internalized the cultural values and realizing the practicality of doing so. Three-quarters of the mothers who did not work but previously had held jobs said they do not wish they had continued the job. The main reason (quoted by more than half of the mothers) is that they want to concentrate on childrearing and that they felt they could not handle home and outside work simultaneously, followed by admonitions that their former occupations were not meaningful jobs anyway (11.2%). Here one can see the obvious manifestation of role commitment and the idea that the maternal role is the most meaningful role for women. Furthermore, many believe that it is necessary for children's healthy development that the mothers stay home. This is *amae* interdependence being affirmed as the core of Japanese pedagogy, which works with role commitment as a pair of wheels to push the vehicle of the maternal role.

Let me introduce some examples. There are fifteen former teachers (kindergarten, nursery school, elementary school, etc.) who answered the questionnaire. These mothers quit their jobs, because, "[A] mother should stay home while her children are young. It seems self-contradictory to look after others' children while putting your own under somebody else's care," "I didn't want others to take care of my child so I sacrificed my job which I had wanted to keep for a lifetime," and "There is a substitute for a teacher, but there is no substitute for a mother." These are particularly telling comments on how strong the mother-child inseparability is, and the significance with which the role of the mother is regarded, given that these mothers were involved in nurturing and educating professions and virtually stated that "the importance of taking care of my own child as a mother for my child and myself far outweighs that of taking care of others' children as a teacher."

In the commitment to the maternal role lies the belief that it is essential for the child's development. Mothers recognize affirmation of that belief in everyday life. A mother who contemplates getting a job for financial reasons, but thinks twice at such a moment: "When my son comes home sobbing from a friend's house – they must have fought about something – he would see me there, feel all better, and go out with his energy all charged up again."

Some have more tragic circumstances that forced more commitment to the maternal role. A thirty-eight-year-old Christian mother talked about the death of her first child. She "took an oath to God that (she) would make a total sacrifice next time she would be so lucky as to be given a child." In a mixture of Christianity and Japanese indigenous beliefs, this mother saw the departure of her infant as an eventual result of her lack of total commitment to the young, and vowed to prove her worth as a mother the next time when she would be given a child. A twenty-eight-year-old mother stated, "Since I've lost my husband to an accident, all I care about is my children." Living with and financially supported by her in-laws, she has no agenda to gain a personal relationship with the opposite sex or her own economic means other than taking care of her two daughters. She has a dream, however, for the future of her daughters: "I want them to become lawyers or medical doctors." Western observers may become pessimistic that this mother's dream may not come true because she is not a good role model for her daughters for such an aspiration. Yet, this mother sees no contradiction or adversarial effect. On the contrary, she believes that raising successful children needs not a mother who wants to carve out her own career but a mother who "devotes totally" – taking direct care of or catering to her children.

The Degree of Maternal Commitment

How much mothers are or think they should be committed to the maternal role draws one's curiosity.

The mothers were asked to rate themselves as mothers out of the perfect score of 100. The distribution is shown in Figure 3.1.

As this was the case of self-rating, ideosyncrasies seem to be at play. No good statistical predictor for the score (age, educational level, family income, etc.) could be found. Let us then examine the reasons the mothers gave for their ratings. When stating the reasons, the mothers tend to stress their weaknesses and negative sides. Among the 169 responses (188 mothers rated themselves but 19 of them did not describe the reasons), 134 mothers cited only negative reasons. The tendency to focus on one's weaknesses may be a manifestation of a strong desire not to settle down into the status quo, but to improve oneself. With this view, it is understandable that great emphasis is placed on effort. The effort to reach the perfect, ideal mother is often recognized positively and it allows some affirmation to the mothers. Nevertheless, effort alone can never bring total satisfaction to the mothers or completion of the job they have undertaken. Rather, mothers have to

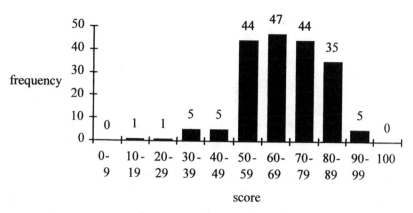

Figure 3.1. Mean score: 62.9.

keep trying very much like a mouse in a wheel. For a mother to say that she has perfected the role is to declare that she has stopped trying and at that moment she falls far away from the ideal mother. In this sense, the mother who gave 90 to herself and reasoned, "I think I am doing my best; however, in others' view I may be inadequate. I want to search for my weaknesses and improve myself, therefore I will leave it at 90," embodies this attitude, with a healthier or more satisfactory outlook.

There are fifteen mothers whose reasoning for self-rating specifically concerns imperfection as a mother. For example, "I cannot do anything perfect" (a 35 score), "I cannot do even half of what I think I should" (a 50 score), "I cannot reach the ideal no matter what" (a 50 score). A few mothers have very little confidence in themselves as mothers. One mother gave herself 10, because she "doesn't discipline the children well and only gets passionately mad at them."

Incidentally, almost half of the mothers who gave the reasons for their own ratings commented on their scolding as being problematic. Thirty-eight mothers stated that they become too emotional or cannot control their emotions when scolding their children. Fifteen mothers said they scold their children too much and/or they get mad at their children too often too quickly. Ten mothers admit they get irritated at times and take it out on the children and scold them. Another ten mothers are influenced by their moods and scold their children for something they may overlook otherwise. Six mothers admit they are nagging, scolding their children continuously. Two mothers said they become hysterical when scolding children.

There are mainly two issues needing to be discussed here. One is the effect of scolding on the mothers' guilty conscience. There seems to be a premise among the mothers that a good mother should never become emotional or lose her temper but should calmly admonish her children. This ideal of the mothers may be related to the Japanese tendency of avoiding overt displays of conflict. Because of this, Japanese mothers may experience severe inner struggle when dealing with uncooperative children. Unlike American mothers who set rules as the authority and try not to lose a battle with their children in power struggles, Japanese mothers try to get their children to understand what the mothers are wishing, which requires tremendous patience. Accordingly, American children break rules and get into trouble with their mothers, whereas Japanese children can expect their mothers to bend rules to accommodate their whining. When the Japanese mothers' patience is finally exhausted, however, *"kanninbukuro no o ga kireru"* (the string of patience bag breaks off), the pressured emotions will burst out to the children who wouldn't understand the mothers' feelings. Japanese children get into trouble with their mothers by refusing to empathize and breaking their mothers' hearts. Violation of feelings is a more serious crime than violation of rules in Japan. Thus, when mothers actually lose their temper in scolding their children, they may have been conditioned to feel tactless, failing to employ a sounder method of discipline, violating the peaceful, agreeable mother-child bond.

The other issue is the possibility that the mothers do indeed frequently and excessively lose control over their emotions when scolding their children. The husband-fathers are absent from home and parents-in-law no longer live with them. The mothers have no one to turn to but must take on a nurturant role and disciplinarian role with which they may be uncomfortable. Isolation with the children at home may cause the mothers to focus on minute details of children's behavior. In addition to the pressure placed on the mother as a single caretaker and on childrearing as the mother's exclusive responsibility, the existence of observers may have something to do with the seeming contradiction between the image of indulging mothers and self-reported "en mama terrible." The Japanese mothers, when being observed, may tend to become more self-conscious. Actually, some mothers confided to me that when there are guests at home, the children know that their mothers would make a maximum effort not to scold them so the children behave especially naughtily, taking advantage of the situation. The mothers, feeling like a pressure cooker and thinking, "I'm going to get you for this," would do just that as soon as the guests have gone.

American mothers may diagnose their Japanese counterparts as frustrated or overwhelmed and advise them to have a time-out from the children and find their own pursuits. These Japanese mothers, however, tend to think that they should take their children's perspectives more and try to understand better why their children are doing what they are doing so that the mothers will not be so angry. Moreover, if the mothers put themselves in their children's shoes, the mothers won't scold the way they do now but will find gentler ways. In other words, devoting themselves more to tuning into the children's feelings, reinforcing the oneness, or having *omoiyari* (empathy) is the mothers' resolution. In this reasoning – being even more involved in their children rather than taking a break from them – the *amae* interdependence appears to take on further intensity.

To the question of an unfit mother, the response was predominantly a "selfish" mother. Mothers who cannot "sacrifice themselves" for the family are regarded as unfit mothers and total devotion to the role seems to be the norm that is held true at any time.

The mothers are strict in criticizing themselves in this regard also. Some mothers said that they are "selfish," dragging their children along during their shopping, doing their hobbies (instead of doing something for the children), having the children adjust to the mother's schedule (rather than the other way around). Many more mothers admitted to being "selfish" occasionally, especially when things get busy or their physical condition is bad. When the mothers feel tired or sick, they admit to skipping household chores. Failing to be considerate to the children or doing poor household work due to an ill condition are both thought to be selfish.

Lock's (1987) observation of medicalization of social and interpersonal conflict among Japanese housewife-mothers, adds another dimension to this attitude. Conflict between constant pressure to perfect the maternal role (which is imposed by both culture and the mothers themselves) and the desire to get away from it may be expressed as physical fatigue or an ill condition, which prevents the mothers from performing their tasks at their usual high level. While this is a convenient excuse for taking a break from the maternal role – though the mother may or may not be aware of it – the mothers express a guilt feeling. It is difficult to speculate whether the mothers genuinely feel guilty; or because they are conscious of the cultural norm of role commitment, the mothers may feel it is necessary to express their guilt for not living up to the expectation.

What Are the Safety Valves?

Dissatisfaction with the maternal role is not expressed in either interviews or the questionnaire, except possibly in the form of physical illness, as mentioned earlier, and the mothers' anticipation for the stage that follows the intense *kosodate* period as will be discussed later. Given their interpersonal environment and the pressure to commit to the maternal role, it may be expected that the mothers should feel isolation, frustration, and underachievement. The question might be asked why these negative feelings did not surface. The answer lies in the convention of the normative ideal. These women are following a Japanese communicative style of putting a good face on their personal situations; were they to admit difficulties and unhappiness to the researcher, they might see themselves as unworthy complainers. So they support conventional ideals in characterizing their personal lives and indeed, this kind of affective support for convention is part of the highly committed *kosodate* mother role itself.

What works as a safety valve other than the aforementioned medicalization of the conflict? One such device might be the anticipation that "This, too, shall pass." Three-quarters of the mothers said yes to the question, "would you like to work in the future?" This result and the fact that the majority of the mothers do not wish they had continued their jobs because they feel they could not handle both responsibilities of home and outside work lead to the following speculation: that the mothers see there is a stage of mothering that requires concentrated maternal attention and that after passing that stage, mothers feel less restricted in staying home and more at ease at diverting their energy and time. Also, as the children grow, so does the financial cost of educating them, therefore, providing extra financial resources for the children becomes a part of mothering. The longer hours the children spend at school both physically and psychologically free mothers from childcare. At the same time, by taking a part-time job,[4] the mothers are able to continue to assume the maternal role upon the children's return to home from school. Thus, without hindering their identity as a mother, the mothers can safely look forward to expanding their daily life.

Most mothers cited children's readiness either in a concrete age or grade level (after their youngest "enter kindergarten," "enter the elementary school," "become second or third graders," "are in upper grades (4th–6th)," "become junior high school students," "senior high school students"), or in more abstract expressions as signaling the time for the mothers to get jobs. Such expressions include: "when (my) hand becomes free from the children," "after the children are grown," "when children can understand,"

---

4   The majority of the mothers stated that this would be their choice. Choice that is convenient for business and industry's perspective as well. The economic structure of Japanese society takes advantage of the internalized norm of women as mothers as the premiere role, and is able to get an ample supply of inexpensive labor without having to pay benefits or guaranteeing long-term employment.

"when children become independent," "when children are settled down," "when the time free from children increases," and so on.

Another safety valve could be the *shikata ga nai* (there is no help for it) mentality, which can be regarded as a common method of suppression of feelings in Japanese culture. To pass the frustration and reach the stage of "*shikata ga nai*" demonstrates the wisdom of a mature person. There is no use in being frustrated when one cannot do anything to change the circumstances without causing friction with the family, which would make things worse. In order to illustrate resolution of conflict, in particular, two separate interviews will be introduced in the following pages.

Mrs. Araki.[5] Mrs. Araki is a forty-year-old, slight woman with short graying hair. She has a husband who is a year older than she, a ten-year-old boy, and a five-year-old girl. Her husband works as an electrical engineer and makes somewhere between nine and ten million yen ($77,000–85,000) a year. The couple graduated from universities. She is currently a full-time housewife who previously worked as a counselor and has been wanting to go back to the job.

Mrs. Araki seemed to be ordinarily a quiet, reserved person. Yet, as she introduced herself to the researcher, she was enthusiastic about having an opportunity to discuss her desire to work as a counselor again. She spoke without having to be prompted throughout the interview. First she recounted the circumstance of her resignation from the counseling job. She had worked as a counselor for four years and was determined to continue her work after her first child was born. Three weeks after the birth, however, the boy was hospitalized for intestinal blockage and in and out of the hospital for about a year. Mrs. Araki said that she could have worked while he was in the hospital; she could have just left him there and delivered her milk. But she couldn't because it was her "first-born baby." "Besides, when he was released from the hospital, there would have been nobody to take care of the baby except his mother; a nursery wouldn't take a sickly child, all the grandparents lived far away and were unavailable." Even though she had hoped for her eventual return to her work, the counseling center filled her vacancy with another person and she thought it was her "mission to raise the child she was given." She gave up trying to get back to her job.

The child's condition varied over the next few years. When the child was well, she would reminisce about the old cases she treated and felt a strong desire to go back to her work but when the child got ill, she could forget her

5 In order to protect the privacy of the informants, pseudonyms are used.

work and concentrate on the child's recovery. By the time the child entered kindergarten, his condition had been successfully treated and Mrs. Araki received words from the clinic where she used to work that there was a job opening. She wanted to "seize this opportunity." "Fortunately or unfortunately," Mrs. Araki said, smiling, "I found out I was pregnant again." She felt "intense conflict." "Why do the chances always have to slip away from me?" she thought then. "If I weren't pregnant, I could work – such a thought really frustrated me. But now I know it is only an illusion. An illusion to think as if you would be able to work without the child." Once the child was born, Mrs. Araki said, she cherished the girl and thought that she could learn a lot of things through childrearing that can be applied to counseling.

"For a woman to be able to continue working, her husband needs to be cooperative. First it depends on his occupation. If he works for a company, you cannot expect him to be home on time." Such is Mrs. Araki's observation that came too late for her. "I didn't calculate that matter before I got married." But in any case, she figures that the majority of Japanese husbands come home late. Especially men like her husband, who is forty-one and has reached a senior position, tend to work even later while allowing younger men to leave for home. She thinks that his upbringing, or more specifically, his mother's influence is important, too. Mrs. Araki's own mother was once working outside the home, so she has no objection to the idea of a working mother, unlike her husband's mother. Mrs. Araki can understand her mother-in-law's feelings, even though it is not favorable to her own desire to work. She wants to show her respect to her mother-in-law's feeling and her husband's; he is capable of only limited cooperation, since he was brought up by his mother after all. Mrs. Araki summed up her feeling about her current situation vis-à-vis the job as "*shikata ga nai*" (there is no help for it). She sees that those women who can continue to work have not only professional jobs but other conditions satisfied: understanding and helpful in-laws and cooperative husbands. About other mothers in general, Mrs. Araki voiced some suspicion: "Many mothers go to culture centers nowadays. I wonder if they are truly satisfied. It seems to me they take courses (not to pursue their own interests) to search for friends. Maybe it gives some pleasure, temporarily." After a little pause, she continued, "But you have to continue one thing while raising young children to develop your hobby into *ikigai*. When children get older, they go to *juku*,[6] which are expensive, then mothers start working part-time. They may say,

---

[6] After-school private tutoring places.

'for children's sake,' but what it boils down to is just killing time." She added, "Mothers now have no clear goals of their own and therefore get obsessed with their children."

Displayed in Mrs. Araki's story of job resignation are the feelings of inseparability from her "first-born baby," failure in arranging childcare due to lack of adequate institutions, and unavailability of extended family members. Half-forced by social conditions, Mrs. Araki entered full-time motherhood and accepted her new role with commitment (her "mission"). Nonetheless, she admitted experiencing the frustration of not being able to work as a counselor in the past when she was pregnant with her second child. But she did not display her frustration any more, at least not during the interview. Rather, she shrugged it off, saying, "*Shikata ga nai.*" Mrs. Araki's earlier usage of the word "illusion" also underscores this feeling. In addition to affirming maturity in not fighting against the circumstances, Mrs. Araki finds comfort that her experience as a mother is not a waste when she resumes a counseling job in the future. It seems that finding meaning in motherhood not only for its own sake but for the purpose of excelling as a counselor is Mrs. Araki's way of resolving the conflict that has arisen from her career interrupted by motherhood. Affirming the maturity and wisdom brought through motherhood, Mrs. Araki nevertheless feels compelled to draw a line between herself and other mothers, who appear to be lacking "self" and personal goals, and as a result of being obsessed with their children. These downsides of motherhood can be avoided, as Mrs. Araki does, by having career goals. Thus her desire to go back to work and the demands of motherhood are somewhat successfully integrated in Mrs. Araki.

Mrs. Yamamoto – longing for freedom. Mrs. Yamamoto is a thirty-five-year-old mother of two boys, aged six and four. She teaches piano to children at home. Her husband is forty years old and works as a salesperson. The combined family income for the 1992 fiscal year was in the range of five to six million yen ($43,000–51,000). They both graduated from college.

Mrs. Yamamoto, a short but energetic woman wearing a Harvard sweatshirt, was eager to talk to the researcher about her frustration over not being able to expand her hobby and work – learning and teaching the rhythmic method (a method designed to teach music through body movement). She explained:

I wanted to start swimming lessons after my younger son entered kindergarten. Then I was asked to be on the P.T.A. board and had to give up on going to the swimming pool. I also planned to increase my working hours in the fall asking for help with child care from my mother who lives not far away. However, my father injured his leg and my mother, who had to take care of him, became unavailable. So my plan to work also fell through.

Mrs. Yamamoto spoke of the turn of events in a fast tempo, laughing as if her stumbling at each of her plans was some sort of comedy. In the end, however, she became quiet. Asked by the researcher how she felt about her plans, Mrs. Yamamoto said, "It's not the right time. I feel frustrated, but I keep telling myself, `It's not the right time yet.'"

Still, she seemed to wonder if there should be alternatives for her other than accepting life as it is. Her recent encounter with an American stewardess through a group called "Home Hospitality," which invites foreign visitors to Japanese homes convinced her that "Japanese husbands are doing less than their American counterparts." She learned that the stewardess's husband was taking care of their two grade-school students while the mother was away. He would come home at 4:00 in the evening to look after the children. Mrs. Yamamoto was "surprised" and at the same time "couldn't help being envious." She figured Japanese fathers work too much and went on to assess her own husband.

Compared with the general standard, my husband is a family man; sometimes he washes dishes and he takes care of the children while I'm gone for a conference twice a month. But I know there are husbands who are doing much more. Well, but it's also true that many husbands do much less than my husband. In any case, Japanese men overwork.

Then Mrs. Yamamoto started to talk about her experience in the United States when she was a college student and learning the rhythmic method at a summer school. She said that she really had a wonderful time then and that she would like to do a similar thing in the future. "I would like to go to study abroad – either in Switzerland or the U.S. – when my children become high school students and are able to take care of themselves while their mother is gone." She said firmly, "My *ikigai*, hobby, and work all revolve around the rhythmic method."

Like Mrs. Araki, Mrs. Yamamoto has a strong desire for her personal goals and tries to resolve the conflict, however less successfully. Mrs. Yamamoto tries to accept the fact that her husband, like the majority of Japanese men, cannot be counted on to do household work or childcare. But her exposure to American culture makes it harder for her to accept it as an unchangeable social custom. Having her own mother nearby also made it difficult for Mrs. Yamamoto to shoulder the childrearing responsibility totally. It has been always a possibility in her mind that she could relegate at least partial responsibility to her mother in order to create more time to devote to her own activities.

Furthermore, it may be harder to make a positive connection between the rhythmic method and motherhood, whereas experience as a mother can be readily valued in counseling. While Mrs. Araki reminisces about her old cases and ponders different approaches, utilizing her experience gained as a mother and setting up almost imaginary training sessions, Mrs. Yamamoto longs for the day when she can be free from her childcare responsibility and act on her desire to learn more about the rhythmic method, just like in her single days.

Such a condition may be causing considerable frustration, which may be reflected in her own assessment as a mother. She rated herself 50, because she often finds herself unable to control her angry emotions toward her children. Her own mother has criticized Mrs. Yamamoto, saying that she is too harsh on her children, to which Mrs. Yamamoto responded that her mother is too permissive. In the questionnaire, she chose the lifestyle, "Do what I want to do as long as not causing trouble to my family," which may represent her compromise in balancing her passion for the rhythmic method and the motherhood responsibility.

3

The anatomy of *kosodate mama* has been examined, and some criticisms or questions readily come to mind.

Is *kosodate mama* an Urban Middle-class Model?

Is *kosodate mama* an urban middle-class model, who can financially afford to stay home and tend to the children? Yes, it is an urban but not necessarily a middle-class model. Because of the lesser degree of education they receive, working-class mothers do not often reach the position for which maternal leave is provided. Their husbands may not be liberal enough to share household work and/or childcare. Nursery schools typically have rigid hours, which makes it very inconvenient for many working mothers. One mother observed nursery schools are "for people who have 9–5 kind of jobs, like the government." These circumstances are portrayed in the following interview.

Mrs. Shioda. Mrs. Shioda is a twenty-six-year-old housewife and her husband is a thirty-year-old construction worker. They live with their children, a three-year-old boy and a two-year-old girl, in a publicly subsidized apartment building. Mrs. Shioda graduated from high school and Mr. Shioda graduated from junior high school. Mrs. Shioda has worked various jobs for three years but quit working at the time of her marriage. She has experience of working as a waitress and as a server at the wedding receptions at a wedding hall, among others, and thinks a job at a wedding hall would give her *ikigai* in the future, though at this point, "extra money" is the real attraction. She does not know, however, when she can start working. Mrs. Shioda spoke of her friend's experience. "One of my friends started working as a life insurance salesperson after her child entered kindergarten. But the child often became sick and she had to stay home to take care of the child. This friend finally quit the job." Mrs. Shioda continues,

> Actually I thought about working, too, like as a cosmetic saleslady or something. I could send applications for my children to the nearby nursery school (which has longer hours than a kindergarten) and start working. I was really serious but I talked myself out of it.

Asked why she gave up the idea of working, Mrs. Shioda said,

> Even if my children were at a nursery school, when they get sick, and at their age, they get a cold or tummy ache, this or that, I would have to take a day off and care for them. So I have decided it's better not to start working only to quit after a short while like my friend. Besides I heard that it's going to be easy (to go to work) after children enter school and so I shouldn't hurry.

There are mothers, of course, who need to bring in extra money, no matter how little it is. These mothers often opt for *naishoku* so that they can work while keeping an eye on their young. Torn between the two tasks at hand, however, they may be forced at times to pay less attention to the children's needs. Wrote one such mother, "I still remember when my son started to talk. One of his first words was 'mommybusy.' I felt like I was being stabbed in my heart." She realized how frequently she had turned down her toddler.

This example testifies to the fact that there are indeed class differences in Japan, and, in a strict sense, that full-time housewife-motherhood or *kosodate mama* is a middle-class model, even though the idea has permeated into the working class (quitting work at the time of marriage, for example) and the difficulty of finding a job that is compatible with childcare responsibility (and back-up childcare in case of a child's sickness) keeps many of them in full-time motherhood.

Are There Any Working Mothers?

Yes, there are. Because most mothers who have jobs work part-time while their children are at kindergarten, as a group, they do not show much difference from stay-at-home mothers, except in a couple of points. Some of the former group feel sorry for their children when they cannot attend various school events, and wonder if their mothering is inferior to their full-time mother counterparts in the sense that their attention has to be divided. All but a few underplay the significance of their jobs in their lives. The mothers with part-time jobs often stated that their work is an extension of their hobbies or helping their husbands' business. In other words, they regard their part-time jobs as not conflicting with but inclusive in the framework of the full-time housewife-mother.

There are two mothers who work full time (or eight hours a day): a dentist and a nurse. The former lives around the corner from her parents' home, which is also her place of work. She works for a total of eight hours a day; nonetheless, her work schedule is spread out through the day to accommodate the time for childcare. Her first session starts at 9:00 (after her children have gone off to school or kindergarten) and ends at noon. Then she goes to kindergarten to get her child and spends early afternoon with the child. She goes back to work at 2:00, works until 4:00, then goes home and prepares dinner. Her mother takes over the childcare. After her third and last session, 5:00–7:00, she goes home. She feels responsible for continuing her work because she is the heiress to her family practice and thinks that being a working mother is a good influence on the children; they may feel the need to be self-reliant. The nurse mother lives with her mother. The nurse mother leaves for work at 7:00 in the morning and comes home at 6:00 in the evening. Sometimes she has night shifts also. She has been working as a nurse for eleven years and answered the question, "How long would you like to continue the job and why?": "For a long time, because I am proud of my job and I need my income to help the mortgage payment." She also shows, however, other feelings in the response to a question on personal goals. She wrote, among other things, "In the near future (if possible), I would like to quit my job and become a full-time mother for my children. Right now, I am too dependent on my mother (who lives with the family) for childcare." Her case exemplifies the condition to which many mothers refer as ideal or even the only possible way for a mother to be able to work full time: cohabitation with the mother who helps around the house and a good job (a job that requires certain qualifications and not easily replaceable). But even then, this mother hovers around the idea of becoming a full-time mother. Her remark, "I am too dependent on my mother," came not out of the concern that her relationship with her own mother might be strained if she would continue "burdening" her mother, but rather from the internalized cultural value of being a fit mother.

Getting help from one's own mother is regarded as a very desirable, almost necessary condition for a woman to work full time. Two *amae* relationships are in play; one between the grandmother and grandchildren and the mother and her grown-up daughter. Any lack of *amae* given by the mother to her children is compensated by the grandmother, and the mother's wish to work is supported by her own mother. For a mother to have a job may be regarded as a willful choice, for which her mother has to fill the void.

A couple of issues regarding the mothers' attitudes toward occupations need to be addressed. The fact that this research was conducted with mothers who had kindergartners, not nursery school students, has a lot to do with the predominant representation of full-time housewife-mothers. Kindergartens, however, are much more common institutions for three- to five-year-olds in Japan (making it more difficult for mothers to continue their jobs), and, therefore, it can be assumed that the model of *kosodate mama* represents a considerable population among Japanese mothers. Another is the issue of social desirability. Had it been research of women's careers rather than the mother's role, more ambitious, positive attitudes toward careers may have been forthcoming.

Is Conflict with the Maternal Role Not Voiced at All?

As has been discussed, the conflict mothers have with the maternal role is not openly stated. Instead, to feel conflict is presented as the evidence of selfishness or immaturity in a mother. One mother, however, seems to go beyond. Meet Mrs. Kamotani.

Mrs. Kamotani. Mrs. Kamotani is a thirty-one-year-old housewife. She lives with her husband (thirty-six years old, a product engineer), three boys (aged eight, six, and one), father-in-law (sixty-three years old) and mother-in-law (fifty-eight years old). She graduated from high school and her husband graduated from graduate school. The combined family income for the 1991 fiscal year was in the range of six to seven million yen ($51,000–60,000).

When called by the researcher to arrange a meeting, Mrs. Kamotani responded that she would be actually too busy for a meeting but that she would be willing to talk to the researcher for a while on the phone. The reason why she is usually busy is because she is an active member of a religious group called *jissen rinri kosei kai*, or Practical Ethics Righteous Association. Mrs. Kamotani devotes at least a few hours each day to the *jissen rinri kosei kai* activity, including the morning gathering that starts at 4:00 A.M. and "volunteer work" (which is virtually a recruitment of new members) in the afternoon.

She spoke of her motivation to join the group as follows: "When my oldest son first entered kindergarten, I worried about him all the time. Is he listening to the teacher? Is he doing all right? and so on." Her worry worsened when she saw him taking off his underwear while asleep.[7] The thought that came to her mind was, "Is he going to be a bully? Or worse, a rapist?" One day somebody from *jissen rinri kosei kai* advised Mrs. Kamotani, when she was suffering from a neurosis (according to her own account), that since the mother and child are connected through an invisible thread,[8] she was sending poisonous gas by worrying about the child. Mrs. Kamotani immediately bought this logic and the person further convinced her to practice ethical behavior as dictated by the group.

Mrs. Kamotani said that ever since she joined the group three years ago, she stopped worrying about her children. According to her, though "the real reward" will come years after, some benefits are already visible. As an example, she said, "Many children yawn at school or kindergarten on Mondays from fatigue from outings on Sundays. But not my children (because they never go out) and it is better that way, for my children are able to pay attention to what the teachers say."

In the questionnaire, Mrs. Kamotani wrote that her *ikigai* was trying to do things to please her husband, while her other's *ikigai* were children or hobbies. She chose lifestyle b, "To give preference to the children and home but sometimes enjoy myself." She is critical of other mothers who concentrate on the children and forget about the husbands. On the contrary to such families, which are like a "mother-child home," Mrs. Kamotani says she always shows her respect to the husband-father. "Whatever we do, we consult with him first." About her membership of *jissen rinri kosei kai*, however,

[7] Japanese boys, as well as girls, wear underpants and pajamas/nightgowns at night.
[8] The idea of an invisible thread between a mother and her child may sound very natural to Japanese people, who have a tradition (though fading now) of keeping the umbilical code in a special wooden box. And the *amae* psychology seems to be represented in a very graphical (however imaginary) way as an invisible thread.

she knows that her husband wants her to quit but he keeps quiet about "what his beloved wife does." As for the in-laws, she said that they also dare not voice their disapproval for they obtained their bride or daughter-in-law against her own parents' will. She wrote that she has been criticized by her parents-in-law for things she "no longer remembered."

Her zealousness for the religious activity seems to have outgrown her initial motivation – to stop sending poisonous gas to the children – and consumes her time on weekdays and weekends. Her husband, according to the questionnaire responses, spends no time interacting with his children (except thirty minutes on a weekend with the mother present). As a result of no family outings or activities, the children are not tired on Mondays, which she counts as a benefit of her religious work. Although Mrs. Kamotani maintains that she is doing it for her children and her future grandchildren, in whose generation it is believed that her devotion will be generously rewarded, it appears to be a rationalization on her part.

There also are contradictions in Mrs. Kamotani's behavior, such as claiming that her *ikigai* is pleasing her husband but her personal goal is to get the whole family to attend the meeting of the religious group, of which her husband does not approve. Mrs. Kamotani's religious activity can be viewed as a perfect outlet for her anger. Recall her "rapist" remark on her son, which may show her own aggression. Fearing her aggression toward her children might destroy them by "sending a poisonous gas," she joined the *jissen rinri kosei kai*, where she found her niche. Under the name of religion, she can get out of the house and leave the family behind. In other words, she can rebel against her husband and parents-in-law; the religion provides a shield. Her parents-in-law's criticism would no longer hurt her. To her husband, she can maintain that she is a good wife because she is devoting so much time to gain benefit for their children and grandchildren. Thus, Mrs. Kamotani's conflict in motherhood is being resolved within the very framework of motherhood – devotion to the family – however superficially.

CONCLUSIONS

In Japanese society, there are many advantages to being a full-time mother, which is in accordance with social sanctions and the internalized cultural value of commitment to this role. It is in agreement with the mothers' need for *amae*, inseparability from their young and the general belief that a child needs the mother to be home for a normal childhood, which helps to justify the intensity of the mothers' commitment to childcare.

Few career opportunities offering prospects for women's advancement, a scarcity of childcare facilities, frequently absent fathers among nuclear families, and so on, are manifestations of the current socioeconomic conditions that help to shape this full-time maternal role. Through all of this, few mothers openly express their dissatisfaction with this status quo. This cultural convention of the totally committed mother is reinforced by the mothers' acceptance of their personal situations and anticipation of the change that would allow them to branch out after the children reach a certain age. Thus, the *kosodate mama* is a product not only of prevalent socioeconomic conditions and cultural values but also of the involvement of the mothers who pursue moral virtue through their attitudes and activities as committed mothers. Role commitment in Japan requires a positive, effective attitude toward the norms, sometimes resulting in perfectionism, extreme self-criticism, and self-sacrifice.

There are a few issues that might be suggested. One is that the maternal role may have to be differentiated according to the children's age/developmental stage. In other words, the cultural convention of a committed mother may have relevance in real life only for *kosodate* mother (i.e., mother of a preschool child). Another is that the mothers' anticipation of the next stage in which they hope to expand beyond the maternal role works conversely to reinforce the intense commitment to childcare during the *kosodate* period. The third is that the change may exist only in the mothers' imagination for the future. In other words, the kind of change that the mothers are hoping for – continuing to enjoy and devote themselves to the children but at the same time carrying out meaningful and financially gainful work, deriving *ikigai* from sources both inside and outside the home – may never materialize.

The data used in this research were expressed in verbal form. Therefore, it is difficult to understand what the mothers "really" feel or to what extent their expressed feelings are "true." With the issue of social desirability and Japanese dualism of *honne* (true feeling) versus *tatemae* (social expectation) in mind, it is possible that the mothers may have deliberately brought their responses in line with the public norms, but that seems to be part of their normal functioning outside the research situation. Finding ways to clarify this aspect of Japanese women's experiences is one among many that are left for future research.

REFERENCES

Azuma, H. (1986). Why study child development in Japan? In H. Stevenson, H. Azuma, & K. Hakuta (Eds.), *Child development and education in Japan* (pp. 3–12). New York: W. H. Freeman and Company.

Befu, H. (1986). The social and cultural background of child development in Japan and the United States. In H. Stevenson, H. Azuma, & K. Hakuta (Eds.), *Child development and education in Japan* (pp. 13–27). New York: W. H. Freeman and Company.

DeVos, G. A. (1973). *Socialization for achievement.* Berkeley: University of California Press.

Doi, T. (1973). *The anatomy of dependence.* Tokyo: Kodansha International Ltd.

Imamura, A. E. (1987). *Urban Japanese housewives: At home and in the community.* Honolulu: University of Hawaii Press.

Kumagai, H. H. (1981). A dissection of intimacy: A study of bipolar posturing in Japanese social interaction – amaeru and amayakasu, indulgence and deference. In *Medicine and Psychiatry, 5,* 249–72.

Lebra, T. S. (1976). *Japanese patterns of behavior.* Honolulu: University of Hawaii Press.

Lebra, T. S. (1984). *Japanese women: Constraint and fulfillment.* Honolulu: University of Hawaii Press.

Lifton, R. J. (1967). *The woman in America.* Boston: Beacon Press.

Lock, M. (1987). Protest of a good wife and wise mother: The medicalization of distress in Japan. In E. Norbeck & M. Lock (Eds.), *Health, illness, and medical care in Japan: Cultural and social dimensions.* Honolulu: University of Hawaii Press.

Vogel, S. H. (1978). Professional housewife: The career of urban middle class Japanese women. In *Japan Interpreter, 12*(1), 16–43.

Wakai K. (1990). Reading picture books for the first time. In *Library Newsletter No. 5.* Sapporo: Hokkaido University Kindergarten. [In Japanese]

FOUR

Japanese Mother-Child Relationships

Skill Acquisition Before the Preschool Years

Shusuke Kobayashi

Ethnographic studies on Japanese family life have suggested that the acquisition of basic social and communicative skills during early childhood take place in the context of a close emotional bond between mother and child, with the mother avoiding confrontation in order to encourage attunement to her wishes. The present study was designed to test this hypothesis and describe how skills can be taught in early childhood without conflict between mother and child. This study specifies the maternal strategies and speech patterns involved and presents how the mothers are sensitive to their children's reaction to their controlling effort and how their childrearing ideals are reflected in their interaction patterns.

Videotaped observations were made of ten urban middle-class Japanese mothers with their twenty-four- to thirty-eight-month-old children during snack time at home. Microanalysis of interactive sequences and maternal explanations showed: (a) Mothers prefer indirect verbal instructions to direct ones, often using the latter only when the former have not worked, and (b) Mothers believe that they should not oppose the child's will to insure spontaneous compliance with maternal instructions that will be experienced by the child as voluntary rather than coerced.

While these findings support the hypothesis generated by ethnographic studies, there are findings to which ethnographic reports have paid little attention, due to their emphasis on culture-specific aspects of childrearing patterns: (a) Japanese mothers do use direct verbal instructions, though they do so in a sensitive way, without making them sound imposing, and (b) Some indirect maternal strategies marked as culture-specific are not observed ubiquitously in actual mother-child interactions.

The findings indicate that for the understanding of the subtle negotiation between mother and child during skill teaching, it is important to analyze the implications of Japanese concepts of childrearing used in mothers' explanation of their own controlling effort, rather than to use the framework of Western dichotomy of discipline versus indulgence. The findings also suggests that the American hypothesis about the positive effects of firm parental control on the child's competence in socialization skill and internalization of values is not applicable to the Japanese childrearing practices.

CULTURAL MEANINGS OF MOTHER-CHILD RELATIONSHIPS

Since early reports on Japanese life appeared (e.g., Benedict, 1946), it has been claimed that the Japanese mother-child relationship is close and that the Japanese mother is indulgent toward her young child. This strong emotional bond has been explained as mutual dependency (Vogel, 1963), interdependence (Caudill & Weinstein, 1969; Lebra, 1976), and *amae* or sweetness in dependency (Doi, 1973). The Japanese mother seems to attempts to foster her young child's emotional dependence on her through close contact in cobathing and cosleeping and through avoidance of denying the child's wishes, while she herself experiences emotional satisfaction from such practices.

At the same time, however, Japanese school children are well disciplined in the sense that they are compliant and polite and that their behavior is well regulated (Benedict, 1946; Lanham, 1956). In preschool, Japanese children develop various habits appropriate to group behavior including self-reliance, conformity, and control of egoistic tendencies, and before they enter preschool, their mothers prepare them for preschool life by teaching them basic skills (Hendry, 1986; Peak, 1991).

In trying to understand the process of the Japanese child's skill acquisition, the coexistence of maternal indulgence and maternal attempts to regulate the child's behavior has posed a puzzling discrepancy to Western observers who are familiar with the image of Western mothers teaching their children skills while encouraging their emotional independence and who also believe that "indulgence" is incompatible with teaching and learning. Then, how does the Japanese mother facilitate her preschool-age child's acquisition of skills for self-sufficiency and interpersonal communication without endangering her strong emotional bond with the child? What specific maternal strategies does the Japanese mother use in this training, which seems to be difficult psychological experiences to both her child and herself?

In trying to discuss these problems, the ethnographic studies on Japanese childrearing patterns have generated the hypothesis that the basic strategy for childrearing in Japan is to establish a close relationship with the child and try to get the child to understand instead of imposing the mother's will (Vogel, 1963; Lebra, 1976; White, 1987). In Japanese childrearing, discipline is not imposed on the child but learned by the child spontaneously. In order for such learning to take place, the mother teaches only when the child is in a cooperative mood. The mother's aim is to establish a close relationship with the child so the child goes along with suggestions without asking questions. The techniques the Japanese mother uses for the child's skill acquisition by relying on this close emotional bond include appealing to the child's empathy, teasing, and praise.

This explanatory model is congruent with the cultural ideal of interpersonal relationship in Japan, that is, harmonious conformity, which expects the individual to be sensitive to others' needs and act upon them spontaneously. Against this cultural background, Japanese children's early learning takes place in the context of an emotionally interdependent relationship with their mothers, and this learning pattern is also used, though modified accordingly, between the teacher and student when children enter school (Rohlen, 1983; White, 1987).

It seems that in Japanese children's early "indulgence," mothers do not simply spoil their children. On the contrary, the "indulgent" Japanese mothers are preparing their children for their later social life by teaching them the importance of emotionally interdependent relationships.

These explanations tend to be rather general, however, failing to account for either how culture-specific strategies are actually used or how the mother is sensitive to the maintenance of the indulgent atmosphere while regulating the child's behavior. First, the contents of maternal strategies are situation-specific. In order to avoid opposing the child's will and to maintain an interdependent relationship between herself and her child, the mother has to be sensitive to the child's reaction to her controlling effort; she has to interpret the child's behavior, decide how to respond to it, and if her attempt fails, she has to modify her strategies (Grusec & Kuczynski, 1980; Minton, Kagan, & Levine, 1971; Schaffer & Crook, 1979, 1980). Second, as skill teaching seems to take place in an indulgent atmosphere, how does the Japanese mother distinguish discipline from indulgence? The examination of the mother's awareness of her role in the child's skill acquisition will shed light on meanings of discipline and indulgence in the context of Japanese childrearing practices.

Thus, the specific research questions of this study were: (a) The Pattern of Strategies: What specific controlling strategies does the Japanese mother use? How are her strategies related to her effort to control the child's behavior without direct confrontation with the child? and (b) The Mother's Emphasis on the Emotional Bond: How clearly is the Japanese mother aware of the importance of the emotional bond with her child during skill teaching? How does she distinguish indulgence from discipline?

My interest is to incorporate into a detailed description of maternal behavior the mother's explanation of her own behavior and psychological experiences at a specific moment of the interaction. The mother's own explanation will at least reveal the mother's awareness of her own emotional state and beliefs about childrearing, which seem to influence her behavior in interpreting and regulating the child's behavior.

PROCEDURE OF OBSERVATION

In order to observe the mother-child interactions in a relaxed and naturalistic situation, I observed mothers and children having snacks at home. At preschool, children are expected to have lunch and a snack every day, and thus eating properly is an indispensable skill for their preschool life. The subjects were ten pairs of mothers and their twenty-four- to thirty-eight-month-old children living in a suburban area of Tokyo. The children were five boys and five girls, all first-born. The average age of the child was thirty-one months. These children had not had experiences of preschool, either *yochien* or *hoikuen*. Because my research questions were based on the ethnographic studies focusing on the urban middle-class families, I chose wives of white-collar salaried men with at least a college degree. The mothers had college or junior-college degrees and came from middle-class families. These mothers were what Vogel (1978) calls "professional housewives," devoted to the care of their husbands and children. The mothers' age varied from twenty-five to thirty years, the average being twenty-seven years.

Observation was conducted in the summer of 1990. The mother-child interactions were observed either in the kitchen or in the living room. The whole sequence during the snack time was videotaped. The length of observation varied, ranging from nine to twenty-three minutes, the average being fourteen minutes. The videotaped interactions were transcribed into detailed narrative description. Then, the episodes showing the mother's attempt to control the child's behavior were singled out from the entire scene. In this research, "skill teaching episode" is defined as an instance in which the mother is trying to modify the child's behavior, regardless of the degree of success. Each episode deals with at least one specific skill such as eating neatly and saying greetings. To examine the mother's controlling effort, examples of both success and failure in gaining compliance were analyzed, rather than the successful techniques per se.

Then, a few days after the initial observation, the videotaped interactions were shown to the mothers individually at home. They were encouraged to comment on what they saw. I asked them both questions to help clarify their comments and the questions I had prepared while transcribing and reviewing the initial interactions. I also asked them to explain their beliefs about childrearing at a more general level. The mothers' comments were tape-recorded and transcribed.

SKILLS INVOLVED IN THE SKILL TEACHING EPISODES

The skill teaching episodes (ninety examples in total) observed during the snack time fall into the three categories according to the aspects of the mother-child relationship, which a skill contributes to: (a) Hygiene: skills for the child's own healthy development; (b) Conventional skills: skills for interpersonal communication; (c) Practical skills: skills for the mother's convenience. Although specific skills emphasized by the mothers differ among children, depending on the mothers' expectations about the child's skill acquisition and/or the level of the child's skill acquisition, most frequently stressed skills were eating neatly and consumption of food (Table 4.1).

Table 4.1. *Skills Involved in the Skill Teaching Episodes*

Category	Skills	Examples		(%)
Hygiene	digestion	1	(1.11%)	29
	try various kinds of foods	3	(3.33%)	(32.22%)
	consume all the served food	25	(27.77%)	
Conventional skills	greeting before eating	2	(2.22%)	31
	courtesy to the guest	13	(14.44%)	(34.44%)
	table manner*	16	(17.77%)	
Practical skills	eat neatly	28	(31.11%)	30
	help oneself**	2	(2.2%)	(33.33%)
Total		90		(100.00%)

Notes:
* eating with utensils, sitting properly
** starting to eat by oneself, going to the bathroom without being reminded

Table 4.2. *Frequency of Controlling Strategies Used by Mothers*

Strategies							
Explicit Strategies							
Command						75	(39.68%)
imperative: V + *nasai*	4	(2.12%)					
imperative: V + *te*	28	(14.81%)	54	(28.57%)			
obligation: V + *naito dame*	4	(2.12%)					
obligation: V + *naito*	7	(3.70%)					
prohibition	11	(5.82%)					
Request			9	(4.76%)			
Instruction/Generalization			12	(6.35%)			
Suggesting Strategies							
Preference/Permission			9	(4.76%)	26	(13.76%)	
Suggestion			17	(8.99%)			
Inferred Strategies							
Direct Control Measures						88	(46.55%)
positive:							
cheering/encouragement	3	(1.59%)					
soothing	2	(1.06%)	22	(11.64%)			
negative:							
teasing/shaming	11	(5.82%)					
disapproval	5	(2.65%)					
provoking fears	1	(0.15%)					
Indirect Control Measures							
questions:							
reminder/suggestion	9	(4.76%)	66	(34.92%)			
rhetorical question	15	(7.94%)					
hint/rationale	42	(22.22%)					
Total						189	(100.00%)

Note: V = verbal stem.

Two mothers with whom the observer joined the interaction as a guest were concerned about the child's courtesy to the observer. Half of the teaching episodes in these two cases were about serving the guest foods and/or drinks. These mothers stated in the interview that greeting and entertaining guests are important skills to be mastered before the child goes to kindergarten.

Table 4.3. *Explicit Strategies*

Strategies	Features	Examples
Command		
Imperative	v + *nasai*	*Chigauno ni shinasai.* (Choose a different one.)
	v + *te*	*Kore tabete.* (Eat this.)
Obligation	v + *naito dame*	*Chanto suwaranaito.* (You have to sit properly.)
	v + *naito*	
	v + *nakya*	
Prohibition	v + *dame*	*Kore wa dame.* (You cannot do this.)
	v + *ikenai*	
Request	v + *kudasai*	*Yamete kudasai.* (Please stop it.)
Instruction/	v + *suru*	
Generalization	v + *shinai*	*Sonna koto shinai no.* (You won't do that.)

Note: v = verb.

MATERNAL STRATEGIES FOR SKILL ACQUISITION

The analysis of the mothers' controlling strategies focused on not only what kind of strategies the mothers preferred to use but also how such strategies are related to the mothers' efforts to avoid direct confrontation with their children when controlling their behavior. Therefore, the observed controlling strategies were categorized by degree of directness: (a) explicit strategies that allow very little psychological space to the listener (Table 4.3); (b) suggestive strategies that allow more freedom of response than explicit strategies (Table 4.4); and (c) inferred strategies in which demand is not

Table 4.4. *Suggestive Strategies*

Strategies	Features	Examples
Preference/Permission		
positive	v + *ho ga ii*	*Koko ni oite ii no.* (You can put it here.
	v + *te ii*	= Put it here.)
negative	v + *nai ho ga ii*	*Sonna koto shinakute ii no.* (You don't
	v + *nakute ii*	have to do such a thing. = Don't do such a thing.)
Suggestion	v + *yoo*	*Motto tabeyoo ne.* (Let's eat more. = Eat more.)
	v + *tara*	*Ato ni shitara.* (How about doing it later? = Don't do it now.)

Note: v = verb.

Table 4.5. *Inferred Strategies: Direct Control Measures*

Strategies	Examples
Positive	
Cheering/Encouragement	*Okasan mo taberu, issoyo ne.* (Mom will also eat, [we are] together. = Eat it.)
Soothing	*Ii no, ii no, ii no.* (It's all right, all right, all right. = Don't pay attention to other things.)
Negative	
Teasing	*Okasan shiranakatta wa, sonna tabekata aruno.* (Mom didn't know there was such a manner to eat. = Eat neatly.)
Shaming	*Hazukashii!* (Ashamed! = Don't do that.)
Disapproval*	*Kitanai!* (Dirty! = Don't do that.)
Provoking fears	*Sonna koto shitara ojiisan yonde kuru.* (If you do such a thing, I'll call Grandfather. = Stop doing that.)

Note: * Disapproval takes the similar form to rationales but is distinguished by its strong emotional tone.

Table 4.6. *Inferred Strategies: Indirect Control Measures*

Strategies	Features	Examples
Question		
Reminder/Suggestion	*v + wa?*	*Itadakimasu wa?* (did you say "itadakimasu"? = Say "itadakimasu.")
	v + suru?	
	v + shita	
Rhetorical question		*Dare ga sonna koto shirotte itta no?* (Who told you to do such a thing?)
Hint/Rationale		*Kore oishii noni.* (This is tasty, though. = Eat more.)
		Moo sanji made oyatsu nai yo. (No more snacks till three o'clock. = Finish eating it now.)
		Ochichatta, ochichatta. (Dropped, dropped. = Don't drop it./Pick it up.)

Note: v = verb.

clearly expressed and makes the listener guess the demand (Tables 4.5 and 4.6). The degree of directness indicates how explicitly the mother's imperative intent is expressed.

Although the three groups are clearly marked in directness and explicitness, it is not the purpose of the present analysis to precisely rank-order each strategy according to degree of directness. Thus, the order of strategies summarized in tables do not correspond to the order of the degree of directness. Each maternal strategy was identified by its discrete grammatical features, especially inflections of verbs. When necessary, especially when identifying inferred strategies, I examined not only the context in which a particular maternal utterance was made but also the tone of voice of the utterance and the mother's intention explained by the mother herself in the interview. The frequency of behavior control strategies refers to the number of incidents of the ten mothers' use of strategies during skill teaching episodes (Table 4.2).

Explicit Strategies

The high frequency of the mothers' use of explicit strategies might sound inconsistent with the general image of the Japanese mother who controls the child's behavior in a subtle and implicit way. How then does the Japanese mother use explicit strategies?

The answer is that the Japanese mother uses explicit strategies in such a way that they do not sound as imposing as when she uses them directly; she prefers to use an explicit strategy only after an implicit one was not effective, and pairs commands with hints and suggestions. Moreover, she is sensitive to the child's reaction to her imperative intent and flexibly changes her strategy according to the child's response. Thus, even when using explicit directive strategies the Japanese mother does so in a subtle way.

This subtle way of persuasion is exemplified by the following episode. A mother told her twenty-nine-month-old daughter to pick up cookies from the can and place them onto the plate. The child did as she was told. Then, she picked up a brown cookie from the plate but she returned it to the plate. The mother's expectation was, as she told me later, that the child would recognize what she liked and eat it. The mother knew that the child liked chocolate cookies.

MOTHER (Picking up a brown cookie) This [cookie] has chocolate.
CHILD (Laughing) Waaa!

MOTHER Do you want the one with chocolate? Do you want a white one?

CHILD (No response.)

MOTHER (Putting down the cookie on the plate) Take one (*Saa ikko totte*). (Pushing the plate to the child) Hurry up and eat this (*Kore hayaku tabenasai*).

CHILD (Picks up a brown cookie and brings it to her mouth.)

In this example, the mother used imperatives: "Take one," and "Hurry up and eat this," after she repeated her expectation implicitly by a hint ("This [cookie] has chocolate") and two suggestive questions and found that they were not effective. From the viewpoint of the child's acquisition of communicative skills, by pairing the implicit and explicit strategies, the mother consciously or unconsciously provides her child a chance to learn how to understand others' subtle messages (Clancy 1986).

The mothers' frequent use of the imperative, verb + *te* also indicates their preference for not sounding imposing even when they have commanding intent. While this directive is a milder form of the imperative, verb + *nasai*, it may be categorized also as an informal request based on its form. In terms of directness, verb + *te* sounds less imposing than the imperative, verb + *nasai* and the formal request, verb + *kudasai*. It may be speculated that it is its form as informal request that made the mothers use the verb + *te* form quite often; with an imperative intent, they can express it in a milder form than imperative and can make it sound less imposing than formal request. It is hard to know, however, if mothers, let alone children, regard this form either as request or command.

By contrast, in spite of, and because of, its politeness, the formal request, when addressed by the mother to the child, sounds not only imposing but also emphasizes the emotional distance between the speaker (mother) and the listener (child). In the following example, a mother used a formal request to let the child know her seriousness. In the middle of the snack time, the child was getting bored and put a piece of dried fish into the milk:

MOTHER (In a small and harsh voice) Who told you to do such a thing?

CHILD: GRANDFATHER TOLD ME TO DO IT. I WON'T [BEHAVE].

MOTHER (Holding the child's hand quickly) Please stop it. Dirty! (*Yamete kudasai. Kitanai!*)

CHILD (Grins.)

MOTHER If you're going to do that, you shouldn't even eat.

CHILD (Looking down on the bowl, and eats the dried fish.)

The mother expressed her strong disapproval of the child's behavior by a rhetorical question in a small but harsh voice, "Who told you to do such a thing?" Then the child answered that it was his grandfather, and then said, "I won't [behave]." It seems that he was in an *amae* (presuming on others' benevolence) state, taking for granted that this much self-indulgence would be allowed by her; he responded to the mother's question in a playful way, mentioning the grandfather who apparently had nothing to do with the present interaction. Then the mother employed a strategy more clearly marked as command, a formal request form. By saying "Please stop it," the mother let him know her seriousness. Because of its formality, this must have been a strong statement to the child. Moreover, as if to confirm her seriousness, the mother immediately employed another strategy, an appeal to the child's feelings; she uttered "Dirty," the direct expression of her annoyed feeling at the child's behavior.

Suggestive Strategies

Suggestions were often followed by the mothers' utterances, which served as reasoning and encouragement. It seems that since the suggestion is not as explicit as the command and thus gives the child freedom to follow it, the mother wants to add some words to it to make sure her intent has been understood by the child. A mother suggested to her child that he should stop eating cookies by saying, "Let's make this the last one, OK? (*Kore de-oshimai ni shimashoo ne*)." Then she explained to him that if he did not stop eating, he could not have lunch, by saying, "Because you won't be able to eat your lunch." The child answered, "Yes," and put away the plate of cookies.

There is an interesting episode in which a mother emphasized the sense of togetherness with her child by suggesting that the child should eat. Kimiko, a twenty-five-month-old girl, was paying attention to a visiting child and was not eating noodles. Her mother said, "Mom wants to eat it, too. Kimiko will eat, too. Mom will eat. Look, together. (*Okasan mo tabeyo. Kimiko mo tabeyo ne. Okasan mo taberuyo ne. Issho ne*)." The child then started to eat. The mother explained about her utterances:

s. k.   Why did you say, "Mom wants to eat it, too. Kimiko will eat, too"?
MOTHER   Because she won't eat if she eats alone. Because she is content (*nattoku suru*) if everybody eats the same thing, I don't make her eat alone. [Do you think] it is strange?
s. k.   No.

MOTHER I'm teaching her we are together [when eating] and we are eating the same thing. I'm teaching. If I do so, she will eat because we are [doing] the same.

s. k. You do this in order for the child to concentrate on eating?

MOTHER Partly so, I think. . . . I don't think through each action every time.

When emphasizing the sense of togetherness in making the child eat, the mother did not deliberately plan to do so, although she was aware of its effect and could explain when asked its meaning. The emphasis on togetherness during the interaction seems to be so natural to her that it comes to her without thinking of it as a possible strategy she should use. These strategies seem to be effective because the suggestion itself (*shiyoo*, equivalent to "Let's" in English) emphasizes the sense of togetherness and is not imposing, allowing the child freedom to comply. It is also because this suggestion form was followed immediately and so naturally by the mother's encouragement, "Look, together," which seems to appeal to the child's feelings; the child does not feel that she is being requested to perform an action alone, but feels that the mother is willing to help her in her task.

Inferred Strategies

To analyze inferred strategies, I used two categories: (a) direct control measures, and (b) indirect control measures. Strategies categorized as direct control measures are used to control the child's behavior by either expressing the mother's feeling or eliciting the child's feeling, either positive or negative.

Whereas direct control measures are associated with strong emotional experiences of either the mother or the child, indirect control measures including questions and rationale/hint, are subtle and least imposing among maternal strategies. Thus, it is up to the child to infer the mother's intent, let alone how to respond to it. The mothers used this subtle method quite often although the children did not always understand the mothers' intentions.

Direct Control Measures. Whereas direct control measures were the most often used strategies of two mothers, five mothers did not use them at all. These two mothers' frequent use of these inferred strategies (eight times in one observation session for the mother of a boy and ten times for the mother of a girl) may reflect personal preference or habitual use. The frequency of teasing/shaming (eleven examples) is outstanding. Four out of five mothers who used any strategies categorized as direct control measures used teasing/shaming at least once.

Teasing is an *amae*-oriented strategy, making use of the child's emotional dependence on the mother and the child's anxiety that his/her *amae* relationship with the mother might be endangered. I define teasing as the mother's introducing in a playful manner a clear untruth, for example, asking the child if she can take his/her food. Teased by the mother, the child feels that the mother is denying his/her *amae* toward her by presenting the statement which is obviously untrue to the mother's intent and undesirable to the child. Teasing is threatening to the child all the more because the mother teases him/her in a playful manner when the child is feeling helpless.

The following example shows how teasing works in correcting the child's behavior without explicit command. A mother teased her twenty-five-month-old son four times during the observation. The child was sitting on the chair with his body facing the wall, not the table. The mother told him directly to sit properly, and the child answered with the repetition of "*hai* (yes)." The issue here is a lesson that the child should not repeat "*hai*" when he is told to do or not do certain things:

MOTHER Sit properly.
CHILD Yes, yes. (*Hai, hai.*)
MOTHER You should answer with only one yes (*hai*). Yes, yes (*Hai, hai*), you are good [at saying "Yes, yes."]
CHILD No, I'm not.
MOTHER You are.

To the mother's command, the child complied, half-seriously, expressing his negative feeling toward the mother's command, by repeating to her "*hai*." This is a bad-mannered answer; the repetition of "*hai*" conveys a sense of reluctant agreement and lack of seriousness. Moreover, his reluctance to the mother's command is against the ideal of *sunao,* an image of the child who internalizes the mother's wish as his own and does his best to achieve it (White & LeVine, 1986). To this answer of the child, the mother mimicked the child's answer and teased that he was good at answering that way. The child immediately protested against her teasing. Instead of explaining to him why the repetition of the answer is bad mannered, the mother chose teasing. It is because, sensing the lack of seriousness in the child's answer, she wanted to let him know that it is an unpleasant experience to be responded to half-seriously. Thus she chose a strategy of appealing to the child's feelings rather than reasoning, expecting that the child would learn how unpleasant it was to be answered with *"Hai, hai."* The child responded to this teasing as the mother might have expected; annoyed by the mother's teasing, an untrue statement that he was good at saying *"Hai, hai,"* he protested against the mother's remark. To this protest of the child, the mother teased back, as if to confirm her former teasing, having seen its effect on the child. The mother's utterances followed those of the child so smoothly that, as she later explained, she herself did not regard her teasing as a strategy when actually teasing him.

Contrary to expectation, there was no example of appealing to the imagined reactions of other people such as, "People will laugh at you." Because, in Japanese interpersonal relationships, to be sensitive to other people's view is important, the mothers sensitize the child to how other people regard the child's inappropriate behavior (Lebra, 1976). It was expected that the mothers would use the observer as the third person to whose views the child had to be sensitive.

And, yet, there was an episode in which a mother used the child's grandparents as authoritative figures. As Clancy (1986) explained, Japanese mothers use a third party as an authoritative figure, "distancing themselves from actual imperative" (p. 234). In this episode, to make her thirty-five-month-old son stop waving his legs under the table, the mother tried to invoke fear in him by mentioning imaginary anger of his grandparents, "If you do that with your legs, I'm going to call Grandfather and Grandmother. Shall I call Grandfather and Grandmother? I shouldn't call them?" Although the mother's voice sounded serious, the child did not show any reaction. Since the grandparents were not living with them, as authoritative figures they did not seem to be threatening to the child.

Indirect Control Measures. The mothers quite often tried to control their children's behavior by asking questions. By reminding children that they have not done the expected task, mothers correct children's behavior without direct command. Although mothers apparently know that their children neglected a task, they ask children questions such as "What about a greeting?" as if they were not sure if children did it or not. Thus, when children remind themselves that they have not done an expected task and now do it, they do not seem to feel pushed by the mother; they were just reminded by the mother, and they are doing the task on their own initiative.

Only two mothers used this technique, but one mother used it four times during one observation. At the beginning of the snack time, a boy started to eat without saying the greeting. Then, the mother reminded him that he did not say the greeting:

MOTHER Did you say *itadakimasu?*
CHILD (Looking at the mother) *Itadakimasu.*
MOTHER Did you say *itadakimasu?*
CHILD *Itadakimasu.*
MOTHER You did it wrong, right? Aren't you supposed to put your hands together?
CHILD (Clapping hands) *Itadakimasu.*

By the second question, the mother wanted to remind the child that he did not clap his hands when he said the greeting. But she used a rather indirect method to do so. Instead of asking, "Did you clap your hands when saying the greeting?" she simply repeated her first question, "Did you say itadakimasu?" She wanted the child to recall by himself that he had forgotten to clap his hands. Only when the child failed to guess based on her indirect message did she point out that he had forgotten that part of the ritual.

When using hints to control the child's behavior, the mother expects the child to figure out what the mother's directive intent is. The use of a hint is effective when the mother wants to modify the child's behavior without explicit commands. Because, however, in the hint the mother's intent is not clearly expressed, it seems hard for the young child to guess the mother's intent expressed as a statement of a simple fact, for example, "The tomato is tasty." By contrast, mothers of older children used hints successfully when correcting their children's behavior. In the following examples, hints (underlined) served as directives:

The guest [should be served] first. . . . The guest is first, isn't he? [The foods are] the guest's gift.
(Message: Don't start eating. Wait until the guest starts eating.
Result: The child waited until the guest started eating.)

＊　　＊　　＊

CHILD This smells funny, this one.
MOTHER It's the smell of the cheese.
CHILD Take the cheese off.
MOTHER Cheese, this is cheese. The cheese is tasty.
(Message: Eat cheese. Result: The child tried cheese.)

＊　　＊　　＊

MOTHER You can start eating any part [of the watermelon]. [But] the green part is the skin.

CHILD (pointing at the skin): Can I eat this part?

MOTHER *This part might taste bad.*

(Message: Don't eat this green part. Eat the red part. Result: The child ate the red part.)

In these examples, the children behaved as the mother expected when hints were given to them.

One mother seems to use a certain type of hint often enough for the child to respond to it promptly:

MOTHER When the child's mouth is white after drinking milk, I say that [the child] is Mr. Santa with mustache (*ohige no Santa san*). Then the child wipes his mouth. He wipes his mouth when I say, "[Your] mouth is [that of] Mr. Santa with mustache," rather than saying, "Wipe your mouth."

S. K. What if you say, "Wipe your mouth."?

MOTHER I think, if I say, "Do it," he will wipe. But I don't want to use the form, "Do it." . . .

She uses this form occasionally because she believes that the hint is more effective than the direct command which she herself does not want to use. It is apparent that "Mr. Santa" sounds familiar and friendly to the child. When the child is not in a cooperative mood, however, the mother does not want to use this hint because she is afraid that this playful hint might allow the child to have his own way:

S. K. Here, you told him directly to wipe his mouth, instead of mentioning Mr. Santa as you did before.

MOTHER It is because he started to play with the towel.

S. K. In that case, is it better to tell him directly [to wipe his mouth]?

MOTHER Yes. If I said something like Mr. Santa with mustache, he would be all the more playful.

S. K. So, you change [your strategies].

MOTHER Yes, but I don't change [my strategies] so consciously.

It seems that the mother uses appropriate controlling techniques depending on the child's psychological state so flexibly that she herself does not feel that she chooses her strategy. Optimal strategies seem to come to her naturally.

In this study, the rationale is defined as the mother's implicitly expressed statement which the mother expects the child to infer as to the reason why a certain behavior is desired or undesired. Although the rationale is as implicit as the hint and requires the child's inference of the mother's intent as the hint does, the rationale is distinguished from the hint for its being paired with mother's explicit directives. Explicit directives such as obligation and prohibition are often followed by rationales:

Kore wa dame. (Don't [eat] this. – prohibition)
Ochita kara. (Because it was dropped.)

∗ ∗ ∗

Saigo made tabenakya. (You have to finish it. – obligation)
Kona ga ochiru kara. (Because [otherwise] you drop flakes.)

These examples suggest that the mothers expected their children to understand that they had to modify their behavior not because it was the mothers' own wish but because there was a good reason for their modification of behavior. Although the present study does not provide the data to examine directly how much the mothers expected their children to understand the basis for their command when they used rationales after commands, it seems that the mothers had some expectation that at this age the child understands the mother's reasoning.

THE MOTHER'S SENSITIVITY TO THE CHILD'S REACTIONS

The Patient Persuasion for the Child's Spontaneous Compliance

When controlling child's behavior, the mothers wanted the child to comply spontaneously, not as a result of the imposition of their will on the child. Therefore, the mothers were reluctant to make the child comply at once by using strong commands. When the child did not comply at once either willfully or from not understanding mother's expectations, the mothers preferred to persuade gradually; first mildly, and, if necessary, more strongly, but trying not to make the child feel imposed upon. Indeed, they employed controlling strategies of different levels of explicitness according to their children's response to their expectations.

As a method of patient persuasion, the repetition of less explicit directives such as suggestions, hints, and questions seems effective, without making the child feel imposed upon. In eleven episodes, the mothers repeated the same implicit strategies, having waited for the children's responses to their initial use of the strategies.

A mother offered her thirty-eight-month-old child some more food in a form of a suggestive question, "Another helping (*Okawari wa*)?" but the child did not show a positive response to it immediately. The mother did not continue to persuade the child. Instead, she waited for a while and repeated the offer again:

> The mother asked the child if she wanted another helping. Holding the spoon at the level of her face, the child said that she would leave the food, and moved deeper into the seat. Then the child took the plate close to her mouth and ate the spaghetti. The mother said, "Another helping (*Okawari wa*)? Let's eat some more. I'll give you Mother's." But the child did not answer. They continued to eat. Looking down on the child's lap, the mother said, "*Wa wa wa wa!*" Then she wiped the child's lap with the towel and also the child's jaw. The child laughed and shook her head. While drinking water, the child giggled. Then, looking into the child's face, the mother asked the child, "Another helping? No more? Are you full? Really? No more snacks." The child stopped drinking water, and said, "*Hun?*" The mother said, "No snacks till three. Do you eat a little more?" The child looked in front of her and then turned her head to the mother and nodded. The mother asked, "[Do you] eat?" and the child nodded.

In the middle of this episode, the child dropped the food on her lap, which apparently caused the mother a problem because she had to wipe the dirty spot on the child's clothes and her jaw. The mother did not show any negative feeling toward the child, however, as she later explained, being afraid that if she had reproached the child's carelessness, the child would not eat any more. Then, after a while, the mother repeated an offer in the form of suggestive questions ("Another helping?"; "Do you eat a little more?") and a hint ("No more snacks"), to which the child responded positively.

These strategies are indirect ones, leaving the child the freedom to comply or not; the child did not comply the first time the mother hinted and suggested that the child eat some more. But the mother's offer was so patiently repeated that finally the child came to understand the seriousness of the mother's expectation. As the mother later explained, at the end, the child must have thought that she no longer could say no and that if she resisted, the mother would have scolded her. It seems that the child was not feeling forced by the mother when the mother was repeating her expectations in a subtle way; she laughed when the mother wiped her jaw, and later giggled, drinking water. In this rather indulgent atmosphere, the mother was successful in persuading the child patiently without making the child feel forced. The mother's comment in the interview shows that when persuading the child patiently, she was aware that commanding the child would not work because the child might have resisted her straightforwardly expressed demand.

The Mother's Effort to Avoid Going Against the Child's Will

The mothers informed me that when controlling the child's behavior, they are reluctant to go against the child's will because once the child resisted, the child would not comply. Thus, they have to be sensitive to the child's reaction to their controlling efforts. Especially when the child has started spontaneously to show some mastery of expected skills, the mother seems to become careful not to discourage child's newborn willingness to demonstrate a skill by imposing her will.

An episode of a thirty-five-month-old boy and his mother's comment on it illustrates the mother's effort not to go against the child's will and her preference for the child's compliance with her minimum control. The boy has already started to demonstrate an expected skill, that is, going to the bathroom by himself.

> MOTHER Kenchan, do you have to pee? (*Oshikko wa?*)
> CHILD (Eating nuts) Hmm.
> MOTHER You don't want to pee? Really? What would happen if you peed here?
> CHILD [Because] I don't want to pee.
> MOTHER You don't, do you?

The mother's first question, "Kenchan, do you have to pee? (*Oshikko wa?*)" was to remind the child of going to the bathroom and did not take a form of full question with verbs (i.e., *Oshikko wa deru no, denai no?*), thus allowing the child to avoid saying yes or no immediately. "Hmm" is neither yes nor no but a mere acknowledgement of the mother's speech addressed to him. This does not indicate that the child did not understand the mother's question, because, as the mother informed me later, this question, "Do you have to pee?" had been often repeated to him by the mother. Although the mother later confirmed that she took this answer as "no" at this point, she was not certain of the seriousness of his answer and asked again if he meant it. This time, she asked more explicitly, "You don't want to pee? What would happen if you peed here?" To this last question, the child, seeming to feel obliged to give a clear answer, gave her an answer with a tone of protest in it. He must have sensed the mother's negative feeling in her second question. His answer, "[Because] I don't want to pee." may be interpreted as "You don't have to ask me what would happen if I would pee here. I'm sure I don't want to pee." To this mild protest of the child the mother responded with a confirmation of his answer in a gentle manner, "You don't, do you?" as if to soothe him, although it was the child's indifferent response to her initial question, which made her ask the second question.

In the interview, this mother explained that recently she came to expect the child to go to the bathroom spontaneously rather than to remind him of the necessity of going to the bathroom. A few weeks before the observation, the mother and the child made a weekend visit to the mother's friend who had a three-year-old daughter. The girl went to the bathroom by herself when necessary. The mother recalled that her son, inspired by the girl's self-sufficiency, went to the bathroom, saying, "I'll go, because older sister does so," and he could dress himself without any help. The mother called the child's newly born willingness "*kyososhin* (competitive-mindedness)," which in this context may be interpreted as competitiveness in self-efficiency. She explained: "Before that, everybody asked, 'Ken, do you have to pee?' But after we went there (her friend's house), it changed." In the above episode, however, the mother still had to remind the child of going to the bathroom. It seems that this child's going to the bathroom by himself without being reminded had not become a habit and that therefore the mother still had to remind him. Thus, at this transitional stage of the child's mastery of this specific skill, the mother was careful not to push the child too much so as not to make him feel imposed upon.

THE MOTHERS' BELIEFS ABOUT CHILDREARING

The Ideal of the Sunao Child

The mothers' goal was to bring up a *sunao* child who internalizes the mother's expectations and straightforwardly tries to fulfill such expectations. A mother uses the word "*sunao*" to describe an ideal child:

s. k. What do you mean by a *sunao* child?
MOTHER Sunao. . . . Childlike child (*kodomo rashii*)? Childlike child? The

sunao child is a child who is a straight arrow (*seikaku massugu*) and well intentioned.

s. k. Do you want [your daughter] to be *sunao* when she grows up?

MOTHER Yes, if possible, I wish [she would] grow up to be a *sunao* person.

s. k. What do you think is important for you to make her a *sunao* person?

MOTHER Because the mother is the closest to the child, she serves as a role model. So the mother should also live a *sunao* life without being double-faced (*ura omote naku*).

Both *"seikaku massugu"* and *"ura omote naku"* refer to straightforward devotion to a task in an almost selfless manner. It seems that the concept of *sunao* has such a basic value in this mother's everyday life that it is not an easy task for her to explain it.

Another mother, describing a child of her friend, used the word *"sunao:"*

[He is] a good child. *Sunao*. When scolded, he knows why he was scolded. "Why did the mother scold me? I did something wrong. Although my sister started the fight, I'm her elder brother." See, he knows what is right and what is wrong.

She refers to the boy who, when scolded, knows why he deserves scolding without being told. Because he knows what is expected from an older brother and that what he did was wrong, when scolded he admits his misconduct and would not protest against the mother's scolding. A *sunao* child accepts the mother's disapproval straightforwardly as if it were the child who is disapproving his/her conduct.

The mothers seemed to believe that in order for the child to develop his/her *sunao* mind, they should help make the child feel like doing spontaneously what they expected from him/her. In other words, anything that makes the child do a task reluctantly should be avoided. Thus, the mothers, by suggesting or hinting, provide the child with chances to perform an expected task as if it were his/her own decision. The suggestion and hint also serve to sensitize the child to others' needs. Because the *sunao* child is expected to mind-read what others expect him/her to do, the mother's frequent use of suggestion and hint helps the child to know what is expected from him/her before it is told directly.

The mothers' negative image of the repetitive use of command is expressed in *"kuchi urusai,"* *"yakamashii,"* and *"shitsukoi"* (all meaning "fault-finding" and "nagging"), adjectives used when mothers explained the nature of the command. In their explanations, mothers' negative image of direct command is contrasted to their preference for suggestion which leads to the child's *sunao* compliance. A mother recollected:

> He complied in a *sunao* manner when I suggested he do something, and I did not have to tell him to do this and that in a fault-finding (*kuchi urusai*) way.

Instead of commands and harsh words, the mothers use praise (*homeru*). The praise is used not only when the mother wants the child to do things but also when the child behaves as expected. When praised for his/her spontaneous behavior, the child seems to learn the value of spontaneous compliance.

The Mother's Emphasis on the Emotional Bond

In order for the child to mind-read the mother's expectation and behave accordingly at the mother's suggestion, there must be a strong emotional bond between child and mother. The mothers' emphasis on their emotional bond with the child during the skill-teaching episodes is symbolized in a mother's use of the words, "*ittaikan* (togetherness)" and "*ninin sankyaku*" (three-legged race)." She thinks that for successful teaching, a relaxed atmosphere in which both the mother and her thirty-two-month-old daughter share a sense of "togetherness" is essential. This mother was watching the child having difficulty in picking up sliced cucumber with chopsticks. She explained, reviewing the videotaped sequence:

> I ate cucumbers, too, because by eating [the same thing] with the child, what should I call it, together (*issho ni*). . . . eating together . . . . what do I call it? Yes, togetherness (*ittaikan*), yes, togetherness, or satisfaction (*manzoku*). Yes, I did it that way. When eating [cucumbers] with the child, we make [the same kind of] noise together. How should I say this, we were both eating the same thing. [When eating] I was not so conscious of my intentions. But, now, watching the video, I think probably I had that intention. . . . But I think it would be a different story if we were three (including the father). I can do that (to share the sense of togetherness with the child) because we are by ourselves.

The mother thinks that there is a special kind of emotional exchange between the mother and the child. With this emotional support from the mother the child seems to feel that her effort toward skill mastery is shared by the mother although it is impossible to know if the child feels that she is in a "three-legged race" with her mother when she is engaged in the skill acquisition.

Another mother explained as to how to develop an emotional bond with the child:

> MOTHER First of all, before being strict with him, I think it is important to be united with the child emotionally. So, if the child wants to *amaeru* [to the mother], [the mother] should [accept it] wholeheartedly; [for example,] hug him if he asks her for hugs. I think it is only after that (the mother and the child being united emotionally) that you can be strict with him. If you always scold him, such a relationship cannot be established.
>
> S. K. Then, how do you establish such a relationship?
>
> MOTHER Although it depends on how much time the mother can spend with the child, the child will understand if the mother shows she is sincere by playing with the child. The child will attach himself (*natsuku*) to the person who plays with him wholeheartedly.

"To be emotionally united with the child" may be interpreted as an emotionally interdependent relationship in which the child's *amae* is encouraged for the emotional satisfaction of both the mother and the child. With an emotionally close relationship, it does not seem difficult for the child to accept the mother's expectation as the child's own, even though, as this mother emphasized, the mother's expectation is a strict one. In other words, in the *amae* relationship in which the child and mother are "emotionally united," the child's goal and the mother's goal become one.

The child's excessive *amae*, however, is not accepted positively by the mother. At the same time, the mother blames herself if she allows her child to show too much *amae*, presuming on the mother's limitless tolerance toward his/her demand. A mother explained that she disapproved of her son's *amae* when he was preparing at home for kindergarten life, because at kindergarten the teacher, having many children as her charges, cannot accept his *amae*. Of course, a moderate amount of *amae* toward his teacher is desirable, so that the child, as with the mother, will have no difficulty in internalizing the teacher's expectation as his goal. The *amae* toward the teacher should be more restrained than to the mother, however, because the teacher cannot accept every child's full-blown *amae*. The mothers described as "*amayakasu* (let the child *amaeru*)" their failure to reject their children's excessive *amae*. "*Amayakasu*," the verb form of *amae*, in this context, may be translated into English as "spoil."

The mothers are sensitive to the distinction between spoiling and *amae*, especially when the children start to prepare for kindergarten life. In the following account, a mother distinguishes her soothing her son from mere "*amayakasu*," when he had a temper tantrum after being scolded by her. The mother knows that when the child is out of temper, he will be soothed if he is drawn back into *amae* relationship with his mother. She thinks that her attempt to soothe the child does not constitute spoiling:

> When the child is at a certain age, for example, school age, he can control [his emotion] when he is being difficult (*guzuru*). At that age, it is all right to scold him when he is not being good. . . . But before that stage, for ex-ample, at the present stage, if scolded for something, it has a lasting ef-fect on him; he might keep crying for a long time, or grizzling (*guzuru*) for over an hour. [But on such occasions] if I go to him and hug him, he will be happy, or at least somewhat content again. On such occasions (when the child is being difficult) the parent should not be overly forgiv-ing, but at the same time, should help the child work through his emo-tions, so as not to spoil (*amayakasu*) the child.

Note the defensive tone of the mother's description of the soothing, which she was afraid might be labeled as "*amayakasu*." To her, it is not spoiling to cuddle the child even when the child has a tantrum, being scolded for his own misbehavior, because she knows that the child cannot be trained un-less she keeps him in a good mood.

Another mother used the word "*kawaigaru* (cherish and love)," to de-scribe her effort to keep her child in a cooperative mood when controlling the child's behavior.

MOTHER I don't separate discipline (*shitsuke*) and being indulgent (*amayakasu*). I mean, I try to make the child understand what I want her to do, while loving her (*kawaigarinagara*), saying, "Big sister. Good girl." . . . Loving her, so that she can understand what I want her to do. . . .

s. k. What do you mean by being indulgent (*amayakasu?*)

MOTHER It is to accept all the demands of the child, whatever her de-mands are.

s. k. What about discipline (*shitsuke*)?

MOTHER Meaning? Its meaning is . . . to teach the child how to tell what is good and what is bad.

To this mother, a moderate amount of indulgence is *"kawaigaru,"* a Japanese concept of loving and cherishing pretty things with no negative connotation. Although she clearly distinguishes being indulgent (*amayakasu*) and discipline (*shitsuke*), she seems to believe that indulgence and discipline go together as long as indulgence does not go beyond the point of *"kawaigaru."* To her, *"kawaigaru"* is indulgent enough for the child to feel emotionally close to the mother and identify the mother's expectation as his/her own, but at the same time, is not spoiling enough to allow the child to have his/her own way. In other words, both discipline and moderate indulgence are indispensable factors for success in controlling the child's behavior.

CONCLUSIONS: SUBTLE NEGOTIATIONS BETWEEN MOTHER AND CHILD

In this section, I shall reconsider my research questions to review to what extent the present findings support existing hypotheses about the Japanese mother's role in the child's skill acquisition. Then, I shall present the implications of the findings to the field of child development and education in cross-cultural context.

The Mother's Choice of Strategies

First, how is the Japanese mother's emphasis on the emotional bond with her child reflected in her interaction patterns during the skill teaching? The present findings suggest: (a) the mothers frequently used indirect strategies, especially hinting. Even when commanding children, they preferred softened forms of command to direct imperatives; (b) the mothers tended to use implicit directives first and then explicit ones if the child did not respond as expected. They rarely used explicit strategies alone. If they use commands they paired commands with less explicit strategies such as the explanation of the reason why certain conduct of children should be stopped or modified; and (c) The mothers were sensitive to children's reaction to their controlling attempt and modified their strategies flexibly instead of imposing their will when the child did not comply at once. For example, they repeated indirect strategies patiently until the child complied.

It should be stressed that the mothers used imperatives and informal requests as often as suggestion and hinting. Even then, when mothers used commands, they avoided using direct command forms, choosing milder imperative forms such as informal requests, and pairing the explicit and implicit forms of directives. By contrast, in the existing research, explanations about the Japanese mother's emphasis on the emotional bond as a way of controlling her child in most cases stress mother's use of indirect strategies of appealing to the child's feelings, hinting, and suggestions. Few studies provided explanations about the Japanese mother's effort to use imperatives without making them sound imposing.

For example, Lebra (1976) listed such culturally salient controlling strategies as threat of abandonment, praise, teasing, ridicule, embarrassment, and appeal for empathy. By contrast, the present study shows examples of teasing and shaming only, even though the specific context of observation in this study, that is, the mother-child interaction in front of the observer in a limited period of time, is taken into account. It may be speculated that Lebra's list of controlling strategies stand out as culture-specific methods even though they are not observed as often as more direct strategies: that is, the sensitive way the Japanese mother uses commands, as described in this study, was overlooked because commanding did not attract as much attention from ethnographers as indirect strategies that are clearly marked as culture-specific.

By contrast, Conroy et al.'s (1980) Japan–U.S. comparative study shows that when controlling the child's behavior, Japanese mothers would often use an imperative approach which roughly corresponds to the use of commands in the present study. Conroy et al. state that Japanese mothers are likely to indicate persuasion as an alternative approach in the situations in which imperatives are inappropriate. They do not explain, however, what kind of imperatives the Japanese mothers actually use nor how they actually use "imperatives." Such a description of the Japanese mother's frequent use of the imperative approach is contradictory to the general image of the Japanese mother who prefers indirect methods. If we pay careful attention to the process by which Japanese mothers actually use imperatives, however, we will find that their frequent use of command is not against the cultural norm of indirect modes of communication. Although the command is quite a common method to control the child's behavior both in the United States and Japan, the Japanese mother does command in a culture-specific way, modifying the form of commanding so as not to make her commands sound imposing.

The Mother's Awareness of Her Role

Second, how clearly does the Japanese mother distinguish indulgence from discipline? The findings from the observation of the mother-child interaction and the interview with the mothers support the general hypothesis that the Japanese mother teaches the child only when the child is in a cooperative mood. Although the skill training takes place in a relaxed atmosphere, the mother's effort to gain the child's spontaneous compliance, while maintaining a relaxed atmosphere is rather strategic. By encouraging the child's *amae* toward them, they are not merely spoiling their children. The mothers are fully aware that going against the child's will does not work, but only results in the child's stubborn resistance. The mothers explained that in order to obtain the child's compliance, it is essential to keep the child in a cooperative mood so that the child complies spontaneously, not feeling imposed on by the mother. Thus, the child's *amae* toward the mother during skill teaching should be encouraged as long as it does not go beyond a certain point.

The mothers seem to be aware that in child training, indulgence and discipline are two indispensable factors for the success of teaching. When asked, mothers could explain meanings and effectiveness of their strategies, especially their reluctance to use direct strategies. But when actually engaged in the interaction, they did not have to use these strategies deliberately. The choice of optimal strategies and the combination of them seem to come to them naturally.

Thus, what is crucial to the mothers in the child's skill training is how much indulgence should be tolerated and when discipline should be given. Because the mother herself seems to enjoy interdependent emotional relationship with the child, it is not an easy task for her to control the child's behavior without endangering a close emotional bond with her child. A mother explained, for example, that she did not distinguish *amae* and discipline when actually engaged in skill teaching although she contrasted *amae* and discipline clearly in her definition of these concepts. The distinction depended on a specific situation, because the child's reaction to the mother's controlling effort indicated how strongly the mother should push her child toward the modification of his/her behavior and when the child's excessive *amae* should be denied. Hence, it is not only the mother's controlling intent alone but also the child's reaction to it which determines the strategy the mother actually uses. In order to keep the child in a cooperative mood, the mother responded to the child's reaction quickly and flexibly, so that she did not have to define her controlling effort in a particular episode as either discipline or indulgence.

When analyzing the Japanese mother's controlling effort, the Western dichotomy of discipline versus indulgence becomes an inadequate framework in which to describe her emotional experiences during skill teaching, especially the emotional bond with her child. For example, a mother explained that the secret of the success in teaching is to teach her child to feel emotionally close to her and internalize her wishes as the child's own, but is not indulgent enough to allow the child to have his own way. The skill teaching in Japan takes place in a subtle negotiation between the mother and child. As a mother explained, teaching the prepreschool-aged child skills for self-sufficiency is like participating as one team in a three-legged race.

Implication to Developmental Issues

This study also offers evidence to test the validity of hypotheses about the effect of the firm parental controlling on the child's social development. In the field of Western developmental psychology, researches were conducted to examine what aspects of parental behavior foster the child's acquisition of self-sufficient skills. Among them, Baumrind's (1966, 1967) studies on parenting pattern and child competence indicate that an authoritative parenting pattern is related to the child's high competence in socialization skills. In her research, authoritative parents who attempt to direct a child's activities in a rational manner and are responsive to the child's needs were found to be the most effectively promoting the development of compliance, independence, purposiveness, and achievement orientation in girls and social responsibility in boys. Coopersmith's (1967) study of self-esteem also points out the positive effects of a parent's high demandingness and high responsiveness on the child's competence in socialization skills. Coopersmith found that firm rule enforcement accompanied by warmth and democratic family decision making was associated with high self-esteem, whereas power-assertive parenting was associated with low esteem. Coopersmith's firm control corresponds to Baumrind's authoritative parenting.

The attention to the cultural difference in parenting pattern between the United States and Japan, however, has led to the question about the validity of applying parenting patterns generated in American psychology to the analysis of the Japanese childrearing practices. Indeed, Baumrind's and Coopersmith's hypotheses about the positive effects of firm control on the child's internalization of values do not fit the hypothesis of ethnographic studies that the Japanese mother prefers indirect control strategies to firm, rule-oriented strategies. Lewis (1986) points out: "Japanese mothers apparently do not make explicit demands on their children and do not enforce rules when children resist; yet diverse accounts suggest that Japanese children strongly internalize parental, group, and institutional values" (p. 192).

As the "diverse accounts," Lewis refers to Nakane (1972) and Vogel (1963, 1979), but these studies do not present concrete examples. As concrete examples, the findings from the present study support this analysis of Lewis; it shows that the Japanese mother controls the child's behavior successfully in a indirect and subtle manner, although it does not provide the direct data to examine how the child internalizes parental values.

Second, research on parental control and its outcome indicate that characteristics of the child's personality which American society regards as positive include self-reliance, social responsibility, independence, achievement-orientation, and vitality. Although it may be safely assumed that the Japanese mother also wants a child to embody these values, meanings of "self-reliance," "social responsibility," and "independence" may have different meanings between the United States and Japan. The "independence" of the child seems to mean to the Japanese mother physical rather than emotional independence from her; while the mother wants her child to be self-sufficient, she may want to maintain an emotionally interdependent relationship with the child. As an image of a "socially responsible" child, the mothers in this study pointed out the "*sunao*" child who experiences a sense of self-fulfillment by complying spontaneously with the adult authority, while, in the United States, this image of a child is unlikely to represent the desirable social skills.

REFERENCES

Baumrind, D. (1966). Effects of authoritative parental control on child behavior. *Child Development, 37*, 887–905.

Baumrind, D., & Black, A. (1967). Socialization practices associated with dimensions of competence in preschool boys and girls. *Child Development, 38*, 291–327.

Benedict, R. (1946). *The chrysanthemum and the sword: Patterns of Japanese culture.* Boston: Houghton Mifflin.

Caudill, W., & Weinstein, H. (1969). Maternal care and infant behavior in Japan and America. *Psychiatry, 32*, 12–43.

Clancy, P. (1986). The acquisition of communicative style in Japanese. In B. Schieffelin & E. Ochs (Eds.), *Language socialization across cultures* (pp. 213–50). New York: Cambridge University Press.

Conroy, M., Hess, R. D., Azuma, H., & Kashiwagi, K. (1980). Maternal strategies for regulating children's behavior: Japanese and American families. *Journal of Cross-Cultural Psychology, 11*, 153–72.

Coopersmith, S. (1967). *The antecedents of self-esteem.* San Francisco: W. H. Freeman.

Doi, T. (1973). *The anatomy of dependence.* Tokyo: Kodansha.

Grusec, J., & Kuczynski, L. (1980). Direction of effect in socialization: A comparison of the parent's versus the child's behavior as determinants of disciplinary techniques. *Developmental Psychology, 16*, 1–9.

Hendry, J. (1986). *Becoming Japanese: The world of the preschool child.* Honolulu: The University of Hawaii Press.

Lanham, B. (1956). Aspects of child care in Japan: Preliminary report. In D. G. Haring (Ed.), *Personal character and cultural milieu* (pp. 565–83). Syracuse: Syracuse University Press.

Lebra, T. S. (1976). *Japanese patterns of behavior.* Honolulu: The University of Hawaii Press.

Lewis, C. (1986). Children's social development in Japan: Research directions. In H. Stevenson, H. Azuma, & K. Hakuta (Eds.), *Child development and education in Japan* (pp. 186–200). New York: Freeman.

Minton, C., Kagan, J., & Levine, J. (1971). Maternal control and obedience in the two-year-old. *Child Development, 42,* 1873–94.

Nakane, C. (1972). *Japanese society.* Berkeley: University of California Press.

Peak, L. (1991). *Learning to go to school in Japan: The transition from home to preschool life.* Berkeley: University of California Press.

Rohlen, T. (1983). *Japan's high schools.* Berkeley: University of California Press.

Schaffer, H., & Crook, C. (1979). Maternal control techniques in a direct play situation. *Child Development, 50,* 989–96.

Schaffer, H., & Crook, C. (1980). Child compliance and maternal control techniques. *Developmental Psychology, 16,* 54–61.

Vogel, E. (1963; 1971, 2d ed.). *Japan's new middle class: The salaryman and his family in a Tokyo suburb.* Berkeley: University of California Press.

Vogel, E. (1979). *Japan as number one: Lessons for America.* Cambridge, MA: Harvard University Press.

Vogel, S. (1978). Professional housewife: The career of urban middle-class Japanese women. *Japan Interpreter, 12,* 16–43.

White, M. (1987). *Japanese educational challenge: A commitment to children.* New York: Free Press.

White, M., & LeVine, R. (1986). What is an *ii ko?* In H. Stevenson, H. Azuma, & K. Hakuta (Eds.), *Child development and education in Japan* (pp. 55–62). New York: Freeman.

PART III

GROUP LIFE: THE YOUNG CHILD IN PRESCHOOL AND SCHOOL

FIVE

Learning to Become Part of the Group

The Japanese Child's Transition to Preschool Life[1]

Lois Peak

How do the Japanese become group-oriented? Contemporary anthropologists agree that cultural behavior and attitudes are a product of socialization rather than heredity or accident. Yet the actual experiences through which Japanese children learn to be group-oriented have not adequately been described.

Most descriptions of Japanese society have generally assumed that group behavior and attitudes are learned in the Japanese home. Children learn how to interact with others by practicing with their siblings and parents in the "small society" of the family and through observing how their parents interact with outsiders. As the child matures, this behavior becomes elaborated and generalized to a larger social setting.

Although this process undoubtedly occurs to some extent in Japan, Japanese popular wisdom does not view child development in this way. For Japanese children, just as for adults, the home and the outside world are very different settings which require different interpersonal behavior and attitudes. This gap between *uchi* and *soto* frequently has been treated in descriptions of Japanese adult society.

Uchi and *soto* differ for Japanese children just as they do for adults. There is a profoundly important difference between the way that children should

Lois Peak is an employee of the U.S. Department of Education. However, the research and analysis presented in this chapter were conducted in her private capacity. No official support by the Department of Education is intended, or should be inferred.

[1] A longer version of this article was first published in *The Journal of Japanese Studies*, Vol. 15, No. 1 (1989). A shortened form of it is published here with permission from the *Journal*.

feel and behave at home with mother and the way that they should behave in preschool and elementary school. Because the two environments are so different, Japanese believe that it is the school's responsibility to socialize children in group behavior. By observing the transition from home to pre-school, we have a window on the first major experiences in acculturation to group norms for individuals in Japanese society.

Japanese teachers do not expect a student to arrive at school with either a well-developed set of social and interpersonal skills or a good under-standing of the limits of appropriate behavior in a social context. Similarly, mothers do not believe it to be their duty to manage their children's be-havior at home according to rules similar to those the children will experi-ence in the classroom. The two environments are naturally and properly discrete; the behavior appropriate for a child at home is not the same as the behavior appropriate at school and vice versa.

Japanese explain the reason for this difference in behavioral expectations simply: the school is *shudan seikatsu*, whereas the home is not. *Shudan* (group, collective) *seikatsu* (daily life, living) means literally "life in a group." By examining the implications of this apparently trivial but to the Japanese fundamentally important difference between the two environments, we be-gin to understand something of the deep structure of the behavior that Japanese cultural norms prescribe as appropriate to each setting.

As a participant in *shudan seikatsu*, children must learn that their own de-sires and goals are secondary to those of the group. A certain degree of *en-ryo* (Lebra, 1976, p. 41) or restraint in expressing one's own feelings and a diffident self-presentation are appropriate. Children must develop a will-ingness to participate enthusiastically in group activities and must interact smoothly and harmoniously with others. Selfishness, or excessive assertion of independent desires and wanting to have things one's own way, is termed *wagamama*. Although it is an understandable aspect of human na-ture, it must not be allowed to influence individual behavior in a group set-ting. Individuals are expected to assume these appropriate attitudes and behavior, almost as one would a suit of clothes, for the duration of their ac-tive participation in the group. Once alone or at home again, one can relax and let real feelings and preferences show.

This chapter will examine Japanese children's transition between these two worlds, focusing on the difficulties children experience as they enter preschool society. Through this, we can better understand the Japanese cul-tural construction of norms of group behavior and deviance. We can also glimpse some aspects of the subtle nature of Japanese individuals' psy-chological accommodation to the expectations of group society.

METHODOLOGY AND FINDINGS

This study attempted to achieve a balance between in-depth investigation of a few schools and less detailed comparison of many schools. Every possible attempt was made to choose representative preschools and the families for study, while still working within Japanese cultural norms, which necessitated an introduction to potential field sites through the personal network of a mutual acquaintance. Schools that employed experimental or atypical teaching methods or that were locally regarded as of high quality or particularly noteworthy were carefully avoided.

The initial eight months of fieldwork were conducted in a private preschool *(yochien)* in a middle-class residential neighborhood in downtown Tokyo. Parents who sent their children to this school lived in modest condominiums or apartments within the neighborhood. Most fathers worked as "salarymen" in medium-sized companies or as local shopkeepers.

The second ten months of fieldwork took place in a private preschool in "Mountain City," a fictional name for a regional city of four hundred thousand people located in the mountains of central Honshu. The occupations of the parents whose children were enrolled in this preschool were approximately evenly divided into three types: university-educated bankers temporarily assigned to Mountain City and living in company housing; white-collar workers with high school educations who were from the area; and others from Mountain City who had a high school education or less and were self-employed in service occupations, such as barbers or taxi drivers.

These field sites were initially chosen on the assumption that childrearing patterns and preschool education might be different in Tokyo and in a smaller regional city. No significant regional differences were observed, however, in the nature of the child's transition from home to school life.

Because this study focused on children's adaptation to group life, classroom observations focused particularly on the transitional periods at the beginning and end of the school year. During the middle of the year, briefer observations and teacher interviews were conducted in other local schools to determine how representative the two schools that were the main focus of the study were. I have had extensive prior experience in Japanese early educational settings and speak Japanese.

In both Mountain and Tokyo preschools, the newly entering three-year-old class was observed during the entire school day for the first one and one-half weeks of the school year. The entire third week was again observed intensively and periodic follow-up observations were made throughout the remainder of the school year. In addition, I attended and recorded all scheduled events for new students, such as application interviews, school observation day, opening ceremonies, and year-end events for graduating students such as farewell presentations, prospective visits to elementary schools, and graduation ceremonies.

Data from classroom observations were collected using a portable cassette tape recorder and handwritten field notes. Observations focused on training in classroom routines and on incidents of misbehavior and student discipline. The tape recordings of teachers' and students' speech were then reviewed and disciplinary incidents transcribed from the cassette tape and synchronized with the field notes that recorded physical behavior and nonverbal activity.

In addition to classroom behavior observations, at the end of each school day, teachers were interviewed concerning their teaching and behavior management objectives for the day. Incidents of discipline and behavior correction were reviewed and teachers were asked to explain what had occurred and why they had dealt with it in a particular way. This combination of observation and teacher explanation proved extremely valuable in learning how Japanese preschool teachers understand the psychological dynamics of children's behavior and the methods they use in its control.

In addition to classroom observation, maternal interviews were conducted. Seventeen mothers whose three- or four-year-old children were newly enrolled in Mountain Preschool were interviewed during the third month of the school year. The interviews were designed to determine the degree to which parental expectations and socialization were congruent with the expectations of the preschool and how each child had managed the transition to preschool life. Lasting from two to three hours each, the interviews were scheduled in the mothers' homes at their convenience and conducted by the investigator in a friendly and open-ended fashion. All interviews were tape-recorded and later transcribed verbatim in the original Japanese.

What is the nature of the difference between the environment of the home and that of *shudan seikatsu* for Japanese preschool children? The mother of a girl in the three-year-old class in Mountain Preschool described the difference in this way:

> I can see that at home she's more relaxed and vivacious; maybe you could even say she throws her weight around a little bit. Somehow I think that she's more open and free. When she goes to preschool, I can feel her *enryo* to the other children and the teacher. Even in her childlike way, she keeps her wings pulled in more than she does at home. [Could you give

some concrete examples?] At home she'll say "I'm going to do this" or "Let's play like this." Even if I say "No," still she'll say "But I want to." But if she's told "No" at preschool, she'll just stop immediately. I guess that's what's called *enryo*. [What do you think about that?] I think that's as it should be. As long as you have to relate to other people (*hito to kakawaru*) you have to act based on other people's feelings too. (Where do you think she learned how to do *enryo*?) From participating in *shudan seikatsu*. In a *shudan* environment there is no other way that things can be. It's not something you can teach with words. It just comes from experiencing that environment.

Learning to keep one's wings pulled in and to display proper *enryo* is the basis of the somewhat cautious and restrained self-presentation that is fundamental to *shudan seikatsu*. Other informants agreed with this mother that these attitudes are learned in the *shudan* setting, and not from parental instruction or family example. Within the give-and-take of peer relationship in a group environment purposely lacking the understanding indulgence of the home, children learn that their *wagamama* (personal desires) must be placed secondary to the activities and harmony of the group.

By definition, life within the family is not *shudan seikatsu*, although from an American point of view it might be described as a smaller group from which the child learns rules and roles that will be later applied in the larger society. Without exception, however, Japanese teachers and mothers denied that it could be described as a small *shudan*. In contrast to the English concept of "group," the defining characteristic of a *shudan* is not the number of people involved but the expectations governing their interpersonal behavior. In this sense, the family is not a small *shudan*, because the expectations for interpersonal interaction are different. Within the family, one can drop the strain of *ki o tsukau* (holding oneself carefully) and freely express one's own feelings, however self-centered, and expect understanding and indulgence of one's personal desires. In fact, the right to expect such indulgence of *amae* (dependency) is the primary characteristic of an intimate or private environment, and without it a Japanese family would not be considered worthy of the name.

Becoming a well-socialized member of the *shudan* does not imply that a child's behavior in the family should undergo similar change. It is considered unremarkable that children and adults display self-reliance, cooperation, and perseverance at school and still remain dependent, assertive, and impatient at home. Such a personality is termed *uchi benke*, and carries no connotations of opprobrium. Indeed, the conspicuous display of *amae* behavior in the home is an important method of affirming intimacy and trust and providing family members with the chance to indulge such desires and, thus, to demonstrate love and affection. Learning to participate in the *shudan* implies learning to switch between two codes of behavior – one appropriate to participation in the family and one appropriate to the outside group.

The mother of a 3.4-year-old boy[2] who had recently entered preschool observed:

> I want him to be able to understand the difference between home [*uchi*] and the outside world [*soto*] so if he becomes an *uchi benke*, it can't be helped. It might even be said we sort of encourage him to be like that. It's proper that his behavior in the outside world be better. No one's a good boy in both places. If he's a good boy at home, I think he'll probably do bad things on the outside. So it's good if he acts *wagamama* [selfish, willful] toward me rather than doing it on the outside.

Indeed, the cultural assumption that the nature of human relationships is basically different at home and outside the family is reflected in the Japanese language. The words that Mountain City mothers used to describe their children's relationships to or interaction with outside people were clearly differentiated from words or terms referring to relationships within the family. As reflected in the words of the mother quoted above, *taijin kankei* (interpersonal relationships) and *hito to kakawaru* (relating to other people) were used to refer almost exclusively to relationships with individuals outside the family. The more simple and direct *ani to issho ni iru* (being together with older brother) was typically used to refer to relations with family members.

Even the word *hito* (people) is usually used to refer primarily to nonfamily members. This is an important distinction not usually drawn in reports of Japanese childrearing attitudes and behavior. For example, the injunction *hito ni meiwaku o kakenai* (don't cause trouble for other people), is frequently quoted as one of the most important goals of Japanese early socialization (see, for example, White, 1987, p. 96). In fact, however, *hito* is not assumed to refer to family members. This is summarized beautifully in one of the interviews:

> [What is the most important thing you try to teach your children?] Not to cause trouble for other people [*hito ni meiwaku o kakenai.*] Not to do things

---

2 All ages for children are given in years and months. Thus, this boy's age is three years and four months.

which will cause people to dislike them [*hito ni kirawareru koto o shinai.*] Those things absolutely must be avoided. [In saying "people" *(hito)*, you mean?] People outside the family, of course.

The legitimated causing of *meiwaku* or trouble for intimate others and the willingness to "let oneself go" to the point of exhibiting demanding and selfish behavior is the basis of *amae* and within the context of the Japanese family is interpreted as a sign of trust and affection.

This discontinuity in behavioral expectations and styles of interpersonal interaction demarcates the Japanese worlds of *uchi* and *soto* (see Lebra, 1976, pp. 112–13; Vogel, 1963, p. 276). Most mothers desire to maintain a certain degree of *amae* (dependency, willfulness) in their child's behavior toward themselves and other family members, while expecting the child to learn to display *enryo* (restraint) toward peers, neighbors, and others outside the family. This means that for most Japanese children, entrance to preschool is the first time they encounter the expectation that their behavior must undergo a radical change.

PROBLEMS IN ADJUSTING TO GOING TO PRESCHOOL

Given the large discrepancy between Japanese children's lives at home and the expectations and routines of preschool life, it is not surprising that many children experience difficulty in adapting to the new environment. During the first month of school, passive withdrawal, tears, temper tantrums, and refusal to attend school are common. For the purpose of discussion, children's difficulties in adjustment have been divided into two categories: problems manifested at home in unwillingness to go to school, primarily crying when dropped off at school in the morning, and problems manifested at preschool, in tantrums, noncompliance, or difficulty in conforming to the expected routine. The first section will discuss the problems manifested at home, and the following section will discuss those manifested in the classroom.

Unwillingness to Attend Preschool

How common were adjustment problems among the new three- and four-year-old students at Mountain Preschool? During the individual interviews, each mother was asked to describe how her child had initially felt about entering preschool, how the child's feelings and reactions had changed over the first six weeks of school, and any problems or difficulties that had been encountered. Based on the mother's description, each child's adjustment was categorized as easy (never cried or refused to go to preschool), somewhat difficult (cried or refused to go to preschool for a period between one and six days' duration), and difficult (cried or refused to go to school for a period of seven days or longer).

Table 5.1 suggests that adjustment problems were not uncommon among children in Mountain Preschool. Two-thirds of the children experienced some difficulty and one-third cried or refused to go to school for a week or longer. Within each cohort, ease of adjustment does not appear to be strongly related to age at entrance, but there is some tendency for four-year-olds to have less difficulty in the adjustment than three-year-olds. This agrees with the widespread opinion of Japanese preschool teachers that new four-year-old classes are somewhat easier to manage than three-year-old classes.

Japanese mothers and teachers feel considerable reticence about discussing difficulties or problems with each other. This reticence exists despite many institutionalized vehicles for easy communication: the parent-teacher message book, brief greetings when dropping the child off and picking him or her up each day, and frequent large-group mother-teacher meetings. A large volume of detailed information concerning the child is exchanged through these channels. For example, some daycare centers require the mother to take her child's temperature each morning and record it in the message book, along with a description of the child's morning bowel movement. In turn, the teacher records the characteristics of any bowel movements occurring at school and how well the child consumes his lunch.

Although mothers and teachers frequently assert that they desire close and open communication, in fact, problems are rarely discussed. Even when children have daily difficulties and frequent tantrums in class over a certain issue, such as dressing themselves, teachers rarely mention the problem to the mothers. Similarly, when children have obvious difficulty adjusting to preschool, crying and refusing to attend, parents rarely discuss what happens at home frankly with the teacher. Both parties' preferred method of handling the situation is to hope that each will somehow notice the other's difficulty, either on parent observation day, or when the mother drops the child off at school in the morning. Most wait for the problems to disappear of their own accord, or wait to raise the issue obliquely in the parent-teacher conference after a number of weeks have passed.

During the first weeks of school, the apparent purpose of the mother-teacher communication is to smooth the child's adjustment to the new set-

Table 5.1. *Mountain Preschool Children's*
Ease of Adjustment to Preschool (1984)

	Easy	Somewhat Difficult	Difficult	Total Students
Three-year-olds				
No. of children	3	3	4	10
Average age	3.6	3.7	3.5	3.6
Four-year-olds				
No. of children	3	1	2	6
Average age	4.6	4.2	4.2	4.4

ting. In fact, however, the vast majority of adjustment problems are never discussed between mother and teacher. This could be due to two reasons. The first is that most mothers and teachers take a long-term view of the child's behavior. This is epitomized by one mother's comment, "He's crying over a little thing today, but as soon as he gets over it, he'll start going to preschool happily again."

The second probable reason involves the Japanese cultural norms of interpersonal communication.[3] Although the espoused goal of mother-teacher communication is the exchange of relevant information for the immediate benefit and assistance of the child, a more fundamental and important goal is the establishment of a positive and harmonious relationship between the mother and the teacher. In Japan, issues that can lead to potential conflict are assiduously avoided in polite social relations. Although contact is frequent and cooperation is prized, person-to-person conversation is maintained within the boundaries of well-defined, safely innocuous topics, such as the child's physical health. Direct discussion of problems or interpersonal conflict is embarrassing and potentially threatening to the maintenance of long-term social harmony. Thus the espoused goal of communicating frankly in order to assist the child's transition to preschool is sacrificed to an unwritten but more fundamental goal of preserving social harmony between mother and teacher.

The following excerpt from an interview with the mother of a boy who was 3.6 years old at the time he entered preschool was typical of the six

[3] I am indebted to Professor Robert LeVine of the Harvard Graduate School of Education for suggesting this interpretation.

children who were classified as experiencing a "difficult transition." This mother also did not discuss her child's problems with the teacher.

> [How did Shingo-kun feel about entering preschool?] At first he didn't know what kind of a place it was. He went just thinking that it was simply a big place to play with a lot of friends. The first day he went happily. After that he cried really hard every morning for about two weeks. When I'd try to put his uniform on him, he'd scream and cry and then throw himself around like he was crazy. He'd try to escape and run from room to room boohooing and I'd have to run after him and catch him and hold him down while I put his clothes on him. Nothing I could say would settle him down. I'd have to forcibly strap him into the bike seat. Sometimes the only way I could get him into his clothes in the morning was to lie to him, saying we were going to the supermarket. When I'd drop him off at preschool, he'd still be crying, but after I left, it seems he'd always give up and go along with it. When I'd come to pick him up, he'd be smiling.
>
> [Do you think he was primarily unhappy about parting from you, or did he dislike preschool?] I think he didn't like preschool. [What did you think he didn't like about it?] I wonder what it was? I didn't think about it too much. Probably being at home was more relaxing. After he gets up in the morning he always watches TV and hangs around all day. He probably didn't like to have to go whether he wanted to or not. At preschool he has to follow rules, and being one among so many people is tiring. Probably it was that, because he was used to pretty much doing what he wanted to at home.

Although mother-teacher discussions of individual children's specific problems were carefully avoided, the general expectation that problems would arise and eventually be solved was expressed in numerous forms during the matriculation ceremony. As a Mountain City teacher said in her opening remarks: "The beginning will be a little difficult for everyone, for you mothers and especially for the children. . . . Gradually they will become accustomed to it." The Mountain City director observed: "I understand that new mothers will have many worries. . . Don't worry if your child cries a bit at preschool. Learning to overcome difficulties makes children's hearts strong."

It requires considerable patience, optimism, and detachment to apply this classic advice to one's own child as each morning he must be forced, screaming, into a bicycle seat. In time, however, the problems eventually *do* disappear. By the third month of preschool, the mothers reported that all children had adjusted to the new environment and looked forward to attending preschool each morning.

Separation Anxiety

Given the importance attached to the mother-child bond during the preschool years in Japan, it is interesting that children's transition problems are almost always described as initial dislike of preschool, rather than unhappiness at being away from their mothers. Japanese teachers, mothers, and informed opinion concur that the primary problem is adjustment to *shudan seikatsu*, not separation from the mother. Of the ten mothers interviewed whose children had some difficulty adjusting during the transition, only one characterized the problem as being related to separation anxiety, and she eventually described the separation problem as her own rather than the child's.

[How did Rumi-chan adapt to preschool?] She was fine except she cried three or four times during the first week. Each day she was fine until we got to the preschool gate. Then she'd realize that I was going home and start crying. I was really surprised because I hadn't expected that *she'd* cry. She was so sad, so sad, to see me go. As soon as I'd gone, it seems she always stopped crying and was okay again, but the moment of parting was really sorrowful. I'd fib a little, telling her I'd wait there for her, or to run off and play with her friends, but no matter what I told her, it didn't work. Sometimes there was nothing to do but have the teacher forcibly pull her away and carry her to the classroom. Other times she'd finally accept it and say through her tears, "Mama, be *sure* to come back and get me." During those four or five days, she always went in to preschool with tears streaming down her face.

[Do you think she cried because she felt sad at leaving you, or because she disliked preschool?] I think it was the parting that was sad for her. [How did you feel when she cried and didn't want to leave you at the preschool gate?] I felt sad too. You know, she's my youngest and last child, and I have a strong feeling that I don't want to let go of her yet. When she's gone, then there's nobody left at home with me. [How was it when your two older children went off to preschool?] It was much easier. They weren't quite so attached to me [*oya ni taisuru omoi go tsuyoku nai.*] They adapted to preschool without a minute's difficulty. I was frankly happy to get them into preschool, because I had three small children on my hands then, and I was ready to let go. With Rumi, she's my last, and although of course I'm glad she's enrolled, and she has a perfect attendance record, I still kind of wanted to keep her at home. I'm much closer to her [*kawaisa ga chigau.*] You know, they always say one's youngest child is the most adorable [*suekko ga kawaii*]. So I'm sure that somehow, she can sense my feelings, and she knows somehow "Mama needs me," so she wants

to do what she can to stay by my side. I'm sure she has that feeling somewhere in her mind.

It has frequently been reported that Japanese children rarely experience
a separation from their mothers until they enter preschool. Much has been
made of the supposed psychological impact of the reported practices of virtually never leaving the mother's side during the early years of life and of
never having been left in another's care (see, for example, Taniuchi, 1982).
Unquestionably, paid babysitters are rare in Japan and it is a cultural ideal
that mothers remain at home with their children during the early years. Interviews with Mountain Preschool mothers, however, suggest that we may
lack important information about Japanese mothers' normative as opposed
to ideal childcare practices during the preschool years.

Almost all of the Mountain Preschool's three- and four-year-old children
had experienced numerous brief separations from their mothers by the
time they entered preschool. Most mothers were straightforward and un-
apologetic about the fact that they often left their child to play at a friend's
house if they had errands to do, or so that the children could enjoy each
other's companionship. Furthermore, almost all mothers were in the habit
of leaving their preschool children at home unattended to "watch the
house" *(rusuban suru)* while they went to the supermarket or on various errands for thirty minutes or so at a time. At the extreme end of the spectrum
of fourteen mothers queried was one who had recently taken a part-time
job and routinely left her four- and seven-year-old children at home alone
for two to three hours, or dropped them off to play unsupervised in a
nearby park if her brother's wife who lived in the neighborhood was unable to look in on them. Table 5.2 shows the various kinds of separation experienced by the Mountain City preschool children.

Perhaps the reason that difficulties in adjustment to preschool are seen
primarily as a problem of adapting to school life rather than shock at separation from mother is that most Japanese three- and four-year-old children
are already used to being apart from their mothers for several hours at a
time. Furthermore, as Mountain City mothers explained, if a child feels secure *(anshin)* about his relationship with his mother, brief separations will
not be too difficult. If mother explains that she will come back to pick him
up, the child will trust the mother to return.

The strong bond of indulgence and trust that Japanese mothers share
with their preschool children undoubtedly provides a strong feeling of psychological security. Also, children's frequent experience of being left alone
or in the care of others provides first-hand experience that mother will re-

Table 5.2. *Extent and Type of Mountain Preschool Children's Separations from Mother before Entering Preschool (1984)*

Never Left Apart from Family Member		3 children
Always in mother's presence	1	
Left only with resident grandmother	2	
Left at Friend's House		12 children
Left to "Mind the House" Alone		11 children
Left alone before entering preschool	7	
Left alone only after preschool	4	
Left at Temporary Nursery Room		2 children

* Some children appear in more than one category. N = 14*

turn. Japanese mothers did not appear to be too concerned about the potential impact of separation on children's adjustment to preschool. Usually the only precaution they felt necessary was to explain to their children that they would return soon to pick them up. The primary difficulty was believed to lie in adjustment to group life.

PROBLEMS IN ADJUSTING TO CLASSROOM LIFE

Analyzing classroom adjustment problems is somewhat more difficult than identifying reluctance to attend preschool, in part because of the need to differentiate between isolated incidents of inappropriate behavior and actual adjustment problems. Clearly, not every incident of inappropriate behavior constitutes an adjustment problem. For the purpose of this analysis, adjustment problems have been defined as consistently inappropriate patterns of behavior, which reveal a fundamental incongruence between the child's feelings and attitudes and the most important rules of classroom life.

Another difficulty in analyzing adjustment problems hinges on the definition of problematic behavior. The behavior that Japanese teachers consider particularly troublesome is different than that considered problematic from another cultural viewpoint. Differences in the determination of what type of behavior is particularly troubling stem from cultural differences in the assumptions regarding the fundamental principles of social interaction and classroom life.

This section will describe how Japanese preschool teachers deal with behavior patterns considered problematic in Japan. It will consider two typical adjustment problems considered particularly troubling to the Japanese:

excessive reliance on the teacher and nonparticipation in group activities. Following these examples of the way some typical types of adjustment problems are managed, we will consider the primary means by which Japanese teachers deal with children's transition problems in general.

Overreliance on the Teacher

As would be expected from our knowledge of Japanese children's comparatively high degree of reliance on their mothers, during the first weeks of school some children expect too much attention and assistance from the teacher. Generally speaking, teachers are remarkably patient and willing to provide practical assistance to children who have difficulty in dressing, toileting, and performing similar activities on their own. Some children go too far, however, refusing seriously to try to do these things for themselves and expecting the teacher to provide the same degree of indulgent assistance and companionship that they have learned to expect from their mothers at home.

Teachers are at pains to establish in children an attitude of self-reliance and a desire to try to perform these tasks by themselves. They also endeavor to turn the focus of the child's desire for companionship away from the teacher toward the other children. Children who cannot do this are said to be *wagamama* (expecting their own way) and to show too much *amae* to the teacher. These children have failed to understand the fundamental difference between *shudan seikatsu* (life in a group) and family life.

Teachers deal with these children's inappropriate expectations in a patient, low-key, but highly consistent manner. Primarily, they turn a deaf ear to the child's requests, verbally acquiescing but being too busy to follow through until the child gives up and tries to do it for himself. Their standard reply to such requests for assistance is "go ahead on your own," "try it yourself," and "hang in there, you can do it," accompanied by a slowness of response. Teachers usually provide active assistance only after the child has honestly attempted to perform the task for himself, or has been made to wait an extremely long time for the teacher's help. Teachers also provide explicit instruction, encouragement, and praise as children gradually become more self-reliant.

Teachers try not to chastise the child or hurt his feelings in this process. They carefully provide only a minimum of assistance, gradually decreasing the child's reliance on the teacher until "independence" and "self-reliance" are achieved. For some children this approach is successful. Some children, however, have an extremely strong expectation that they will be able to rely on the teacher, as they do their own mothers, to perform the various routines of daily life. Japanese teachers describe these children not as lazy or rebellious, but as temporarily lacking the "understanding" that in preschool one must do these things for oneself. A common technique in these cases is to wait for an opportune chance early in the transition period to plant the seed of the understanding that at preschool, one must try to do as much as possible for oneself. This usually takes the form of a protracted battle of persistence that the teacher smilingly and infinitely patiently but inexorably wins. These "battles" involve no harsh words or physical punishment, but rather employ psychological intimidation through the sheer strength of the teacher's will power.

Several incidents of this were observed in various classrooms. One, in which a child who consistently refused to do things for himself was "forced" into trying to put on his clothing alone is reproduced here from the transcript of classroom activity on the fifth day of school in the three-year-old class at Mountain Preschool:

[Children are supposed to be changing clothes in preparation to go home. Several who have difficulty doing this alone are playing here and there, making no move to put on their traveling smocks.]

TEACHER: Hey. I told you to get ready to go home. Why are some people getting ready and some people playing? Why are some people still playing? Tatchan has gotten ready skillfully. (To Katsuaki) Bring your brown uniform. Do the parts that you can do by yourself. *Gambatte* [persevere] when you do it. If you can't do it, ask me "please do it for me." Nobo-kun has done it nicely.

KATSUAKI: I can't. [Stands holding uniform, making no move to put it on.]

TEACHER: [Ignores him, busy with several others' requests to button buttons.]

KATSUAKI: I can't.

TEACHER: If you can't do it, ask me to do it. Say "Please do it for me."

KATSUAKI: I can't.

TEACHER: It's not something you can't do. You *can*. I can't. [He tries ineffectually to thrust his arms into the mass of cloth.]

After encouraging Katsuaki to do it on his own through nine more exchanges, teacher assists other children, then returns to him and says:

TEACHER: Katsuaki-kun, look. It's not ready to wear. Katsuaki. This is the inside, when it's like this. You can't put it on when it's inside out. Turn it right side out. To do that, you put your hand in here [puts arm in sleeve] and grab right here. Now look closely. You're going to do it by yourself in a minute. Then pull it through like this. Now it's right side out. Katsuaki-kun, this is something you must do. This is not the job of your mother or people like that. This is your job that you yourself must do.

Teacher continues instructing Katsuaki through six more exchanges in how to turn uniform right side out.

KATSUAKI: [WATCHING CHILDREN NEAR HIM.] OKAY.
TEACHER: You weren't watching were you? Katsuaki-kun, that's it. It's your turn. Now you do it. What did I do? Show me. You do it.

The teacher persists. Katsuaki looks at teacher's face and tries to pull, bunching the sleeve.

TEACHER: Look here. [Touches Katsuaki's face, then sleeve.]
KATSUAKI: [Stalls, looks around classroom.]
TEACHER: Where are you looking? Look here. [Again touches face, then sleeve.]
KATUSAKI: [Pulls at sleeve with evident irritation.]
TEACHER: It won't work if you do it like that. Watch me, one more time. [Turns sleeve of blue uniform.] Now you do it.
KATSUAKI: [Makes no move to turn sleeve. Looks around classroom.]
TEACHER: Here, do it yourself. Take a hold here, turn it inside out by pulling it all the way out. Use your hand.
KATSUAKI: [Looks at teacher's face. Makes no move to touch garment.]
TEACHER: Take a hold, here. [Indicates sleeve, firmly.]
KATSUAKI: [Tries to stand up to leave.]
TEACHER: Hey, hey, hey. [Pulls him down.] You're going to have to do it by yourself.
KATSUAKI: [Tries ineffectually to put inside-out garment on his shoulder.]
TEACHER: You're supposed to turn the sleeve right side out, not put it on. Weren't you watching?
KATSUAKI: Don't look at me.
TEACHER: I will look at you. How did I do it? Hold right here [puts his hand inside sleeve]. Hold tightly. Now what did I do? Do it.

KATSUAKI: [Goes limp and starts to cry.]

TEACHER: Okay. Cry if you like. You have to do it yourself. Or if you can't, say, "Please do it for me."

KATSUAKI: Mama, mama [crying].

TEACHER: You have to put it on, by yourself. You've done it before. You can do it.

KATSUAKI: [Gets up and runs to corner of classroom where he stands with eyes closed, crying.]

TEACHER: [Follows him holding uniform. Kneels before him so he's boxed into corner.] Try it again. One more time.

KATSUAKI: [Crying harder.] Wa! Mama, mama.

TEACHER: You have to do it. Turn the sleeve like you did before.

Katsuaki continues to cry and makes no movement to touch garment. Teacher remains patiently insistent.

TEACHER: Watch. [Turns sleeve for him.]

KATSUAKI: But that's inside out.

TEACHER: No, it isn't. Now it's right side out.

KATSUAKI: [Wails.] Mama!

TEACHER: See, on the inside are all of these things. [Shows seam facings.] Now put it on by yourself. [Gives him uniform. Turns to class.] It's not time to go out to your mothers, yet. Everyone wait a little longer. [To Katsuaki:] You've still got a long way to go. Hang in there [*gambatte*].

KATSUAKI: Wa! [crying] I can't.

TEACHER: Yes, you can. Where do you put this arm through?

KATSUAKI: [Puts arm out waiting for teacher to thread uniform on it, still crying hard.]

TEACHER: [Holds uniform open, Katsuaki inserts one arm.] Put it on. [She drops uniform, so that it lies on his back, one arm in the sleeve.]

KATSUAKI: [Still sobbing, holds other arm out in front, waiting to be dressed.]

TEACHER: Why won't you do it for yourself? The other sleeve isn't out here. It's around in back.

KATSUAKI: [Tears running down face.] Where?

TEACHER: [Holds back of garment open and guides his hand.] Here. Can you get it in? Hang in there [*gambatte*]. There it is.

KATSUAKI: I did it.

TEACHER: Now you've become able to do it [*dekiru yo ni natta*].

KATSUAKI: I did it all by myself! [Smiles brightly through tears.]

TEACHER: Yes you did!

KATSUAKI: I could do it!

TEACHER: If you can do that so well, I wonder if you can handle buttons, too?

KATSUAKI: I can do buttons, too.

TEACHER: Of course you can.

KATSUAKI: Before I couldn't.

TEACHER: You couldn't, but because you tried hard, now you can. You did it all by yourself. That's because you tried to do it [*yaro to omotta*].

During her attempt to get Katsuaki to "understand," the rest of the class had been abandoned. As there was no assistant teacher in the room, after the nine-minute incident was over, many children had to be collected from the schoolyard and hallways, where they had wandered out of the classroom. Despite the very strong pressure focused on Katsuaki, the teacher never once raised her voice or demonstrated any physical signs of impatience. She smilingly but unyieldingly demanded that Katsuaki make a good-faith attempt to put on his smock by himself. The degree of assistance she actually rendered was not the issue at stake; the goal was to get Katsuaki to actually exert some effort himself. Katsuaki's feeling of joy at his new-found attempt at self-reliance demonstrated that obviously a breakthrough had been made. As the teacher later described the incident:

Because Katsuaki's mother always put on all of his clothes for him, Katsuaki didn't really understand that at preschool, this is something he has to do for himself. He also didn't have confidence that he could actually do it alone. I've been looking for a chance to help him understand these things. Today, although he cried, he finally actually tried to do things for himself and he realized that if he tries, he can do things for himself. That's why he was happy. It's a big thing for him.

Thus we see that overreliance on the teacher is one issue that Japanese teachers consider important enough to force children to the point of tears, if necessary. Establishing in children a self-reliant (*jiritsu*) and "independent" (*jishu*) attitude is fundamental to creating a distinction between the *amae*-based world of the home and the group life of the preschool. Making a sincere effort to perform one's own role and master proper personal habits of daily life is one of the most important fundamentals of *shudan seikatsu*. Overreliance on the teacher is in direct opposition to this.

Nonparticipation in Group Activities

Because of the strong emphasis on group activities in Japanese preschools, refusal to join in group activities is a comparatively serious form of inappropriate behavior. Nonparticipation takes two forms: passive withdrawal and refusal to stop playing to make a transition to the next activity. Nonparticipation is one of the most commonly discussed types of behavior problems in Japanese preschool teachers' professional literature. Perhaps this is not only because group activities are a keystone of Japanese preschool life, but because unwillingness to participate is particularly threatening to preschool teachers, who are well-socialized members of Japanese group-oriented culture. In all preschools visited, it was one of the most common reasons for putting serious pressure on individual children. Preschool teachers' general professional opinion is that children who "don't yet understand the fun of being together with others" *(minna to issho ni iru tanoshisa ga wakaranai)* should not be forced to join in group activities. Rather, teachers should give these children a little time and wait for the child's natural interest in preschool activities and in being with other children to assert itself. This approach is clearly advocated by the teacher's advice column dealing with transition problems in an article published in the trade magazine *Yoji to hoiku* (Children and Childcare) (1983).

Wait Until He Becomes Acclimated

A-KUN: A four-year-old boy who is not yet accustomed to the group [*shudan ni najimanai*].

QUESTION: A-kun comes to school in the morning and plays out of doors during the morning play period. When it comes time to come inside, he won't come in the classroom. Sometimes he will come if he is in the mood, but he usually complains and resists.

ANSWER: It is best not to force this type of child to enter the classroom. Let him play outside as he likes. Sooner or later he will develop an interest in what is going on in the classroom. His interest will gradually draw him to join the other children. Be sure not to react to this child differently than you react to the others.

In actual practice in the preschools studied, the degree of pressure on a reluctant child to require him to join in group activities depends considerably on the activity the child is trying to avoid. Some activities, such as free play, story time, or desk-based activities are not considered essential for the reluctant child to attend. Others, like the brief formal rituals surrounding morning greetings, daily good-byes, and the beginning and end of meal formalities, are virtually mandatory. If a child is unwilling to join the group for these activities, considerable pressure is exerted.

Following a number of direct requests, teachers often try to lead the child by the hand toward the activity. If this fails, the teacher frequently warns the child that the group will proceed without him. Although to a properly socialized member of Japanese society, such a warning is a serious sanction, this tactic often does not work with children who are new to preschool and have yet to "understand the fun of being together with others." Often during the first weeks of school, the class ceremoniously proceeds without a reluctant member who then happily returns to play.

If a child continues to refuse to participate, the teacher may force the issue, often provoking a tantrum. As we saw in the previous example, the tantrum is faced cheerfully, patiently, and sympathetically. The teacher, however, psychologically outflanks the child who ultimately finds himself the loser in a smiling "battle of perseverance." The following incident, which occurred on the second day of school at Mountain Preschool, was typical.

[All are playing out of doors during morning play period. Teacher tells children it's time to go inside for morning greetings.]

TEACHER A: Let's go in the classroom. Just for a few minutes. Let's go inside and say hello to everyone. Let's go in the classroom and all say good morning together. [Continues in this vein, approaching each child.] Let's go inside. Let's all say good morning together.

TEACHER A: [To Satoshi, still playing with trucks in the sand.] Let's go say good morning.

SATOSHI: I don't want to [*iyada*]. No [*iya*].

TEACHER A: Let's go. [Tries to guide him by hand in small of his back.]

SATOSHI: No! *Iyada, iyada, iyada.* [Breaks into tears, crying *iyada* and stiffens body.]

TEACHER A: [Tries to pick him up and carry him in.]

SATOSHI: [Escapes and runs back to where he was playing with trucks in the sand.] I still want to play.

TEACHER A: You still want to play? Then play. Everyone's going inside. You can play. All by yourself. Okay? All by yourself. Goodbye. [Turns and ostentatiously goes into classroom with the last of the students.]

SATOSHI: [Begins to play again.]

TEACHER B: [After two or three minutes, the assistant principal, who is assisting the regular teacher during the first week of school, comes out to the playground where Satoshi is playing alone.] You're a good boy [*orikosan dane*]. After we say good morning to everyone, we can play again. Okay? Everyone's waiting for you.

SATOSHI: [Immediately starts to cry. Stiffens body, resists teacher's attempt to take him in her arms.] No! *Iyada, iyada, iyada.*

TEACHER B: Well then, let's go and play inside for a minute and come back. Come on, come on, just for a minute. Let's say hello with all our nice friends. Then we'll come back outside and I'll play with you.

SATOSHI: No! *Iyada, iyada* [crying hard, body rigid].

TEACHER B: [Picks up Satoshi who begins to hit and pummel her. She does not react to the blows, but carries him gently but firmly to the shoe cupboard, where she sits on the stoop with him in her lap. He continues to kick and hit her, crying loudly.] Let's put our shoes on, okay? [She tries to put indoor shoes on his feet, but he kicks at her.] Hey, hey. Put your shoes on. [She holds his ankles with her hands, and as he kicks, she plays "push me pull you" with him.] One, two. One, two. You're really strong.

SATOSHI: [Still crying loudly.] No! Don't! *Iyada!*

TEACHER B: Look. Let's play together as soon as we sing a nice song with all our friends, okay? Don't cry.

SATOSHI: No! [boohooing]

TEACHER B: Why? Why? All your friends are inside. It's lonely out here. [Renews a frenzy of pummeling at teacher.]

SATOSHI: No! *iyada!* [Now crying hysterically.]

TEACHER B: [Feigning sudden understanding.] Okay, okay. Now I understand. You want to play some more? Okay. Let's play together. [Carries rigid screaming child back to where he had been playing and sets him down. He lies stiffly against her, screaming *iyada* hysterically.][4] What shall we play? [She picks up a truck and rolls it back and forth.] How shall we play? What shall I do?

SATOSHI: [Continues to cry *iyada* hysterically, and hits ineffectually at her.]

TEACHER B: I thought you wanted to play. Don't you want to play? *Iyada?* Then shall we go inside with our nice friends? That's *iyada* too? What shall we do? Huh? Are you okay? What's *iyada?* Aren't you

---

4 During tantrums, Japanese children rarely run away from the people who thwart them, but lie against them stiffly, often hitting or kicking at them.

feeling well? [She remains squatting, her arm around him, while he continues to cry hard, for two or three minutes. She pats him and dries his face, saying "there, there" (*yoshi, yoshi*) and "Are you okay?" (*daijobu?*) as he gradually calms down to hiccuping sobs. He relaxes against her and she takes him in her arms and pats him saying "there, there" as she carries him to the door where he can see the class. She stands in the doorway holding him while he gradually calms down, his face wet, and hiccuping quiet sobs. After the class has finished morning greetings and is starting to play, the teacher sets him on his feet.] Let's say good morning.

SATOSHI: No [limp and unresisting].

TEACHER B: Let's say good morning, okay? [Molding her body over his, she recites the routine greetings for him, bowing herself, which forces his body to bow.] Good morning, teacher. Good morning, everyone.

SATOSHI: *Iya. Iyada.* [Seems about to cry again, but his resistance is vague and drained.]

TEACHER B: [Laughs.] *Iya?* You still think it's *iyada?* [Laughs again as she picks him up and carries him to shoe cupboard.] Here are your shoes.

SATOSHI: [Picks up shoes and throws them.] *Iyada.*

TEACHER B: [Retrieves them and puts them in front of him again.] Here they are.

SATOSHI: [Throws them again, harder.] *Iyada.*

TEACHER A: [Regular teacher comes over and scoops him into her arms.] Now we can play again. Let's go outside, okay? What shall we play? Shall we play together? [She puts on his outdoor shoes, sets him down outside, and follows him across the playground, where she engages him in sand play.]

This method of dealing with children's direct refusals is common in Japanese preschools. Teachers maneuver themselves so that they do not appear to directly oppose the child, and speak in a sympathetically supportive manner. Indirectly, however, they thwart the child in such a way that he gains neither the satisfaction of victory nor a clear-cut glimpse of what is opposing him. At the climax, the child is reduced to a no-win situation, which has become patently ridiculous even to himself. There is nothing to do but rely on the hand of support extended by the smiling teacher, who then proceeds to guide the child through the activity against which he initially rebelled.

This highly sophisticated form of psychological outmaneuvering has also been witnessed in elementary schools and even in dealing with immature adults in the larger society. It is undoubtedly an unconscious product of cultural habit rather than a studied behavior modification technique. Without meeting anger, physical force, or even clearly definable opposition, the child inexplicably finds himself in the position of conceding defeat. But who has brought him to this position? Certainly not the smiling teacher who hugs and comforts him and offers to play with him. Certainly not the "nice friends who are waiting to sing a song with you." This technique leaves the child without an opponent and therefore effectively undermines his rebellion.

The teacher further attenuates the child's rebellion by legitimating and coopting his angry and defiant actions. If the child kicks her, she ignores the blows or plays "push me pull you," flattering the child that he is strong. If the child wants to remain on the playground, she first pretends not to understand, then acquiesces once the child has lost interest, pleading "What shall we play?" By pretending to misunderstand the issue the child is trying to articulate, his anger and frustration are rendered apparently causeless. Children soon learn that it is ultimately useless to rebel directly against the system.

This technique of dealing with rebellious children is similar to a well-known Chinese folk story of a mischievous monkey. Although the monkey goes to extraordinary lengths to cause trouble for his superiors and ultimately runs away to a far-off land to be free of their authority, one day he awakens, as if from a dream, to realize that no matter where he runs or gambols about, all of his actions have taken place in the palm of Buddha's hand *(doko o abaretemo, oshakasama no te no hira no ue de aru)*.[5] Presumably after realizing the futility of escape, he gives up and conforms to society's expectations.

Japanese preschool teachers do not use this method consciously or calculatingly, nor is it a studied product of their junior college teacher training. Instead, this method of dealing with rebellious tantrums is merely what comes naturally to them. As the assistant teacher (who was also the director of Mountain Preschool) later explained regarding the incident:

> Satoshi still doesn't realize that at preschool, you need to do things together with the group. Maybe today he began to get some idea. At the beginning, many children have this problem. [What do you usually do when one child doesn't want to do what the group does?] Well, wait for them a little bit. But it's best to let them watch what the rest of the group

5 I am indebted to Dr. Shigefumi Nagano of the preschool division of the Japanese National Institute of Educational Research for this insightful observation.

does even if they won't participate. At that moment they feel *iyada,* but through watching they will gradually understand how things are [*junjo o wakattekuru*] and later want to join. Today Satoshi cried and got pretty angry. But he wasn't angry when he went home. Children don't hold anger for very long. They cry, and then they forget. But it's important not to just drop it as soon as they stop crying. It's important to cheer them up again [*kibun o totte ageru*]. [How do you do that?] You can play nicely with them, bring them toys or something like that. If you make them cry, you shouldn't just leave it at that [*nakasetara, nakashippanashi ni shite okanai*]. Children aren't good at changing their own mood [*kibun tenkan*], so you have to help them feel happy again. We'll watch carefully how Satoshi feels when he comes tomorrow. If there seems to be some hard lump [*shikori*] inside him, we'll try to help him understand that preschool is an enjoyable place. It's important that he not dislike preschool.

Japanese teachers see making restitution to children after they have become angry as an important ingredient in securing the child's friendliness and psychological affiliation. To the Japanese mind, the issue is not whether this implies a softening of the teacher's expectations or weakening of authority. The issue is whether the child wants to come to school again tomorrow. Securing an enjoyment of preschool is the crux of the means by which children are assisted in negotiating the transition period.

Learning to Like Preschool

It is extremely important to Japanese preschool teachers that their students like coming to preschool. On the surface, this merely reflects a benevolent wish that the children spend the school day happily. Or perhaps a business-like desire that the private institution not lose enrollees. There is, however, a much more fundamental issue at stake.

Japanese teachers' nonauthoritarian approach to discipline and training in appropriate behavior is ultimately based on the child's willingness to internalize the preschool's standards and expectations as Lewis insightfully notes:

> When questioned about misbehavior, teachers frequently volunteered that enjoyment of school was the key element to good behavior for children. An emotional attachment to the teacher and friendships with children were considered critical elements in the child's enjoyment of school. (Lewis, 1984, p. 82)

Enjoying preschool and feeling an emotional attachment to the teacher are important because they provide the psychological foundation for internalization of the school's values. Unless the child desires to please the teacher and wishes to spend the preschool day happily, Japanese teachers' nonauthoritarian techniques are rendered largely useless. Teachers are correct in identifying "learning to enjoy coming to preschool" as the indispensable first step in the process of adapting to school life.

Helping children "come to understand the fun of preschool life" (*yochien no tanoshisa o wakaraseru*) is almost universally cited as the primary goal of instruction during the first month of preschool. The Ministry of Education's official guidelines for preschool education reflect the psychological importance of this period, as do the instructional objectives of Mountain Preschool. Individual teachers frequently cite "coming to dislike preschool" as the most serious possible occurrence when something goes wrong.

Although the child's initial focus is on the teacher, friendships with other children soon assume a greater importance. "Learning to enjoy being with the group" (*minna to issho ni iru tanoshisa wakaru*) forms the psychological foundation of preschool life. Mothers unanimously described their children's enjoyment of other children as the main reason they like preschool. The mother of the three-year-old boy who reported that she had to forcibly strap him into the bicycle seat to take him to preschool each morning described the reason for her son's eventual adjustment to preschool thus:

> It was the other children, and understanding the fun of playing with them, that finally caused Shingo-kun to stop crying and start to like preschool. Slowly he started to mention some children's names, like Hiroshi-kun or Tomomi-chan. I still don't really know who these kids are, but he has several he regularly mentions doing this or that with. That's what finally made him happy about going to preschool.

As we have seen, Japanese preschool teachers see learning to enjoy other children as an inevitable process. All other children in the school are always referred to as "friends" (*otomodachi*). As the veteran director of Tokyo Preschool explained, there are no children who honestly prefer solitary pursuits, only "those who don't yet understand the fun of playing with others." Learning to live in and enjoy life in a group is a natural and highly satisfying step in Japanese children's development toward social maturity.

CONCLUSIONS

It is appropriate at this point to reconsider the original question with which this article began. How do the Japanese become group-oriented? Although family training may provide some influence, it is clear that the schooling experience plays an overwhelming role in training appropriate social behavior in contemporary Japan. It is the teacher and one's classmates, rather than one's mother, who teach children what it means to be a member of Japanese group society.

Training in the habits and attitudes appropriate to group life is the single most important goal of the preschool experience in the minds of Japanese parents and educators. The objective is to foster the child's enjoyment of participating in group activities. Once the child wants to be part of the group, he will adopt the behavior standards his friends exhibit. By avoiding authoritarian means of shaping behavior, internalization of behavior standards is encouraged.

In this process of socialization to group norms, Japanese children are told that it is because they are members of a group that they must learn to control their egoistic and regressive tendencies. It is not the teacher, or the school rules, but "all of your friends," "everyone else," or "group life" that places limits on children's ability to indulge their own desires. Yet these friends are the same ones with whom children are encouraged to develop a strong attachment and whose companionship provides fulfillment of the human longing for social interaction. Indeed, Japanese parents, teachers, and children agree that the presence of all of these "friends" is the primary pleasure of preschool life.

In Japan, the group is both the unsympathetic force to which the child's ego must submit and a primary source of companionship and fulfillment. It is a diffuse and nonpersonified yet unassailable authority. In a more authoritarian culture, children ultimately submit their egoistic desires to the will of an authority figure, or comply out of fear of punishment for infraction of a rule. The anger and ambivalence this arouses in the child's mind has a clear target, which in fantasy and occasionally in real life may be escaped, resisted, or changed.

Japanese children soon learn, however, that to seriously resist the system is to battle an army of friendly shadows. Authority resides with no one and to change the collective habits of the group requires an insurmountable effort. To escape or rebel is to sever social contact with those who provide daily companionship and the warmth of social life. The most prudent alternative is to learn to accept group habits and expectations and to learn the social behavior required by group life. Perhaps because this identification occurs early in the child's life, Japanese individuals exhibit less ambivalence toward authority than is the case in the United States.

It may be, however, that there remains a deep-rooted element of strain in the Japanese individual's psychological relationship to the group. At the same time that Japanese adults are profoundly uncomfortable when isolated from social life, psychological tension is inevitable in the effort to "keep one's wings pulled in." In comparison to the *amae*-based intimacy and informality of the home, even familiar outside social relationships cause some amount of *ki zukare*, or psychological fatigue. To the Japanese individual, the group both beckons and binds, and it may be that the ambivalence arising from this tension is what establishes what Lebra has termed '*hito*' as the central Alter to the Japanese Ego (Lebra, 1976, p. 2).

In summary, we have seen that the preschool experience teaches Japanese children not only the basic behavior but also the psychological attitudes that govern classroom and later public life. In the process, they internalize many of the norms that make them members of Japanese culture. In this way, learning to go to school in Japan represents the first step in the larger process of learning to become a member of Japanese society.

REFERENCES

Lebra, T. S. (1976). *Japanese patterns of behavior.* Honolulu: University of Hawaii Press.
Lewis, C. (1984). Cooperation and control in Japanese nursery schools. *Comparative Education Review, 28,* 69–84.
Taniuchi, L. (1982). *The psychological transition from home to school and the development of Japanese children's attitudes toward learning.* Unpublished qualifying paper. Harvard University, Cambridge, MA.
Vogel, E. (1963). *Japan's new middle class.* Berkeley: University of California Press.
White, M. (1987). *The Japanese educational challenge.* New York: Free Press.
Yoji to hoiku [Children and childcare]. (1983, April). 29(1).

SIX

Peer Culture and Interaction

How Japanese Children Express Their Internalization of the Cultural Norms of Group Life (Shudan Seikatsu)

Victoria E. Kelly

Previous research has shown that children are able to express their knowledge of social norms and cultural values during interactions with peers. The goal of this study was to systematically examine this process among five- and seven-year-old Japanese children and to clarify aspects of their socialization through their knowledge of those values, social conventions, and cultural traits that define Japanese society.

The major findings of this study indicate that the subjects possessed surprisingly sophisticated interactional abilities that are reflective of many aspects of the Japanese value system as well as of certain social customs and behavioral conventions. In particular, it was found that concepts of empathy (*omoiyari*), "parent-child" (*oya-ko*) stratification, and helpfulness were strongly apparent in the speech and behavior of both five- and seven-year-olds. High levels of coordinated action and cooperation in play were also much in evidence, demonstrating the need for "belongingness" via a clear preference for group and parallel play activities, while the capacity for individual self-regulation – reflective of Japanese kindergarten training toward personal responsibility – was also highly salient in a number of activities.

JAPANESE SOCIAL VALUES AND THEIR RELATION TO INTERPERSONAL BEHAVIOR

Children's use of social norms may reflect their internalization of the values of a particular culture as they are manifested in preferred behavior patterns or the verbal expression of concepts. The value-system in Japanese society has been well documented (Benedict, 1946; Dore, 1978; Vogel, 1963), and its relation to interpersonal behavior patterns also has been the subject of much research (Lebra, 1976; Nakane, 1970). In historic terms, certain aspects of the value-system and contemporary frame of mind may be traced to the Tokugawa (Edo) period (1600–1868), an era in which Japanese society was restructured according to Confucian precepts as interpreted by the Tokugawa government (*bakufu*). In order to maintain their authority, the *bakufu* established a class system dividing society into four general castes, and the strong sense of hierarchy that survives in the present Japanese system of social values is a remnant from this era. Rank-order engenders stability in Japanese social life in that awareness of one's rank is inseparable from a sense of "belongingness" with one's group, and it is group identity that lies at the core of individual consciousness of oneself and others (Nakane, 1970).

The Japanese adherence to group life and activities is immediately noticeable in their institutions overall, which encourage the strong feelings of group identity and loyalty developing from the value placed on human ties. The ability to form good relations with others is viewed by the Japanese as a vitally important personality trait, as they recognize that the life of the individual is inextricably bound to life in a group (*shudan seikatsu*).

Within the group's structure, gregariousness, feelings of "oneness" (*ittaikan*), and positive relations (*naka yoshi*) are viewed as cultural ideals, with great value placed on interdependence, "kindness" (*shinsetsu*), and helpfulness as preferred characteristics of personality and behavior. Interdependence with the members of one's group fosters the ability to give priority to the accomplishment of group goals, while it is widely understood that it is not only permissible but almost *obligatory* to depend on the strength of ties with others when help is needed.

Adherence to group norms and conformity are well-documented Japanese cultural traits much misunderstood by members of more "individualistic" Western societies, who often assume that personal characteristics are forced thereby into a common mold with the end result of a "robot-like" personality. Through their concept of *kejime,* or "ability to distinguish," the Japanese view conformity less as a mechanism for the repression of individual impulses than as the ability to comprehend and act on behavioral requirements that differ according to the social situation at hand (Bachnik, 1992).

In *shudan seikatsu,* individuals do not feel that being or acting "like everybody else" threatens individuality; rather, a sense of belongingness and the competitive urge to always be "in" on activities are sustained by doing so. Within the dynamics of the group, conformity both encourages adherence to group goals and protects each member's right to take part in the decision-making process, while the cultural values of empathy (*omoiyari*) and kindness (*shinsetsu*) are strongly emphasized as components in "getting along with others" as well as desirable personal characteristics. In this context, the ability to scan the feelings of others and to show kindness when it is needed is a vital social skill in a culture based on interdependence.

The giving of empathetic attention to those in need of "talking out" their problems is one form of showing kindness to others (*shinsetsu*), which is also frequently manifested in terms of helpfulness. Doing favors unasked and general "pitching in" are among the ties that bind group life and great emphasis is placed on being helpful to others in Japanese society in general. Persistence (*gaman*) and effort (*doryoku*) are also expected of each group member so as not to "let down" the others in the process of goal achievement. These qualities, it is believed, cannot be imposed on a person, but can only come from within the individual "spirit," and their development is regarded as a personal endeavor. Through these expectations, the Japanese acknowledge that the strength of the group stems from and is dependent on the individualized will of its component members.

EARLY SOCIALIZATION IN THE HOME AND KINDERGARTEN

The unusual intensity of the mother-child bond in Japanese society has been well documented by both anthropologists and sociologists (Beardsley et al., 1959; Lanham, 1956; Norbeck & Norbeck, 1956; Rice and Kobayashi, this volume; Vogel, 1963; Vogel & Vogel, 1961; White 1985). While developing close emotional ties with her child, the Japanese mother "wants the child to be *sunao* (obedient), honestly receptive to adult expectations, and attempts to achieve this through the child's internalization of a desire to conform" (Conroy, 1980; Kobayashi, this volume).

Because the preschool child is too young to understand what is expected of him, the mother relies on indulgence, persuasion, and reasoning in teaching him to *want* to comply. Through the creation of a warm atmosphere emphasizing interdependence and close human ties, she fosters early awareness of the presence and needs of others by communicating the values of empathy and conformity (Clancy, 1986), and relies on affective ties to gain compliance and to "get the child to understand." This emotional atmosphere is crucial to the development of relational attitudes important to the child's ability later in life to form ties with others in group-life situations.

At the age of three, the child is ready to go to kindergarten (*yochien*), an environment radically different from that of home and one in which he will be expected to develop self-sufficiency and control while learning to identify with a peer group consisting of strangers. The transition from home to the outside without disruption of the mother-child bond is the stated function of the kindergarten curriculum, since: "higher expectations or requirements for self-discipline most easily come from a less 'sympathetic' and more objective source outside the family" (Peak, 1987, also this volume).

Studies of beliefs and classroom practices among Japanese kindergarten teachers and daycare givers indicate that their primary concern is the fostering of a *ningen-rashii kodomo* (human-like child) who is empathetic, cooperative, harmonious with others, and persistent (Shigaki, 1983). Interdependence, group-values acceptance, and individual persistence are fostered through a variety of practices both overt and subtle, while the routine of everyday classroom activities is designed to promote positive attitudes toward group life, as the following observation from this study's kindergarten will show:

> At the end of the day, the children put their chairs upon the tables while the teacher played a happy tune on the organ, a signal for the event to begin. While singing a cheerful song about what a nice place their kindergarten is and how much fun they have, the children played patty-cake and *janken* (scissors/paper/stone) with each other. Next they marched around the room in a musical chairs routine, except that the object when the music stopped was to race around and make physical contact with at least one other child and form a group as quickly as possible. Each group then formed a line, hands on each other's shoulders, and repeated the contact game until all the lines became one. Next everyone re-formed holding hands in a large circle, facing each other and swinging hands in time to the music while singing "goodbye everyone, see you again tomorrow" and then repeated a little prayer, "thank you for today." The group broke up to fetch their hats and coats, then returned to their desks and played a game of *janken* with the teacher. Children who matched the teacher's throws were allowed to leave and gradually everyone dispersed.

Personal self-sufficiency in basic skills is also viewed as a necessary component of group life and kindergarten children are encouraged – *never* scolded – to persevere until they have achieved them. The seriousness with which routine-mastery is taken by the children themselves is illustrated by the following excerpt from this study's field notes:

About fifteen minutes before lunchtime, the investigator notices Kimi-toshi, a five-year-old boy, sitting at his usual place and crying quite loudly, unusual here among children of that age. He is surrounded by six or eight other children of both sexes who are patting his head and speaking comfortingly in soft voices while he continues to cry. His *obento* (lunch box) brought from home is neatly set up on the table in front of him. A teacher from the next-door classroom is called, who holds the sobbing child comfortingly, gets him to tell her what's wrong and gradually coaxes him into calming down. She later explained to the investigator that he had gotten out and set up his lunch and was told by the other children that it "wasn't yet time" to do that, whereupon he became very upset and cried. The teacher told him that the "mistake" didn't matter and that it was all right.

Kimitoshi was upset not because he was thwarted in an attempt to eat when he wanted to, but because he had made a mistake in a routine that everyone – himself included – had mastered two years earlier, when they were first-year pupils. His tears were probably caused by both disappointment in himself and shame at his error; even the empathy (*omoiyari*) given by his classmates failed to comfort him. Such potentially high levels of frustration in group-life socialization are typically reduced by a subtle stress-reduction process through which routines requiring self-control are surrounded by tension-relieving or "comforting" activities and symbols, such as the *obento* itself, which is meant to be a reminder of his mother's love (Peak, 1987) and as such is a powerful symbol of *amae* (dependence). The boisterous activities observed during kindergarten free-play times (Peak, 1989) are regarded by teachers as tension-relievers rather than disruptions. In their view, the important thing was for the children to learn to make the distinction (*kejime*) between structured activities where control is required and those in which it is not, through which they learn to distinguish differences in social situations and alter their behavior accordingly.

Self-control and sufficiency as well as feelings of belongingness are further encouraged by the early and frequent delegation of classroom authority to children (Lewis, 1984), while responsibility for each other and for their school is fostered by organized activities such as lunch-serving and school cleaning. Preschool teachers encourage children to work out disagreements on their own (Peak, 1987), which gives them the opportunity to express their understanding of culturally sanctioned pro- and antisocial behavior. Finally, we note that anecdotal evidence in studies of nursery schools indicates that Japanese preschool children are capable of verbally expressing group-sanctioned behavioral norms to both adults and peers (Lewis, 1984; Shiagki, 1983).

DATA COLLECTION AND ANALYSIS

The core areas of research in the present study involve the investigation of values-internalization among five- and seven-year-old Japanese children through an examination of their socially normative verbal expressions and behavior in a peer-group setting. The main focus is twofold: children's understanding of the behaviors and values learned during the transition from home to school, and ways in which children express these values during free-play sessions.

The method for this research was originally developed and tested as a pilot study at the Harvard University Peer Interaction Project for application to cross-cultural research and is grounded in data-based categories; that is, categories of a preconceived or theoretical nature are not imposed on the data but are derived from the nature of the data itself (Kelly-Suzuki, 1983). In the pilot study with an American sample, this method successfully identified the types of norms and values that children understand and implement in their peer interactions. The methodological focus was upon the three basic components: (a) the observational method; (b) peer group interactions; and (c) play as a context for observation. In this research, the method and its essential techniques of video-recording, naturalistic observation, and the use of data-based categorizations were adapted to a Japanese field site.

Observations for this fieldwork were made during the course of same-age playgroups organized and time-limited but otherwise free of adult influence. Data collection consisted of a series of videotaped recordings of thirty-two one-hour playgroup sessions, sixteen of which were of two groups of five-year-olds and sixteen of seven-year-olds equally divided by gender from local schools, and took place in a small urban middle-class field site approximately halfway up the southern coast of Honshu. The videotaping was conducted in playrooms set up in each school and furnished with play materials designed to encourage engagement in fantasy play, creative or constructive play, and structured or rule-oriented play. During the videotaping, the children were allowed complete freedom in their activities without intervention from the investigator except in rare instances of excessive physical roughness, teasing, or other anti-social behavior.

Each tape was reviewed several times for behavioral and speech occurrences by individual subjects, with the criteria for utterance selection based on their *normative content,* defined here as: (a) references to rules, regulations, or social conventions; and (b) forms of speech with normative implications such as "should" "must" or "can't."

With these criteria as a guideline, qualified utterances were transcribed and coded by subject for variables relevant to the basic research questions. Their basic categories are: (a) thematic content of play being engaged in during the course of the utterance; (b) normative reference, defining the issue being negotiated; (c) direct/indirect verbal presentation of the issue, a Japanese-language specific variable that codes grammatical or socially-based circuitousness in approaching the issue; (d) use of honorifics and forms of address in reference to another; (e) level of formality in grammar, verb conjugation, and reference to self; and (f) speaker-addressee gender criteria. The content of these categories is entirely data-based and is, in accordance with past research (Clancy, 1986; Ide et al., 1986) often highly specific to Japanese behavioral and verbal modes of interaction, particularly in terms of certain issues of reference, the indirection variable, and the use of honorifics. These criteria served as guidelines in discovering the ways in which Japanese children manifest their *shudan seikatsu* socialization through socially appropriate behavior, and the modes of negotiation used in given interactions with relationship to appropriate age, gender, and group-life criteria.

The normative utterances emerging in this study were each found to be classifiable within one of the thematic categories of *constructive play, structured play, fantasy play, cleanup activities,* and *physical* or *sports-related play.* Structured play and sports-related play will not be discussed here, as the findings in the first category are salient only to maturation level differences, while the frequency distribution of the second is too low to merit examination. The normative issues of reference in each utterance were found to be classifiable as *coordinated action, rules, institutions, prosocial behavior, logical associations, teaching, possession,* and *turn-taking.*

THEMES OF PLAY AS THE CULTURAL SETTING FOR PEER INTERACTIONS

Constructive Play as an Index of Creativity and Knowledge-Sharing

Constructive play activity, which involves the use of play materials for building and creating in a nonpretend activity, scored high frequency counts of normative references of *teaching* at 14% for five-year-olds and 26%

for seven-year-olds, with the subjects willing to offer and request help in their various projects and enjoying both roles. The thoroughness with which they enacted the role of teacher is particularly noteworthy:

(Fumio and Mariko, both five years old, are at the table making folded-paper origami constructions. Mariko's is a game in which different numbers are written on each fold with messages hidden underneath. The game is played by choosing a number, opening and closing the folds the correct number of times, and reading the message.)

MARIKO: What number?
FUMIO: Number six.
MARIKO: One, two, three, four, five, six . . . it says *baka* (fool).

(Both laugh, and Fumio begins to make a game for himself while Mariko turns aside to show Isamu a paper fan she has made.)

MARIKO: (To Isamu) Is it all right? (*ii?*) Is it okay if I show you how to do this?
FUMIO: (Moving toward Mariko; he is having trouble with his origami and interrupts before Isamu can speak.) How do you do this?
MARIKO: (Leading Fumio back to the table.) You write the numbers one through eight. (Both nod emphatically) Then for this part in the center you do it like this, all right? (*ii?*)
FUMIO: I get it. (Mariko leaves and Fumio works on origami.)

(Soon after, Mariko returns to the table and shows Fumio how to fold.)

MARIKO: The important part, right (*ne*), now here (*ano ne*). It's right here. (Using *desho* form of "is.") Then you finish up quickly, right? (Using *ne* and nodding emphatically at Fumio.)
MARIKO: You can't do it? (Takes Fumio's origami and demonstrates.) You fold it like this, right (*ne*)? Right? (Turning and nodding emphatically to Natsuko, who is watching. Both Natsuko and Fumio nod in acknowledgement.)
MARIKO: When you've finished (using conditional *dekitara*) you turn it around to the back. The back, turn it around to the back. (She leans over Fumio watching carefully.)
FUMIO: Then I write the numbers.
MARIKO: That's wrong. If you don't do it this way from the beginning it won't be any good. This is folded (correctly). (Using *desho* form of "is" and showing Fumio and Natsuko her own origami game.)

MARIKO: This is the way to do it, like this. Fold it, right (*ne*), right here. (She demonstrates with her own origami.)

(Isamu has returned and joins Fumio and Natsuko in watching Mariko demonstrate.)

MARIKO: Like this, like this . . . after that, right (*ne*), on this part, right (*ne*) you write one, two, three, four.

(Fumio finishes making the game and invites Natsuko to play. They play for a moment, then Natsuko starts folding one for herself. Sayoko has also joined in and watches Natsuko.)

NATSUKO: (Taking Sayoko's origami.) Okay? (*ii?*) It's like this (using conditional *daro* form of "is"). Then . . . (Demonstrates.)
SAYOKO: (Watching intently.) I get it, I get it.

(Natsuko continues instruction while Sayoko watches carefully. They finish construction and start playing the game together.)

Indirect forms of speech were quite frequent in these interactions, particularly use of the expression *ii?* and *ne*, as well as the conditional *desho*, all roughly translating as expressions meaning, "Is it all right with you?" and "Right?" on the part of the "teacher," in which "asking permission" to instruct downplays authoritativeness and makes it easier for the learner to accept instruction. Expressions such as these are important elements of verbal interaction among the Japanese as they serve to maintain consensus between group members by inviting input (Clancy, 1986).

Utterances involving *coordinated action* also occurred with very high frequency during constructive play, with 27% for five-year-olds and 23% for seven-year-olds, an expected observation, as these utterances make reference to group behavior leading toward a common goal and ways in which play materials should be used. Such expressions are vital to the success of negotiations in interdependent activities requiring group consensus. The following play episode illustrates the adeptness of these subjects in such negotiations:

(Shohei, five years old, has discovered the dinosaur set, which consists of a large plastic mat marked with trees, land, and bodies of water, two large plastic mountains, and an assortment of toy dinosaurs and cavemen.)

SHOHEI: (Taking the set out.) Hey, we've got this here!

(Saburo helps unfold the mat and takes out the toys while Nori joins the play.)

SABURO: (Brandishing a large rubber snake.) Do we want him to be a sea snake?

NORI: Sea snake!

SABURO: It's a sea snake (He places the snake in the "sea" on the mat.)

NORI: (Taking out the tyrannosaurus.) Where does he go . . . here.

SHOHEI: There . . . no, not there.

NORI: (Pointing to the mountain.) Here?

SHOHEI: It's a forest creature so it should go here. (The tyrannosaurus is placed near the "trees.")

SABURO: The red ones go here. (He groups red dinosaurs together as Aiko joins the play.)

SHOHEI: (Watching Saburo place a small dinosaur next to the tyrannosaurus.) Oh, this is that one's baby so it goes here.

NORI: This is that one's mother. (She places small and large dinosaurs together.)

(Masaki joins the play and everyone gets very busy arranging the dinosaurs and toy animals.)

SABURO: A white horse! (He brandishes a toy horse.)

NORI: (Singing) *"Shiro uma-kun"* ("Mr. White Horse," a pun taken after a popular television commercial featuring a "Mr. White Bear," *shiro kuma-kun*).

SHOHEI: (Puts the white horse on the mountaintop.) He can go there because it's not a volcano.

NORI: What about Mr. Giraffe? (Again uses *kun* honorific.) Where should Mr. Giraffe go? (She brings the toy giraffe to Shohei.) What about Mr. Giraffe?

SHOHEI: The giraffe goes here – there. (He gives it to Saburo and points.) Over there. (Saburo puts the giraffe in the indicated space.)

NORI: These are parents and children, parents and children. (She places groups of dinosaurs together.) This goes here. These are parent and child so they go there. (She examines a dinosaur closely.) Oh, this one's wrong, he has spikes on his back.

(Shohei takes the dinosaur and looks at it.)

NORI: But he has spikes on his back.

SHOHEI: That's okay, we can put him here. (He places it in the group of nonspiked dinosaurs.)

This episode, involving the setting up of toy animals and dinosaurs in groups according to color, type, and perceived family relationships, continued in this vein for some time and was consistently coordinated through a great deal of discussion and opinion solicitation, with logical reasons given for decisions (i.e., "the horse can go on the mountain because it's *not* a volcano").

In this coordinating process, which earlier studies have found to contain abilities and preoccupations typical to this age group overall (Forbes et al., 1982; Kelly-Suzuki, 1983), the subjects also made frequent use of normative utterances involving *logical associations.* These are references to causal connections as indices of reasoning power and the ability to associate ideas and usually serve to categorize objects by characteristics. This thematic category appeared at a rate of 12% for five-year-olds and 8% for seven-year-olds. In the above episode, for example, connections were often expressed in familial terms such as "the big dinosaur is the mother of the little dinosaur" and "the spiked ones go together because they're a family." This reference to the *oya-ko* relationship was not unexpected, as most Japanese social organizations are constructed along quasi-familial lines (Lebra, 1976). What is more interesting about constructive play activities is the way in which the children not only grouped the toys according to characteristics, but clearly preferred whole-group projects or parallel play over solitary activities, often sitting in close proximity to each other. These behaviors, while generalized, may reflect the Japanese preference of group activity as well as the ability of individual members to cooperate within a collective social situation.

Pretend Play and the Creation of Real and Imaginary Worlds

Two types of pretend play activities – defined as play in which toys are used in enactment and/or in which players are in fantasy roles – emerged from this research. The first developed from "fantasy-like" flights of creativity with storylines and characters in completely imaginary settings, while the second is a recreation of social situations based on the subjects' understanding of the "real world" and reflect their knowledge of behavior and conventions in Japanese society. In both types, the defining criterion is the assigning of character parts, creating dialogue and activities for characters represented either by subjects or toys and often by the use of distinct vocal tones.

"Fantasy" pretend play often involved the distribution of "space" in a given play area to individual participants, an activity defined here under normative utterances of *possession,* a form of reference found in pretend play at a rate of 17% for five-year-olds and 14% for seven-year-olds. The following episode, in which three seven-year-olds claimed and assigned "territory" in the toy prehistoric landscape, illustrates how this was done:

(Seiichi, Jotaro, and Masuo have the dinosaur playset set up and are running dinosaurs aimlessly around the mat. Masuo moves his dinosaur over to the mountain but changes his mind when Jotaro and Seiichi follow him.)

MASUO: Oh, my territory is here, my territory is here. (He moves over to a second mountain on the other side of the mat.)

SEIICHI: My territory is from here, all this is mine. (He indicates a "borderline" in his immediate area.)

JOTARO: Mine is from here. (He outlines his border.)

MASUO: You're – I'm from here, you're from there. (He indicates separate areas for himself and Jotaro.)

SEIICHI: My territory starts from here, all of this is mine. (To Jotaro;) You – you're from here to here.

JOTARO: This is our island. (He uses "our" (*bokura no*) to mean his group of dinosaurs and is now engaged in role-playing.) We sleep here, all around here, this is all we have. We don't even have a refrigerator.

In this episode, all used careful hand gestures to mark their spaces and were scrupulously fair in claiming no more than anyone else, behavior that may reflect their understanding that mutually owned materials must be equally distributed. Failure to do so could cause confrontation, which the Japanese prefer to avoid in their social interactions (Azuma, 1986; Lebra, 1976).

The episode continues:

(Jotaro brings a toy pterodactyl to the group of "dinosaur friends" and Seiichi objects.)

SEIICHI: The birds are the only ones who aren't friends.

MASUO: This isn't a bird, it's a dinosaur.

SEIICHI: But these weren't friends with dinosaurs so he can't be a friend.

(Soon afterwards, Seiichi "flies" a toy wild boar towards the dinosaur mountain.)

> JOTARO: (With sarcasm.) Is the wild boar supposed to be a dinosaur?
> SEIICHI: It's okay, he's their friend.

(The three boys start creating "family" groups according to size and color.)

> JOTARO: This is the baby dinosaur, and this is the big brother. This is the oldest brother and this is the youngest.
> SEIICHI: This is the baby, the mother, and the father.
> JOTARO: What? (Pointing to another dinosaur of the same type.) *This* is the same.
> MASUO: No, the white ones are the same, they're the same color.

(Ariko comes to join the game and starts grouping dinosaurs together.)

> ARIKO: Oh, there's two of them, they're the same. (She groups similar toys near a "lake" on the mat.) They go together, they're siblings, siblings. And they're all dinosaurs who drink water.

In this part of the episode, toys were once again divided "logically" by type, color, and perceived friendship or family relations, which could again be indicative of these children's socialization toward cultural values of group orientation and "belongingness."

Such values were very much in evidence in the *prosocial* normative utterances emerging from this study. These utterances, found at rates of 11% for five-year-olds and 18% for seven-year-olds within pretend play episodes, and defined as references to behavior as being "good"/"correct" or "bad"/"incorrect," are indices of the subjects' understanding of socially approved or disapproved behavior, ideas, or concepts. The following episode is evocative of the ways in which the subjects expressed their internalization of such values:

(Ariko, seven years old, is engaged in fantasy pretend play using toy dinosaurs and animals. Jotaro, Masuo, and Seiichi are nearby with dinosaurs of their own.)

> ARIKO: (In a "baby"-like voice.) I don't have a mother! (She holds aloft a small dinosaur and directs the utterance towards the boys.) I don't have a mother! (She uses the masculine *boku* form of "I," having apparently decided on a male role, and speaks in a sad, whiny voice.)

(Seiichi comes and takes the "orphan" dinosaur to his group.)

ARIKO: My friends, my pals. (She gathers together a group of dinosaur "friends," using a babyish voice and the *boku no* form of "my.") My father and mother are gone! Have my mother and father gone? Say, where *are* they? (Directed towards Masuo and Seiichi in a sad voice.)

(Masuo offers a large dinosaur as Ariko's "parent," but she says it's the wrong one.)

ARIKO: Please be my friend, I don't have any mother or father and I'm lonely, so someone please become my friend.
MASUO: Did someone call? (In dinosaur role.)
ARIKO: I did . . . are you my mother or father?
MASUO: You can come with us, we'll be your friends.
ARIKO: Thank you.

(Ariko continues to search for her parents, saying she can "hear their voices." Soon after, at the dinosaur mat, she calls out "the baby has fallen into the sea!," which brings Masuo and Jotaro rushing to the rescue.)

In this episode, the "baby" dinosaur is pleading for help and friendship from the "big" dinosaurs on the grounds that she has no family and is "all alone," whereupon the "big" dinosaurs respond quickly and positively with empathy (*omoiyari*), gathering the "baby" into their group. These actions may reflect the subjects' understanding of the prosocial values of interconnectedness and the need for parent-child ties and indulgence (*amae/amayakasu*) within interdependent relationships, values that in their created worlds always triumph no matter how dramatic the action becomes.

In a related episode, Masuo, Jotaro, Seiichi, and Ariko are gathered around the plastic mountain with dinosaurs, when Masuo suddenly announces that "the baby has been locked up!" At Ariko's exhortation of "everybody!," Jotaro speeds his large dinosaur to the rescue, while Seiichi attacks from the other side. Ariko anxiously inquires about "our child's" welfare and, being assured by Masuo that "he's fine," she remarks happily that "the big animals always protect the little animals."

The second type of pretend play, "real world," was found to be an excellent index of the subjects' capacity for imitative behavior based on the use of expressions and interactive styles, which they have observed among adults. This type of play provides the opportunity to examine their knowledge of attitudes, behaviors, social customs, and institutions as they exist in Japanese society (such as the standardized expressions used by shop-keepers when addressing customers, or the comfortable neighborliness of small family-run stores). Certain aspects of "real world" understanding are expressed in the following episode:

> (Aiko, Yoko, and Masaki, all five years old, are playing "mom and pop" store, with Masaki in the role of "father" and Aiko as the "child." Saburo has been periodically disturbing the game by grabbing "merchandise" off the table, and Masaki finally takes action.)

> MASAKI: (As Saburo takes an item and runs.) Hey you – you're sup-posed to pay! Oh, you're a thief, a thief! (He chases after Saburo and grabs him.) A thief, a thief!

> (Masaki gets Saburo in a headlock and wrestles him to the ground amidst much shrieking, but Saburo gets the better of him and manages to pin him down.)

> MASAKI: That's enough, Azuma. (Using Saburo's family name and breaking briefly out of character.)

> (Saburo complies, but soon after steals another item and tosses it to Shohei, causing a general ruckus to erupt.)

> AIKO: Father, Father! (Directed at Masaki and pointing at Shohei.) A thief!
> MASAKI: If you want that, it's just one piece of candy and you don't have to pay for it. (Shohei "pays" for it anyway.)
> AIKO: A thief, Father!
> MASAKI: I'm the father.
> AIKO: Father, a thief! (She points at Saburo who is stealing again.)
> MASAKI: Eh?! (Using a deep-throated "stern" tone of voice, he goes after Saburo and nabs him.) Hey, you don't live in (belong to) this house! You should come in here and be a customer.

> (Soon after, when Saburo takes a "candy" again, Masaki says "please have one; you live here so it's okay," thus assigning Saburo the role of "family member" and drawing him into the game.)

In this episode, the "father" is attempting to solve a problem by reas-signing the "thief" from "customer," and finally to "family member" – us-ing the expression *uchi no hito* (household member), an expression that car-ries a sense of "belonging" – thus nullifying implications of "stealing" via the concept that group-owned items are to be shared by group members. By being brought into a *shudan seikatsu* situation – with the potential conflict sparked by "stealing" diffused by the need for group cohesiveness implied thereby – the third child cannot be stealing, and consequently is not a "thief." Interestingly, the "father" also avoids further conflict at one point by offering the candy for free, a technique so successful that the "thief" pays for it anyway. The "mom and pop" store scenario of this episode is also interesting, as these small neighborhood establishments are usually the first encounter with the entrepreneurial world experienced by young Japanese children, and was expertly recreated by these subjects.

In these two forms of pretend play, we have seen to a certain extent how these children interpret the world and exercise their imaginations. In doing so, they may be giving possible evidence of their socialization toward *shudan seikatsu* in their expressions of group-related concepts and behavior, and as Japanese culture-members in their maturing understanding of social roles.

Cleanup Activities: Expressions of Mutual Responsibility

At the end of each play session, the children were asked to put away their play materials and to generally set the playroom to rights. While they usually did this with cooperation and efficiency, it was during instances of *non-cooperation* that interesting forms of social pressure appeared.

This category, although undefined as play and numerically insignificant, is nonetheless worthy of qualitative examination since well over half of the category's normative issues of reference – fifty counts out of a cumulative eighty-one – are clustered around the prosocial behavior classification.

These references mostly occurred during disagreements about cleanup duties, frequently taking the form of pressure to share responsibilities and often covert via "mock" indignation expressed in "overacting" with exaggerated tones of voice and language, while occasions of several subjects "ganging up" on another in an exaggerated way to get him to cooperate were also often observed as follows:

(Seiichi, Jotaro, and Masuo, all seven-year-old boys, are playing with a variety of trucks, blocks, and construction straws.)

MASUO: (Pointing accusingly at Jotaro and speaking in a stern, "scolding" tone of voice.) You should clean those [blocks] up because you played with them more than anyone else. (An exaggeration.)

SEIICHI: That's right.

MASUO: ("Glaring" and speaking sternly, pointing at Jotaro.) You're supposed to clean up!

SEIICHI: (Imitating Masuo's tone.) You're supposed to clean up!

(Jotaro, who has been ignoring both other boys, grins, they giggle slightly and the matter is dropped.)

(Masaki, five years old, puts away one or two items when the investigator announces cleanup, then says to no one, "I'm all right, I don't have to pick up any more," then picks up a box of pipestem straws and looks around.)

AIKO: Where does this go? (Referencing another item.)

MASAKI: It goes over here. (He directs Aiko in putting away the item, then puts away his box of straws.)

(Masaki then notices Yoko still sitting at the table working on a picture. He looks around, picks up a tiny piece of lint from the carpet, and strides over to her.)

MASAKI: (Holding out the lint to Yoko at eye level.) Hey, Morita (Yoko's surname) how come you're not helping to clean up? (Uttered in stern, self-righteous tones.)

(Yoko glares at Masaki and then ignores him.)

(On hearing the cleanup announcement, seven-year-old Haruko gets up from drawing pictures and goes to a corner where Akihiro and Nobuyuki are counting play money.)

HARUKO: (In loud, carrying tones.) It's time to clean up. (The two boys pay no attention.)

HARUKO: It's time to clean *up!* (She glances in the boys' direction and emphasizes her words heavily.)

AKIHIRO: I *know!*

HARUKO: If you don't clean up . . . (She leaves the sentence open, using "warning" tones.)

(Akihiro and Nobuyuki ignore Haruko but start putting the money away, carefully grouping them by denomination. Haruko meanwhile gathers up the pictures she has drawn, writing her name on each, and in fact gets so busy that she does very little cleaning up herself.)

In these instances, the *reality* of cleanup activities appears to be less important than the *idea* that everyone in the group is obligated to take part in them. Most Japanese schoolchildren are taught from an early age to keep their school halls and classrooms clean, impressing upon them a sense of responsibility for their schools, group cohesion with classmates, and a sense of "good basic habits of daily life" (Peak, 1987). It is interesting to note, therefore, that many of the accusations against "shirkers" observed here, while stern in tone, were also delivered in a humorous or teasing format that may have served to lighten a situation by taking a circuitous approach to the issue, a provocative and sophisticated social skill that will be examined next.

INDIRECT SPEECH PATTERNS AND THEIR FUNCTION IN GROUP INTERACTIONS

Circuitousness in speech is one of the mainstays of Japanese social interactions, often a requirement if the interaction is to go smoothly and successfully. "For a Japanese to express himself or herself too clearly is impolite. It shows deficient empathy; the listener puts the speaker in the position of having to express his or her own opinions too explicitly. Such an attitude helps avoid confrontation, an adaptation well suited to people destined to live for generations in a restricted area without too much room for mobility" (Azuma, 1986). The individuals sense the possibility of confrontation whenever a forthright expression of their thoughts or desires would constitute insensitivity to the feelings of others, thus upsetting the flow of social interaction. It is in such situations that indirect expressions may be employed. A circuitous approach, in which the feelings of others are scanned before action is taken, is a familiar manifestation of the *honne-tatemae* dichotomy in Japanese social interactions as well as a crucial technique in *shudan seikatsu* management (also see Kobayashi, this volume, for circuitousness in Japanese mothers' speech to children). Indirection is particularly important in situations where politeness is required in the form of *enryo* (self-restraint), a necessary component of Japanese social etiquette in which differences of opinion, conflicting interests, or criticism must be expressed indirectly to avoid confrontation.

The subjects in this study were found to be highly sophisticated in the use of indirection in a variety of ways. The first may be described as "circuitous grammatical structures and fixed verbal formulae," which take the form of the use of certain set conjugations frequently heard in everyday speech. One of the most common is the verb conjugation *desho,* usually followed by a rising vocal tone, which "softens" the definitive *desu* "to be" or "it is" verb. Translating as "maybe" in its future tense, the expression carries less authority than *desu* and conveys both implications of social equality between parties as well as the speaker's desire not to appear arrogantly all-knowing.

A second grammatical convention with indirect implications is the *-ara* verb conjugation, which renders it to the conditional tense and means "if it is (possible) to do (this)." As it is tentative and nondemanding, this verb form implies dependence on the other's good graces, while showing consideration by not forcing one's own priorities on the situation. Indirection also may be expressed through fixed verbal formulae in which "speakers need only to indicate, by means of the right formula, that they are experiencing the appropriate reaction. . . . An important goal of socialization in Japan is to promote the unanimity in feeling that will support the norm of verbal agreement and empathy" (Clancy, 1986). For example, the subjects in this study frequently used the expression *ii desu ka?,* translating as "is it all right" (if I/we do this), which literally asks the other's "permission" to engage in activity, and that often occurred as a mitigation of authoritativeness during teaching/learning situations. Also frequently noted was the expression *ne,* meaning "right?" or "isn't it?" (much like the French *n'est-ce pas*), which implies that the speaker is making very sure that suggestions are acceptable to others in the process of establishing mutual accordance.

The second way in which verbal indirection was expressed is "indirection via word selection and exclusion," a technique that both mediates the conduct of negotiations and involves issues of etiquette. For example, it is correct among the Japanese to address another by using his or her honorific-appended name instead of the direct "you," thus easing potential friction and conveying respect for the other's social identity. Because Japanese personal pronouns may be left out when speaking, the technique of addressing a comment "to the air" also was frequently used, which avoids putting the addressee "on the spot" and averts possible confrontation.

All of these indirect communicative techniques have the common outcome of the maintenance of harmonious group relationships within the structure of communal values. As discussed next, it was found that circuitousness was most often used as a part of coercion or persuasion tactics to influence behavior when group norms were violated.

Peer Pressure and Indirection

Group norms were frequently expressed by these subjects as a form of peer pressure to influence individual behavior through the use of normative utterances related to *prosocial behavior*, a category in which 30% of all indirect utterances emerged. Although the potentially critical nature of these utterances often were tempered by smiles, laughter, and the omission of personal pronouns, it also was usual for speakers to comment on their *own* prosocial behavior, often in very self-righteous tones, while the addressee registered awareness by glancing silently from one accuser to the other with a serious facial expression. In the following illustrations, brackets around a word means that it is in the English-language transcription for purposes of clarity but was not in the original Japanese:

> (Michiko, aged seven, has been playing with construction straws and has left them strewn about on the floor. Masuo sees them and turns to Michiko.)
>
> MASUO: (Smiling and lightly laughing.) If ([you] are through with them [you] should clean up. (Play-kicks in Michiko's direction but gets no response.)
> SEIICHI: (In smug tones, pointedly *not* looking at Michiko.) I cleaned up *my* stuff.
> MASUO: *I've* just now cleaned up.
> SEIICHI: (Very smug.) I didn't even play with it that much.
>
> (Michiko glances from one boy to the other, face serious, saying nothing.)
>
> CHIKAYO: Michiko-chan is the only one who hasn't cleaned up.
>
> (Michiko goes and starts picking up toys, while Chikayo delivers the parting shot.)
>
> CHIKAYO: It's really a mess over there.
>
> (Michiko says nothing as she cleans up. In a moment, Ariko comes and helps her.)

Because the initial criticism here was indirectly addressed via the lack of personal pronouns and direct eye contact, and because even the more direct accusations from Chikayo were softened by the use of Michiko's name instead of a personal pronoun and by not looking directly at her during the utterances, the possibility of confrontation was mitigated and the addressee was given the opportunity to uphold group-sanctioned norms on her own volition.

A more complex episode demonstrates the ways in which indirect tactics are used to prevent a negotiation from accelerating to confrontational heights, while providing both parties with satisfaction:

(Items from the toy cooking set are strewn about the floor in everybody's way. Yoko – five years old – looks at them, then around at the others reprovingly.)

> YOKO: Who got all these out?
> AIKO: *I* didn't get them out.
> NORI: *I* didn't take them out.
> AIKO: *I* didn't get them out.

(Aiko and Nori glance at Yoko briefly with serious expressions and use very self-righteous tones throughout this exchange.)

> ABURO: Matsumoto (Yoko's surname) got them out.
> YOKO: That's a lie! That's a lie, somebody else got them out! (Very indignant tones.)
> SABURO: Well, [you] had them (indicating another part of the room).
> YOKO: What ! [I] did *not!*

(Saburo makes no comment, sits, and pointedly looks in the direction of Nori and Aiko, who are carefully not looking at Yoko. Yoko comes towards the others. By now she is frowning and glaring around at everyone, while they all avoid looking at her except for the occasional quick sidelong glance. Saburo changes the subject and returns to the game of storekeeper he had been previously playing with Nori and Aiko. They ignore Yoko.)

> YOKO: (To Saburo.) As far as cleaning this up is concerned, the person who plays with it cleans up, you know.
> SABURO: I did *not* have it.
> YOKO: (Turning desperately to Aiko.) Ai-chan, I just *took* them out, right (*ne*), the cooking set, right (*ne*), I didn't *have* them, right. (**Have** meaning temporary personal possession.)

(After one quick glance, Aiko does not look at Yoko or answer her.)

> SABURO: It was supposed to be over here. (He comes over to Yoko and gestures in the direction he means.)
> YOKO: Even so, Saburo-kun used it.

(Saburo makes no response and does not look at Yoko. Yoko is glaring angrily around the circle but gets no response.)

YOKO: (Suddenly changing tactics.) It's all right, [I] will pick them up for you.

(With the tones and manner of a martyr, Yoko starts picking up the toys, while letting the others know she is doing them a favor. She puts the toys in the bag, not looking at anyone. The others glance her way with expressionless faces.)

YOKO: Telling Yoko-chan to clean up when [I] didn't get them out. (Looking at no-one, muttering in self-righteous tones which are perfectly audible to everyone.)

(Yoko rattles the bag loudly for emphasis. Nori and Aiko make no response.)

YOKO: (To Nori and Aiko.) You got out this truck, right, all these things (indicating toys strewn about).
AIKO: But I didn't get them out.
YOKO: That's not true.
AIKO: It wasn't [me], it wasn't [me].
YOKO: That's why, everyone cleans up, just what they used. (Self-righteous, looking at nobody.)

(While engaging in "I didn't get it out"/"It goes here" bickering, all three girls put the toys away.)

Overall, indirect speech forms were most likely to appear during interactions in which a sensitive approach to negotiations was needed due to relative uncertainty of reaction. For example, in the area of normative issues of reference, the greatest need for indirect speech was in the category of possession – found here at a rate of 51% within the category – since making personal claims of commonly owned play materials was seen as a violation of group norms. A direct expression of ownership thus has high potential for confrontation, as it lays itself open to immediate challenge. Indirectly expressed claims often took the form of verbal avoidance; for example, resisting giving up a play object by the evasive "I'm still using it" rather than the straightforward "it's mine." Subjects also often directed the attention of another to an alternative toy or directly offered one in place of giving one up, a technique evocative of *omoiyari*, which becomes an overt expression of kindness and consideration. Such an expression would make a challenge of the first party's claim by the second party seem both ungrateful and insensitive; thus, conflict was avoided and the issue was usually settled to the reasonable satisfaction of all. Children as young as the age of five were capable of using these speech forms, confirming an awareness of the basic Japanese values of empathy and consideration for the feelings and social identity of others.

Equally striking in their sophistication are the techniques used by these subjects in making requests, which the Japanese often tender via social and linguistic cues designed to ease the requestee's feeling of obligation while gently steering him into perceiving the requestor's desire clearly enough to offer *voluntary* satisfaction:

> (A small group of five-year-olds are making constructions out of snap-on blocks, and Shohei has run out of a certain kind and needs more. Looking at Yoko's impressive construction, he asks if there isn't one more block. Masaki points out others in the block bag, but Shohei says they aren't the right kind. From this point, Yoko watches both boys, saying nothing.)

> MASAKI: That's the only one of that kind. (Glances around the room as if searching for more blocks.)

> (Shohei glances at Yoko's structure while Nori regards the situation.)

> NORI: Isn't that nice, Yoko-chan is able to make such a large one. (Not looking at Yoko.)
> YOKO: (Looking directly at Nori.) Shall I give you one?
> NORI: But . . . (Not looking at Yoko.) Just one is no good.

> (Yoko takes a block from her construction and gives it to Nori, then gives another to Shohei.)

In this episode, Yoko is indirectly given the opportunity to show generosity and helpfulness to other members of the group, and all are spared any hard feelings which could have arisen during a more confrontational negotiation. Most striking, perhaps, is the group effort put into it, with Shohei receiving help from Masaki and Nori without any direct solicitation on his part, volunteer efforts that reflect the distinctively Japanese cultural understanding that indirect tactics are less likely to lead to open confrontation during a potential disagreement.

HONORIFICS, PERSONAL REFERENCES, AND LEVELS OF LANGUAGE FORMALITY

Japanese linguistic variations are usually dependent on age, gender, family relationships, hierarchical rank in institutions, and the criteria of any kind of relationship in which reciprocity is involved. Thus, learning to speak Japanese involves acquiring an understanding of a myriad of possible social relationships and situations which are dependent on the rank-order of the parties concerned. Research among adult Japanese has shown that "masculine" speech is rougher, more vernacular, and less "beautiful" than feminine speech, which is usually more etiquette-bound, "polite," and "high-class" (*johin*) (Ide et al., 1986). Certain forms of address are also considered correct if the addressee is male, but not if she is female, while first-person singular pronouns differ according to speaker-addressee relationships.

Despite these complexities, the young subjects in this study showed themselves capable of applying the correct forms of address according to gender and, to a certain extent, age, during their peer interactions. For the most part – at rates of sixteen times out of a recorded thirty-five instances of honorifics use by five-year-olds and twelve times out of thirty-two instances among seven-year-olds – they employed the use of the intimate name-*chan* form of address, which would be expected among young coevals of both genders rather than the more mature name-*san* form used by adults. It was also noted that the form name-*kun* – usually restricted to young males – was correctly used when addressed to boys by either boys or girls. By using correct forms of address, these children showed an awareness of the age and gender criteria that are the mainstays of the Japanese status structure, awareness that is vital in a society where personal identification is tightly bound to relative-status criteria and where most groups and institutions contain members of different statuses.

Forms of Second-Person Pronoun Address

One of the peculiarities of the Japanese language is that it is both possible and conventional to directly address another without employing any of the second personal pronouns at all. Correct pronoun use is dependent on differences in social status and indicates an awareness of the personal identity of both parties involved. Consistent misuse of these pronouns is extremely rare in Japanese society; errors such as using a lowering form of address, for example, to one's company president would be certain to have socially disastrous consequences.

In this study, it was found that pronoun use was more the exception than the rule, and, when they were used, stayed within the basic guidelines of speech and gender differences. For example, five- and (but in particular) seven-year-old boys favored the use of the very informal, lowering *omae* form of "you" in addressing both girls and other boys, with use among the older boys totaling at fifty-three out of a possible sixty-one instances of pronoun use, while with one rare exception this form was not used by girls of either age at all. This finding indicates that very young boys have already learned that social convention allows them to use very informal pronouns with peers of either sex, and that girls of the same age have learned not to use such terms under any circumstances. Both genders also made frequent use of the familiar but relatively formal *anata* form of "you" as well as the standard formal *name of other* as terms of address, both of which are more or less standard-equal pronouns and may reflect the subjects' comprehension of same-age social equality.

Whereas pronoun selection by these children tells us something about their knowledge of status and its relation to speech, it is more interesting to note their relatively much greater *lack* of any kind of personal pronoun use. Because the overly direct verbal expression of anything is considered generally impolite by the Japanese, this may be an index of their internalization of an etiquette structure that promotes harmonious group relations through the protection of individual sensibilities.

Gender and Self-Reference

It is in the area of personal gender identification that the comprehension of clear-cut differences in sex-role behavior appears in patterns of speech. In this study, the extreme polarity of male-female references was striking: the very informal *ore* ("I") and slightly more formal *boku* were used almost exclusively by boys of both ages, with thirty-three instances of the former and ninety-eight of the latter out of a total of 139 recorded self-references. In the rare instances when they were used by girls, it was in the context of sex-role reversal during fantasy play when a male character was being enacted. The standard formal *watashi* ("I"), the only personal pronoun usually available for female use, was in fact used much more often by girls than by boys – thirty-four times out of a total of forty-six recorded self-references – and may be an index of behavior appropriate to the peer-group situation in which "equals" speech is acceptable.

These subjects' use of honorifics, forms of address, and self-reference are clear indicators of their growing awareness as culture-members. Aspects of Japanese etiquette, status structure criteria, and individual identity in terms of age and gender embedded in these expressions are illustrations of the strong relationship between speech and social relations in Japanese society, where human ties define not only the spirit of the language but the structure itself.

Levels of Speech Formality in Social Interactions

A second means of expressing differences in social status inherent to the Japanese language – formality levels in verb conjugation and selection – may be less expected in a peer-group situation as it is not specifically gender-dependent. It was unexpectedly found, however, that under certain circumstances differences in formality levels did appear in the speech of these subjects.

The structure of formality levels in Japanese can be divided roughly into three strata – the informal, the semiformal, and the formal. Informal speech is characterized by simple, basic verb conjugations, semiformal speech by more complex endings of the predicate verb, adjective, or copula, and formal speech by more formal equivalents of verbs and nouns (Niwa & Matsuda, 1971). In this study, the primary concern is with informal and semiformal speech constructions and with several of the formal equivalents as we examine the circumstances under which such speech is used.

Generally speaking, in Japanese social interactions that are based on the "insider/outsider" dichotomy, individuals from an "outside" circle are addressed in more honorific forms than are those in the speaker's "inside" circle, as for reasons of etiquette an outsider is automatically assumed to possess higher social status (Niwa & Matsuda, 1971). Because the school group is an inner circle secondary only to that of the family, informal speech used among themselves would be expected, and indeed was found to be the case among these subjects. There were also, however, a number of instances of formal speech use observed in this data, indicating that these young children are both aware of its existence and capable of using it. Primary examples of this appear in role-playing during "real-world" fantasy-play episodes, which are characterized by relationship changes suitable to the thematic episode at hand.

In reality-based pretend play, these children are reenacting what they have observed of adult behavior in their society through the use of those interactional conventions learned thus far in their lives as Japanese culture-members. By doing so, they demonstrate their ability to use the verbal and behavioral skills considered correct in "real" social situations, which includes both the ability to use formal speech and the knowledge of the circumstances under which it is required:

(Masaki, aged five, has the toy cash register out and is playing store. Saburo is his first customer.)

MASAKI: Pachin! (Ostentatiously rings the register bell and imitates its sound.)

SABURO: (Bringing a "merchandise" item.) I'll take this. (Using the polite *kudasai* form of "give me.")

MASAKI: Very good, very good. Let's see . . . that is 10,600 yen. (Using the semi-formal *desu* form of "is.")

(Both boys speak in adult-like tones, with Masaki using the traditional stylized intonations of Japanese shopkeepers.)

MASAKI: That's 10,600 yen. (Saburo counts out the money and pays.) There you are. (Using the stylized *hai dozo*, literally "yes, please" [take it] typically used in such transactions.)

(Yoko comes to the "store" and asks Masaki how many of a certain item he has in "stock.")

MASAKI: Let's see . . . one, two, three, four . . . there are four of them. (Using the semiformal *desu* form of "are.")

YOKO: I just want one. (They conduct the transaction.)

MASAKI: There you are. (Using *hai dozo*.)

MASAKI: (Looking at Saburo.) What do you wish? What do you wish? (Using "singsong" and the semiformal *desu* as verbal copula.)

SABURO: I want this. (Also using *desu* form.)

MASAKI: Let's see . . . this one, right (*ne*) . . . it is 15,000 yen. (Using semiformal *desu* form of "is.") Is 15,000 yen all right? (Using indirect "polite" tactic as well as *desu*.)

(The transaction is completed and the game continues in this vein for some time.)

In their imitation of entrepreneurial activities, these young children reveal considerable social knowledge. Traditional merchandising behavior among Japanese shopkeepers typically follows stylized patterns based on the ancient convention of paying great respect to a customer, who is assumed to have higher status and is addressed through the use of semiformal and formal verb conjugations, substitutions, and standard expressions. We also note the stylized vocal tones based on traditional aggressive merchandising techniques used by competitive entrepreneurs in an effort to "lure in" customers, a phenomenon that may be observed today in many Japanese shopping areas.

Competitiveness was in fact the hallmark of other "merchandizing" episodes noted in this research, with vociferous use of stylized expressions and intonations on the part of "merchants" to get "customers" to patronize their establishments:

(Masaki and Nori, age five, are both in the role of shopkeeper with Yoko as a customer.)

NORI: (Calling out with shopkeeper intonations.) This is a pastry store so there are plenty of cakes.
YOKO: I want some.

(On hearing this, Masaki – who had come over to inspect Nori's "store" – immediately leaps back to his own store area and calls out to Yoko in a booming, stylized voice.)

MASAKI: I am selling cakes, you know! (Using the semiformal *utte imasu* form of "selling.")
NORI: (Immediately joining the competition.) If it's cakes you want there are plenty *here!*
MASAKI: There are plenty *here!*

(Yoko comes to Nori's store and buys cakes.)

NORI: There you are. (Using the polite *hai dozo* in stylized tones.)

(Yoko handles the competition between Masaki and Nori with tact by going to Masaki's store and buying from him, using the polite *kudasai* form of "please give me," while Masaki responds with the correct *hai dozo*, then going back to Nori's store and repeating the interaction with her. This is repeated several times, each time with the expressions required by the etiquette typical of such social situations.)

Recognition and acknowledgement of differences in social status through the above techniques represent a subtle and highly sophisticated verbal skill. Without it, it would be virtually impossible to function interactively as a Japanese culture-member, because its lack would reveal a shocking ignorance of standard social skills as well as of the basic hierarchical structure of the society itself. "For the Japanese . . . the established

ranking order is overwhelmingly important in fixing the social order and
measuring individual social values" (Nakane, 1970). Sensitivity to rank-order and status must be internalized in childhood and behavior differentia-
tion established as a social skill in the early experiences of *shudan seikatsu* if
later interactions in adult social groups are to be successful. The knowledge
of gender- and status-related speech conventions that these children reveal
will form the basis of their continuing socialization as members of a society that is both modern and sophisticated, yet retains hierarchical elements
of its feudal past in its present social order.

CONCLUSION

This research indicates that these five- and seven-year-old children possess
sophisticated interactional abilities that are reflective of many aspects of the
Japanese value system, of certain social customs, and of behavioral conventions. Within the category of constructive play, they demonstrated a
high level of helpfulness during teaching and knowledge-sharing activities
as well as perseverance throughout the process, qualities regarded by the
Japanese culture as characteristic of the well-socialized individual. We have
also seen evidence of the subjects' orientation toward *shudan seikatsu* in
their particular way of organizing toy animals into "family" groups – often
using expressions clearly indicative of the desirableness of interdependence – an activity in which their understanding of the *oya-ko* concept may
be reflected in the specific creation of groups with "parent" and "child"
members. High levels of coordinated action and cooperation also appeared
in this play category, suggesting the sprit of *ittaikan* via the clear preference
for group and parallel activities.

In the "fantasy" context of their pretend play, we again note reliance on
the *oya-ko* concept in these children's creations of "family" groups and role-
playing. The importance of human ties and interconnectedness often were
specifically expressed in prosocial utterances stressing the need for others
through elements of *amae* and *omoiyari* – values encouraged in *shudan*
seikatsu as essential features of a "human-like" person (Lebra, 1976; Peak,
1987, this volume). In the category of real-world play, they demonstrated
their understanding of Japanese social institutions and behavioral customs
by reenacting roles and activities observed in the wider society. Expressions
of prosocial behavior stressing connectedness often appeared in this category in the form of conflict avoidance and resolution, which the subjects
handled with remarkable tact using skills possibly learned during author-
ity-delegation experiences in school.

They also demonstrated their capacity for self-regulation in the context of cleanup behavior, in which they showed no reluctance to remind each other of mutual responsibilities. Most notable – although not unexpected – was their efficiency and cooperation in carrying out these tasks, behavior that may reflect kindergarten training toward responsibility for belongings and the surrounding environment.

In their communication style, these children displayed considerable sophistication through the use of culturally specific indirect speech patterns. This is particularly salient during negotiations involving issues of ownership and sharing, interactions that are relatively sensitive and require diplomatic tactics. The use of indirect speech during such interactions would indicate a growing awareness of the need to avoid conflict and to show consideration for the feelings of others, both essential to the smooth coordination of group life. The ability to discern formal and informal social situations is illustrated in the subjects' use of formal speech patterns during "real-world" replications of social roles, which have inherent and presumed differences in status relative to one another. Many of these utterances and their concurrent behavior patterns include formalisms and speech conventions culturally specific to the Japanese and related to aspects of personal identity inseparable from social roles. Although these episodes are likely to be simple imitations, the accurate recreation of conventions of speech points to an embryonic understanding of the function of status in the Japanese perception of the self and others.

These children also demonstrated a well-developed awareness of gender- and status-related speech conventions through their use of honorifics, forms of address, and references to the self, terms that are often gender-specific and always dependent on the relative social status of speaker and addressee. Their use of such terms is almost without exception accurate and gender-appropriate, revealing an early understanding of these social and linguistic conventions. A quite sophisticated understanding of individual status and its relationship to thematic categories in the larger society is also evident in their use of formal and informal speech patterns, which is almost always socially correct in use and reflects a keen observation of their world on the part of these young subjects.

In closing, it may be interesting to mention at least one notable way in which these findings offer challenges to conventional American views of peer relations and interactions among young children. One of the most important of Japanese cultural values central to interactional patterns is *nemawashi,* or consensus-building toward a common goal. The purpose of this vital social skill is not, as has been assumed by casual Western observers, simply to maintain conformity, but to protect the right of all group members to be part of the decision-making process. Through their use of indirect verbal expressions and emerging sense of *omoiyari* toward others, these children may be demonstrating conflict-avoidance skills based on the function of mutual consensus, as well as a developing sense of respect for the rights of others. The recognition that human ties are much too important to be threatened by petty disagreements that are better defused than allowed to harm the sensibilities of others is one that these young children already appear to be comprehending. This may be a challenge to the popular view that conflict among children is somehow "expected" and thus unavoidable, as these children are clearly able to either mitigate the damage of conflict or avoid it altogether. In this way, they may be expressing social knowledge acquired during the home-school transition in terms of some of the norms and values viewed by the Japanese as components vital to the well-socialized individual, to successful interpersonal relationships, and to the structure of their society.

REFERENCES

Azuma, H. (1986). Why study child development in Japan? In H. Stevenson, H. Azuma, & K. Hakuta (Eds.). *Child development and education in Japan* (pp. 3–12). New York: W. H. Freeman & Company.

Bachnik, J. (1992). *Kejime:* defining a shifting self in multiple organizational modes. In N. R. Rosenberger (Ed.), *Japanese sense of self* (pp. 152–72). New York: Cambridge University Press.

Beardsley, R., Hall, J. W., & Ward, R. E. (1959). *Village Japan.* Chicago: University of Chicago Press.

Benedict, R. (1946). *The chrysanthemum and the sword: Patterns of Japanese culture.* New York: Houghton-Mifflin.

Clancy, P. M. (1986).The acquisition of communicative style in Japanese. In B. B. Scheiffelin & E. Ochs (Eds.), *Language socialization across cultures* (pp. 213–49). New York: Cambridge University Press.

Conroy, M., Hess, R. D., Azuma, H., & Kashiwagi, K. (1980). Maternal strategies for regulating children's behavior: Japanese and American families. *Journal of Cross-Cultural Psychology, 11*(2), 153–72.

Dore, R. P. (1978). *Shinohata: A portrait of a Japanese village.* New York: Pantheon Books.

Forbes, D., Katz, M. M., Paul, B., & Lubin, D. (1982). Children's plans for joining play: An analysis of structure and function. In D. Forbes & M. Greenberg (Eds.), *New directions in child development: The development of planful behavior in children* (pp. 61–80). San Francisco: Jossey-Bass.

Kelly, V. (1989). *Peer culture and interactions among Japanese children.* Unpublished doctoral dissertation, Harvard University, Cambridge, MA.

Kelly-Suzuki, V. (1983). *Assessing children's knowledge of social norms: An observational method.* Unpublished qualifying paper, Harvard University, Cambridge, MA.

Ide, S., Hori, M., Kawasaki, A., Ikuta, S., & Haga, H. (1986). Sex difference and politeness in Japanese. *International Journal of the Sociology of Language, 58,* 25–36.

Lanham, B. (1956). Aspects of child care in Japan: Preliminary report. In D. G. Haring (Ed.), *Personal characteristics and cultural milieu* (pp. 565–83). Syracuse, NY: Syracuse University Press.

Lebra, T. S. (1976). *Japanese patterns of behavior.* Honolulu: University of Hawaii Press.

Lewis, C. (1984). Cooperation and control in Japanese nursery schools. *Comparative Education Review, 28,* 69–84.

Nakane, C. (1970). *Japanese society.* Berkeley: University of California Press.

Niwa, T. & Matsuda, M. (1971). *Basic Japanese for college students* (rev. ed.). Seattle & London: University of Washington Press.

Norbeck E., & Norbeck, M. (1956). Child training in a Japanese fishing village. In D. G. Haring (Ed.), *Personal character and cultural milieu* (pp. 651–73). Syracuse, NY: Syracuse University Press.

Peak, L. (1987). Learning to go to school in Japan: The transition from home to preschool life. Unpublished doctoral dissertation, Harvard University, Cambridge, MA.

Peak, L. (1989). Learning to become part of the group: The Japanese child's transition to preschool life. *Journal of Japanese Studies, 15*(1), 93–123.

Reischauer, E. (1978). *The Japanese.* Tokyo: Charles E. Tuttle Company.

Shigaki, I. (1983). Child care practices in Japan and the United States: How do they reflect cultural values in young children? *Young Children, 38*(4), 113–24.

Vogel, E. F. (1963). *Japan's new middle class.* Berkeley: University of California Press.

Vogel, E. F., & Vogel, S. (1961). Family security, personal immaturity and emotional health in a Japanese sample. *Marriage and Family Living, 23,* 161–6.

White, M. I. (1985). *The Japanese educational challenge: A commitment to children.* New York: Free Press.

PART IV

ADOLESCENT EXPERIENCE

SEVEN

Beyond Individualism and Sociocentrism

An Ontological Analysis of the Opposing Elements in Personal Experiences of Japanese Adolescents[1]

Hidetada Shimizu

In recent years, cultural psychologists have emphasized the contrast between the individualistic premises of American psychology and the sociocentric orientation of non-Western indigenous psychology (Markus & Kitayama, 1991; Marsella, DeVos, & Hsu, 1985; Shweder & Bourne, 1984). Generally, the discussion focuses on the proposed, individually self-contained, and self-transcendent aspects of Western selfhood (Geertz, 1983), and its interpersonally contextual and "other-oriented" (collective, empathic, etc.) counterparts, particularly in India (Dumont, 1970; Shweder & Bourne, 1984) and Japan (Markus & Kitayama, 1991). Others have pointed out methodological and conceptual limitations of an attempt to link directly the two dichotomized essences to the aspects of self that are characteristically psychological and hence less accessible to direct observation and measurement, and to generalize the dichotomy to groups with large populations such as Japanese or East Asians who are contrasted with Westerners (Kusserow, 1999; Lindholm, 1997; Murray, 1993; Spiro, 1993).

Japan provides a particularly illuminating context for this debate. Nearly a half century ago, Ruth Benedict (1946) argued that fear of being shamed in interpersonal relationships (*hito ni hazukashii*) was the main cultural configuration of Japanese behavior, personality, and socialization. Others who followed Benedict's footsteps two decades later elaborated her interpersonal framework of analysis (e.g., Lebra, 1976; Nakane, 1970). Some Japanese scholars extended it as a conceptual basis of their *nihonjinron*, a

[1] Reprinted by permission of S. Karger AG, Basel from *Human Development*, 43(4–5): 195–211. The writing of this article was supported by a National Academy of Education Spencer Post-Doctoral Fellowship.

"theory" of Japanese people's uniqueness (e.g., Aida, 1970; Doi, 1977; Hamaguchi, 1977; Kimura, 1972). Again, some Western scholars refuted the claim of *nihonjinron* as a myth based on little sociohistorical evidence (see Dale, 1986).

In this chapter, I argue that the individualism-sociocentrism dichotomy as applied uniformly (i.e., all or *the* majority of Japanese are sociocentric) and exclusively (i.e., Japanese are sociocentric but not individualistic, unlike Americans who are individualistic but not sociocentric) to Japanese people is methodologically limited and conceptually inadequate to understand everyday experiences of Japanese adolescents. Instead, the two orientations need to be integrated from an ontological perspective that decenters *either* of the two orientations as the primary constituting agent of individual or collective experience, and to recast *both* elements as mutually and dynamically constituting elements of the individual's personal experiences. My aim is not to argue that either the proposed individualistic and sociocentric orientations of American academic psychology or Japanese cultural psychology is invalid, but that each perspective alone is an insufficient methodological and conceptual ground to understanding empathically the *personal* experiences of Japanese adolescents.

CONCEPTUAL CONTEXT OF THE INDIVIDUALISM VERSUS SOCIOCENTRISM DEBATE

During the last two decades of the twentieth century, developmental researchers have turned their attention to the sociocultural origins and contexts of mental functions (Rogoff, 1990; Vygotsky, 1978; Wertsch, 1985). Until then, the majority of American psychologists have formulated theories of human development as based in individuals' *intra*psychological dispositions that are assumed to be universally applicable, transcending individuals' relations with other people as well as diverse sociocultural environments in which they function. The assumption about individuation and individual development as the universal goals of human development, however, is not consistent with goals of individual development in Japan (see Azuma, 1994; Lewis, 1995; Peak, 1991; Rohlen & LeTendre, 1996; Stevenson, Azuma, & Hakuta, 1986, for empirical evidence).

Examples of American theories representing individualistic assumptions with applications that are problematic in Japan include David McClelland's theory of achievement motivation and Lawrence Kohlberg's theory of moral reasoning. McClelland (1961), for example, conceptualized the motive to achieve as "need for achievement," which refers to individuals' incentive to compete against their *own internal* standards of excellence. He theorized that individuals with "independence training" in childhood would have more "need for achievement" in later years than those with less independence training. Kohlberg (1969, 1981) analyzed moral reasoning with its underlying logical structure unfolding as an invariant sequence. In so doing, he argued that moral reasoning operating independently of social conventions and interpersonal relations (i.e., "principled" or "postconventional" moral reasoning) constituted a higher stage than its socially embedded counterparts.

The assumption about individual transcendence as the universally applicable goal of achievement motivation and moral reasoning does not apply adequately in Japan. For example, DeVos (1973), who did intensive research on achievement motivation among the Japanese, showed that the Japanese individual was driven to achieve not only to meet his or her personal standard of excellence, but also to serve the collective obligation and responsibility of the relationship or social group of which he or she was a member. Using Kohlberg's moral dilemmas, Iwasa (1989, this volume) found that although the same proportion of graduate students in Japan and the United States reached the highest stage of moral reasoning, the contents of the Japanese responses revealed principles of interpersonal concerns that overrode abstract oppositions such as life versus property. For example, when faced with the dilemma of whether a protagonist should steal a drug from a pharmacist to save his wife's life, Japanese students tended to say that the man should not steal the drug because his *wife* would feel that theft was more disgraceful than death. From the Japanese perspective, therefore, achievement and morality seem to entail much more than the individual's *intra*psychological concerns; they include concerns for others and interpersonal relationships.

My case studies of three Japanese adolescents' real-life experiences that focused around the issues of achievement and morality, however, defy the validity of *exclusively* individualistic (e.g., McClelland's and Kohlberg's approaches) or sociocentric models (e.g., cultural psychology of *omoiyari*) to account for their experiences. My evidence indicates that the adolescents show both sociocentric and individualistic concerns. Furthermore, while the two elements are in a state of tension (i.e., drawing away from one another), they complement each other in such a way that to achieve the purpose of each (e.g., to be individuated) is to make it conditional to the other (e.g., to participate, be part of the collective). Thus, one cannot individuate without being part of that which he or she individuates *from*, or one cannot participate without being individuated first.

THREE JAPANESE ADOLESCENTS' ACCOUNTS

The interview data were collected in a private, Protestant-Christian junior-high and high school. Being impacted by American-derived Protestant ideals since its inception, it is considered as an Americanized school by local Japanese standards. Joseph High School (pseudonym) in central Japan was founded immediately after World War II to honor the Christian educator, Joseph N, after whom the school was named.[2] Joseph N, the first son of a samurai family, studied at Philips Academy, Amherst College, and Andover Theological Seminary at a time when leaving the country was punishable by death. Many of the teachers, themselves, were educated in Europe and the United States (e.g., Cambridge, Yale, Oberlin), and a good portion of students travel abroad each year. A Protestant service is held each morning. The schoolwide questionnaires indicated that parents described the school's "characteristic features" as Christian-religious education (18%), nonrestrictive and laid-back atmosphere (16%), and freedom (13%). High school students indicated similar views: freedom (22%), Christian-religious education, morning service (11%). Because of these unusual characteristics of the school, I do not intend to treat the school or the students I interviewed, who also were purposefully selected for my interviews, as representatives of adolescents in Japan or students in this school, respectively. The goal of the interviews, therefore, was to attain phenomenological and contextual understanding (*verstehen*) of the meanings of a few selected adolescents' real-life experiences.

My approach followed the *logic of discovery* (Maxwell, 1996) that gives the individual informants, not the investigator, the freedom and authority to determine which aspects of their cultural experience are most salient to *them*. I used a semistructured, open-ended clinical interview technique over time to understand the complexity and depth of each individual's private experiences.

The three individuals were selected on the basis of interest in participating in the series of interviews as well as on the basis of the themes of their accounts. During our first interview session, we talked about general aspects of their lives and themselves (such as past year, self-descriptions, school and home life). In the next interviews, I asked them to "remember" experiences from the past or present, in which they (a) worked very hard at something (achievement), and (b) had to make decisions as to what was the right versus the wrong thing to do (morality). Three, six, and nine months later, fol-

---

[2] Joseph N, a Japanese man, adopted his American name, Joseph, later in his life.

low-up interviews were conducted in which the informants reflected on meanings and implications of their own experiences. I also visited their homes to interview their parents.

YUMI

Yumi is seventeen. She has large, round eyes on a thin face with long, shiny black hair hanging down straight to her narrow shoulders. When I saw her for the first time and asked her to "describe herself," she said, "I think I am *zurui*" – *zurui* means being cunning, hypocritical, or "two-faced" in Japanese. Remarkably, she stayed on the subject of "two-facedness" throughout our four interviews.

Zuru-sa ("Two-Facedness")

Here is how she initially described her "two-facedness:"

> I want to be seen well and liked by everyone. So even when I know a certain thing to be true, I modify and change (my characterization of) it a little, so that I will not say what might be regarded negatively by other people. To put it another way, I "lie."

When I tried to clarify what she meant by "lying," she explained:

> In other words, it's not exactly that I "lie," but I patch things up. . . . Even if it [i.e., what she is saying to others] is not what I really think, I would go ahead and say it because I think to myself, "If I say what I really feel, I could be disliked, or taken wrongly." But when I sense somebody else is doing that, I feel that he/she is *zurui*.

She explained that her desire to be liked by others went back to her childhood. When she was in preschool, her mother always reminded her to be a "good girl" (*'ii ko'*). For Yumi, this meant being kind, sensitive, and dedicating herself for the needs of other people (i.e., *omoiyaru*). One example was picking wild flowers on the way home from school for her mother.

One day, however, her *omoiyari* backfired and gave her a memory she never forgot. While she was in elementary school, she invited one of her neighborhood friends home. Knowing that her friend, who lived in a lower-income housing unit, did not have a piano at home, Yumi told her that she could play hers. The friend came, but the next day she told everyone in the class that Yumi was "showing off" her piano. This experience caught her off guard because she expected that nobody was going to take advantage of other people's kindness. In fact, it hurt her so badly that she decided "not to let anyone dislike her for the rest of her life." Her determination to win everyone's favor kept her from being hurt, but it was producing another problem for her at age seventeen: She was no longer sure if she was being true to her own self. She shared this concern with me as her story of "achievement motivation."

Achievement Motivation

When asked if there was anything she tried or worked on hard in recent years, she told me that she tried her hardest to "be a good girl (*ii ko*)."

> When I was at my relatives' house, I felt it like a reflex that I had to keep smiles on my face and be a good girl. My relatives have this little child, and as soon as I saw him, I felt, "I have to look after him," as if this was something that I always had to do.

After she came home, she told her parents that she volunteered to take care of the child at her uncle's house to remind them that she was a "good girl" (*ii ko*).

> When I came home, I wanted my parents to know what I did. I wanted their approval (laugh). So I hinted at that indirectly by saying, "Looking after the baby was a lot of work." And I hoped to hear them say, "Very good. We'd like to commend you for being such a good girl."

She then felt ambivalent about the way she acted at her uncle's house. She felt, on the one hand, that she took care of the baby because it was "so cute," but on the other hand, she did so because she wanted her relatives to praise her. She was confused as to which one of these two motives was her true motive. She recalled, "I am not what people think of me as (i.e., *ii ko*). I'm cunning. . . . I don't do what I really want to do, but I do what I want other people to think of me as."

Moral Reasoning

During the following three interviews, Yumi continued to talk about being *zurui*. The following episode illustrates the crux of her problem:

> Friend A comes to me and speaks ill of friend B. Then I go along with A and speak ill of B. For example, if A says, "B is selfish," I say, "Yes, she is, isn't she?" On another occasion, I happen to be talking with B, and she says that A is mean. Then, I end up speaking ill of A.

Reflecting the way she acted in this situation, she criticized her own inconsistency: "But come to think of it, I'm the one shifting between the two, so I am the one who is really selfish and mean."

Here is another example of being *zurui:*

> There was a girl who had the flu and was absent today. She's been unpopular among the girls I hang out with for quite some time and getting bad remarks from us. . . . But personally, I had nothing against her. I didn't think she was a bad person, and these trivial things for which they were criticizing her didn't bother me. But, you see, these girls were criticizing her only because she was absent today. . . . My conflict was that I didn't really dislike her in the first place, but when I heard what other people were saying, I began to dislike her, saying, "Yes, she did that to me, too." I mean, these are such trivial things. For example, when I was reading a comic book, she came to me and said, "I want to read it." Then, she snatched the book from me although I was only halfway through. So then I said to myself, "Well, I'll just have to read it later." But today I found out that she was doing that to everybody. They told me, "She always takes things away from you." So although what she did to me didn't disturb me in the first place, when I heard other people talk about it and ask me how I feel about it, I said, "I don't like it." But immediately after that, I asked myself, "Should I be speaking behind her back like this?"

Conflict between "Real" (Honne) and "Official" (Tatemae) Feelings

To be truly honest (*honne*), Yumi wanted to act and speak as she felt. This way, she would be honest and not *zurui*. Yumi felt that being *zurui* was wrong, as she said she often shared with her best friend Kumiko: "Gossiping about someone behind her back is a disgusting thing to do. Let's stop doing that." Asked how she might feel about herself if she stopped gossiping, Yumi said, "Then I'd say 'ah ha, I had the courage not to gossip even when A did it right in front of me.' By telling her, 'I don't agree with you,' I would prove that I was a 'good girl' (*ii ko*) after all." Going along with her peers to be part of them (*tatemae*), by contrast, was an equally important goal for her because "that's the only way you maintain any relationship (*ningen kankei*)." She explained:

> How can I put it . . . you need to be "people-wise." . . . It's like the lesson to be learned if you want to keep your relationships with others. If you say, "I'm not going to talk with anyone whom I don't like," then you'd be only talking with people you like, and by doing that, you are shrinking

your world. It would also mean not getting along with someone in my peer group, and I don't want something like that to happen.

Yumi knew that she was acting superficially to maintain her ties with her peers. She also knew, however, that no one wanted to rock the boat because everyone found it very unpleasant if she had to isolate herself from others because of a disagreement. She said, "Like it or not, that's how we girls stick together."

Overcoming the Contradiction

Yumi admitted that "going to the bathroom with other girls" when she did not wish to or telling one of them that her handbag "looks cute" even though they went against her honest opinion were just as "petty" as they were "important" – that is, very. So by the end of our fourth and last interview session, Yumi decided to remain *zurui*. There were at least four reasons for her decision.

First, what Yumi described as her own *zuru-sa* (being *zurui*) was a nearly universal phenomenon among her female peers. It was fighting against this norm, as Yumi had been, which made a girl "abnormal" among her peers. She said: "[Although being two-faced was not noble], recently I came to realize that many of my friends were doing the same thing. As I looked around, I noticed, 'She is doing it [i.e., being two-faced], and she is doing it, too.'" Thus she asked herself, "If everyone is cunning, why should I be the only one trying to 'solve' this problem? Is it bad to say one thing here and another thing there after all? Maybe it *is* natural and normal to do so."

Second, being "two-faced" was probably the only way for her to remain friends with most of her female peers, albeit fragilely and superficially. Yumi said that saying what was really on her mind always entailed the risk of losing relationships. For example, even a seemingly justifiable cause as asking not to be pressed to go to the bathroom to have some privacy could make her friends feel jealous and irritated. Yumi elaborated the point as follows.

If you jokingly tell someone, "I don't like you very much, so leave me alone," with the slightest hint that you might actually mean that, then you see girls congregating after school and gossiping, "She says things too clearly," or "She's so immature to say things that she really feels." So I thought, "OK, so saying things clearly isn't 'adult-like.' Then maybe I should be just as cunning as everyone, and say one thing here and another thing there."

Third, maintaining superficial relationships at least saved her from being a "loner" among her peers, something that she and most of her peers dread. Yumi explained:

I mean, if you were raised to be on your own all your life, you probably wouldn't mind it (being alone or lonely). But once you are attached to someone, it is very difficult to leave that relationship. So if you grew up being with your friends all the time like most of us, that habit is very difficult to unlearn.

Fourth, and most important for Yumi, she could be totally honest to herself when she was with her best friend, Kumiko. Having Kumiko as her best friend, Yumi told me, was more than enough to compensate for the down side of being *zurui*. Yumi said:

Because I have Kumiko to share the truth, I say, "Having just one true friend is enough." I mean, Kumiko also said this to me. She said, "From now on, I will not share important things with these friends. I'll just joke around with them, and that's all I'll be doing with them. But to you, I tell the truth, and even when I do joke with you, that's because I *really* enjoy doing so." So I told Kumiko, "I feel the same way about you," and I said to myself, "Kumiko is all the friend I need."

In the end, Yumi suggests that there are two types of human relationships. One was like her relationship with Kumiko, in which she could reveal her true self (*honne*). The other was what she now considered the norm of adult relationships, in which she used *tatemae* to get along with others. She explained:

Suppose you are a "salary man" [i.e., white-collar worker], and you privately feel that your boss is a wonderful person. But you don't want to say this to your coworkers – like "What a wonderful guy he is!" – because most of them don't like your boss. So instead of saying what is really on your mind, you tell your coworkers, "What a terrible boss he is," just to create a cheerful atmosphere between you and them, like when you are having a few drinks with them in a bar or something.

She said being *zurui* was not about being right or wrong. Rather, it was about doing what one was supposed to. "I'll just let go," she said with a sigh, "then everything will be all right."

YASUHIKO

Yasuhiko is fifteen years old. He describes himself as "fat" and wears large, black-framed glasses. With his eyes peering through them, he looks like a curious and approval-seeking young child. He talked about being bullied at school and his effort to regain self-confidence.

Developmental Background

Yasuhiko's mother said, "My son had a strong sense of justice ever since he was little. When he saw a child being picked on by another, he would always give a helping hand. But, . . ." she continued, "he was also very shy *(ki ga yowai)*. Playing mostly with his father, and not children of his own age, he became like a little adult who couldn't relate well with children of his own age." Her statement set the tone for the rest of Yasuhiko's story.

Yasuhiko's childhood was relatively trouble-free. Both parents stayed at home, running their family-owned drug store, and his father often took time to play with his son in the outdoors. Growing up as an only child and spending little time with his peers, Yasuhiko had learned to isolate himself and act more precociously than his peers. When the school bus took him to school in the morning, for example, all of his friends would rush into the classroom, but he would take himself to the playground and play alone. When a school music recital was held, he refused to take part in the activity saying, "Who could sing a childish song like that? I'm not singing." His mother explained, "He became so used to the freedom he enjoyed with his father that he felt constrained by the group life of kindergarten."

During the early years of elementary school, Yasuhiko's shyness and precocity began to affect his peer relationships. His peers ostracized him as he, unlike them, came from a private kindergarten. They bullied him by stealing his swimming pants. Yasuhiko simply did not know how to handle the situation, so he concentrated on studying. His teacher did not help him but wrote on the report card, "He acts like a little adult, and refuses to get along with his friends."

Achievement Motivation

Learning that his son was being bullied at school and getting little help from his teacher, Yasuhiko's father sent him to a karate gym. He hoped that his son would "strengthen his body and character" through karate lessons.

Yasuhiko shared his experiences at the gym as his story of "achievement motivation." He said the practices there were "tough," and the coach was "mean." But he put up with the practice because he had two important reasons not to quit.

First, he said he wanted to become "normal" by practicing karate. He wanted to overcome his shyness by being good at karate and feeling more self-confident. He said, "Because I was so quiet, I was always alone. I would be sitting away from my friends. Even in a school picnic, I would be eating alone." He explained that karate made him "feel stronger" and no longer being attached (*amae*) to his father. Second, by being physically and mentally strong, he wanted to help his friends who were also being bullied. He explained that he had a "strong sense of justice since I was little" such that, "If I see someone being treated mean, I'd go and try to help him."

Eventually, he became so strong with karate that he was able to beat even the bullies. So one day, he courageously told the bullies to stop bullying his friend. But the bullies, knowing full well that Yasuhiko was a precocious isolate, waited the opportunity to turn the tide against him. When Yasuhiko threatened the bullies that he might counterattack them with karate, the bullies told their classmates, "Look, he is the one who's going to bully us with karate. Everyone, we got a bully here. Say it, everyone, 'bully! bully! bully!'" Because no one rallied behind Yasuhiko, he "became" wrong and unfair in everyone's eyes – the bully.

Being Bullied

Yasuhiko came to Joseph High School because he "heard it was a good school without *ijime* (bullying)." Ironically, the grade in which he was enrolled had bullies who abused some of their classmates, including Yasuhiko. On the day of our second interview, the bullies "put paint on his back just for kicks." Yasuhiko could find no apparent reason for this except the bullies were "simply dumping their frustration upon someone who was weaker than they." Because he failed to use his karate skills constructively, he quit going to karate gym. He gained weight, and this time, his bullies were much larger than he and there was little chance that he could beat them. He could no longer protect his bullied friends, either. As a result, he became withdrawn and contemplative. Asked to talk about an example of his achievement behavior after he came back from summer vacation, he said that the question was difficult to answer because he was motivated very little during this time.

"During the summer vacation," he continued,

I kept myself in my room with curtains closed and lights on. And my mother, who used to dream of becoming a doctor and studying medicine, said what I was doing was something that a neurotic patient would do. I didn't know if what I was doing was right or wrong. I mean, I had no purpose or goal in my life, and that's why I don't know what to do in my life.

In our third, and last interview, Yasuhiko told me that the bullying became even worse after he came back from the summer vacation. One time, he was "beaten up pretty badly" because,

I told my friend not to lend my comic book to a guy because he keeps it too long. Then my friend spilled the beans – and I thought he was really stupid to do this. He told the guy that I said these things about him. Anyway, then the guy came up to me and said, "You told him not to lend this book to me, didn't you?" And he beat me up.

Yasuhiko told me that the boy hit his ear with a book so hard that his ear started to bleed. He was even more bothered that his friends were bullied more severely than he. He felt ashamed because of, "my inability to stop the bullies, my lack of strength, to be specific. I feel so miserable when I think how strong I was once, and how weak I am now. It really makes me cry."

Moral Reasoning

By this time, Yasuhiko was convinced that the bullies would never change, so he decided to remain silent:

I just think that people are who they are *(hito wa hito)*, and there's no sense in trying to change them because some of them are really hopeless. I mean, there is a limit for how much a person can change. Some people never change.

Although giving up on the bullies, Yasuhiko defended firmly the victims' right to receive *omoiyari* (his story of morality). He said that the bullies were utterly inexcusable. They should at least realize "where to draw the line. They could do whatever they wanted, but they should never cause troubles for other people." He explained:

I think that every person is entitled to live a "normal" life. But all I'm concerned with is that one should not cause trouble for others. . . . I mean, that's what we call "morality" is all about. If someone breaks it, some other person's life will go wrong. You must know this, and never cross the line. I'm saying that it will do little harm to poke at someone's head, but he should not do it until it hurts. There is a limit in what you can say to other people, too. You can say whatever you want to, but shouldn't hurt other people.

To make his point, he drew two lines, indicating "point zero" and "the boundary set up by society at large." Each individual stands on "point zero" with his/her own sense of moral values, facing another line set up by the society. What "crossing the line" means is different for each person, but "the line no one can cross is that of causing trouble for others." His morality may not be abstract but has a principle of its own: Everyone can set his or her own limit to behavior as long as he or she does not hurt other people's feelings.

TAKESHI

Takeshi is an eighteen-year-old high school senior. He is tall for a Japanese boy (about 5′ 11″), and muscular. Takeshi introduced himself to me as a kind and gentle person, but he did so only reluctantly as follows:

There is a difference between what other people think and what I think of myself. I think it [my kindness] is rather "normal" because I'm only talking about such things as helping someone carrying a heavy load. In that sense, I don't think my kindness is unique to me.

Takeshi is a hardworking person who is also critical of himself. One reason for his self-criticism was his perceived failure to carry out his expected role in school (soccer club) and his family (as the first son).

Soccer Club

For his story of achievement, he talked about being on the soccer team for almost six straight years. First, he told me that he could not get up on time after he moved far away from school. He then began to leave the team practices early. He said, "I had very little time to sleep, then, the practice was very hard, and I was defeated by this inner weakness, and I began to skip the practice and went home early." He even considered quitting the soccer club and joining the ski club whose practice was less demanding. But his father told him, "Once you've decided to do something, you'd better stick to it." So he stayed on the team.

Meanwhile, he was still not able to get up on time in the morning. Noticing his "lazy life style," his grandfather told him, "You'll never amount to anything if you stay that way. Change your life style." So Takeshi "got [his] daily schedule straightened out" and was eventually able to "stop skipping the practices, and much to [his] surprise, began to like them." He explained his experience as follows: "I was quite mad at myself when I couldn't do what my grandfather told me to . . . but when I was finally able to stick to what I decided to do for myself, I really felt good."

After Takeshi stopped skipping soccer practices, another temptation beckoned him: a chance to be on a school trip to go to America. He said he "always wanted to go abroad" and expand his horizons; however, "the soccer club had a strange tradition that once its member went abroad, he would no longer be 're-accepted' as a member of the club." He asked the coach if he could go to America without quitting the club, but the coach said, "No, if you want to go, you must quit the club." Being rather "scared of the coach, he didn't push him further." Although he felt "troubled" by "the strange tradition," he decided to stay in the soccer club and not go on the trip because:

> People who quit the team tend to be indecent people. Most of them are headed for bad things. That's why people say, "There hasn't been one proper person who dropped out from the soccer club." I knew that I would never be such a person even if I quit the club. But I just did not want to be labeled like that.

Fixing Broken Bathroom Switches

What follows is Takeshi's story of "moral reasoning." At his school, a group of delinquents destroyed light switches for no apparent reason. Instead of blaming the delinquents for their wrongdoing, Takeshi criticized his own attitudes to it. He said, "I lacked the courage to say [to the delinquents], 'Stop it.' Instead, I told the teacher who [it was who] broke the switches and left things up to him." This teacher began to fix the switches by himself without confronting the delinquents. Takeshi joined him. He told me a few reasons why he thought helping the teacher was the right thing to do.

First, he said that it would "cost nothing" for him to fix the switches. He said, fixing them wasn't "such a big deal. When I see something broken, I try to fix them anyway." He said the teacher who fixed them "did it all the time," whereas he had "done it only three or four times."

Second, he felt fixing the switches was the right thing to do in order to maintain the good reputation of the school. He explained: "When we have guests, I don't want them to see the school properties being broken and think, 'This school looks great on the outside, but this is how it really is on the inside.'"

Third, he said confronting the offenders was not as a wise decision as it seemed because,

> Even if you don't like this person, it might not always be the case that your friend doesn't like him, either. If you tell your friend that you don't like this person, you might discover that two of them are close friends. I don't want to harm my friendship like that. . . . I didn't go as far as "losing" the friendship, but when I had this person I didn't like and told my friend A how badly I think of him, he said, "I didn't know you were that kind of person to say something like that." Then I felt that I lost A's trust in me.

Finally, he heard from his mother who worked as a nurse at Joseph High School that most of these offenders were from troubled homes, and it would be right to treat them with sympathy. He told me:

> She says that these students often come to see her at her office, and she has favorable opinions about them. She praises them saying that they may not be good all the time, but they could be quite good at other times. Now if they have been in an adversary position against me, they would feel uneasy about seeing my mother. I think that these kinds of people tend to be attracted to someone like a school nurse who treats them gently, listens to their problems, and keeps their secrets. So if they are in an adverse relationship with me, they'd feel uncomfortable about going to my mother's office, and in that sense, they would lose somebody they really can talk to. So although they destroy school properties, I feel sympathy toward them if they become unable to go to my mother. The other thing is that if they can't do that, they may get very frustrated and start breaking windows or something. So it would be better to leave them with somebody who takes care of them. . . . If we can put up with them, they may still have an opportunity to improve. . . . Some people have a certain complex about themselves. And to point out such a complex in front of others is definitely not in line with the "human way."

ONTOLOGICAL ANALYSIS OF THE RELATIONS BETWEEN THE SOCIOCENTRIC AND INDIVIDUALISTIC SELVES

Many scholars of Japan with as diverse backgrounds as cultural anthropologists (Benedict, 1946; Kondo, 1990; Lebra, 1976; Nakane, 1970), psychological anthropologists (DeVos, 1973; Hamaguchi, 1977), social psychologists (Cousins, 1989; Markus & Kitayama, 1991), developmental and educational psychologists (Azuma, 1994; Lewis, 1995; Stevenson et al., 1986), psychiatrists (Doi, 1977; Kimura, 1972), and linguists (Clancy, 1986; Travis, 1998; Wierzbicka, 1996) have used a contextual – collective and empathic – framework of analysis to analyze Japanese culture, people, or behavior. Looked at from this point of view, what American psychologists refer to as achievement motivation and moral reasoning – principally individualistic concepts – may be recast in Japan as primarily sociocentric concepts. My in-depth interviews with three Japanese adolescents show, however, that both exclusively individualistic and sociocentric frameworks are methodologically limited and conceptually inaccurate for understanding the adolescents' *private* experiences. From their phenomenological perspectives, the two orientations complement each other in that each element is finite (imperfect), and, therefore, has to depend on the other to actualize its potentiality.

My goal is to look into and understand the three adolescents' *subjective* experience in a phenomenological analytical framework. I turn to the existential-phenomenologist Martin Heidegger (1996) and existential-theologian Paul Tillich (1951), who spoke of the nature of human existence – that is, "being in the world" (*Da-sein*) – along with its intrinsic "finitude" and accompanying anxiety (*angst*). It is both relevant and illuminating to make a reference to their notions of "finitude" and "anxiety" as implied in the adolescents' life experience.

Heidegger spoke of the nature of being in the world and its intrinsic limitation and imperfection, or "finitude" (Heidegger, 1996). Extending this view, Tillich spoke of finitude as the state of confronting and longing for that which was a definite end or essence (Tillich, 1951, p. 189). He explained:

> Being, limited by nonbeing, is finitude. Nonbeing appears as the "not yet" of being and as the "no more" of being. . . . Selfhood, individuality, dynamics, and freedom all include manifoldness, definiteness, differentiation, and limitation. All categories of thought and reality express this situation. To be something is to be finite. (Tillich, 1951, pp. 189–99)

Of particular relevance to my discussion is Tillich's explanation of "finitude and its ontological elements," because I shall discuss the concepts of sociocentricism and individualism as such ontological elements. Tillich wrote:

In every polarity each pole is limited as well as sustained by the other one. A complete balance between them presupposes a balanced whole. But such a whole is not given. There are special structures in which, under the impact of finitude, polarity becomes tension. Tension refers to the tendency of elements within a unity to draw away from one another, to attempt to move in opposite directions . . . everything is an embracing but transitory unity of two opposite processes. Things are hypostasized tensions. (Tillich, 1951, pp. 198–9)

Our own ontological tension comes to awareness in the anxiety of losing our ontological structure through losing one or another polar element and consequently, the polarity to which it belongs. . . . This can be seen in terms of each of the polar elements. Finite individualization produces a dynamic tension with finite participation; the break of their unity is a possibility. Self-relatedness produces the threat of a loneliness in which world and communion are lost. On the other hand, being in the world and participating in it produces the threat of complete collectivization, a loss of individuality and subjectivity whereby the self loses its self-relatedness and is transformed into a mere part of an embracing whole. Man as finite is anxiously aware of this twofold threat. Anxiously he experiences the trend from possible loneliness to collectivity and from possible collectivity to loneliness. He oscillates anxiously between individualization and participation, aware of the fact that he ceases to be if one of the poles is lost, for the loss of either pole means the loss of both. (Tillich, 1951, p. 199)

While the three adolescents show both sociocentric and individualistic psychological and behavioral orientations, there are elements of a dynamic of opposing psychological forces (of wishes and fear, etc.) – tension and ambiguity – that bring the two orientations into a single focus. The tension is the source of anxiety (*angst*) as well as self-transcendence (courage).

FINITUDE OF SELF AND OTHER ORIENTATIONS AND THEIR DYNAMIC INTERRELATIONSHIPS

As Tillich noted, "self-relatedness produces the threat of a loneliness in which world and communion are lost" (Tillich, 1951, p. 199). The threat of loneliness is an immanent possibility or reality for the three adolescents: Yumi's quest for self-honesty implies the possibility of peer rejection; Yasuhiko's pursuit of principled justice creates resentment by and retaliation from the bullies, and Takeshi's personal dream of traveling abroad would entail the loss of "respect" from his teammates and subsequent expulsion from the team.

By contrast, sociocentrism or "being in the world and participating in it produces the threat of complete collectivization, a loss of individuality and subjectivity whereby the self loses its self-relatedness and is transformed into a mere part of an embracing whole" (Tillich, 1951, p. 199). The loss of self to the collective is also a concern for the three adolescents: trying to be accepted by her relatives and her peers, Yumi fears losing self-honesty. Being a "daddy's boy," Yasuhiko struggles to establish a more individuated "adolescent identity" among his peers. Trying to attend to feelings and needs of others (of his mother and delinquents), Takeshi is forced to forsake personal goals and desires.

Finally, in the polar structure of individualism and sociocentrism, "each pole is limited as well as sustained by the other one. A complete balance between them presupposes a balanced whole. But such a whole is not given." In other words, a person's orientations toward self- (individuation) and other- (participation) relatedness is never in a perfect harmony. It is a *tense* harmony, which is "an embracing but transitory unity of two opposite processes" (Tillich, 1951, p. 199). Oxymora such as "unkind empathy," "noisy isolation," and "lonely crowd" illustrate the dynamic tension inherent in the adolescents' experiences. For example, to wear an empathic "face" on the surface to cover up the act of speaking behind somebody's back is an "unkind empathy" (Yumi). To be alone in one's own room wishing to join others is a "noisy isolation " (Yasuhiko). Finally, to be a member of a group (soccer team) that denies one's personal dream (to go abroad) is to be in the "lonely crowd" (Takeshi). Also in the domain of moral reasoning, there is no clear line separating selfishness and observed "moral" conduct. For example, as Yasuhiko noticed, many people overlooked *ijime* for fear of being bullied themselves. Yumi said that many girls felt it acceptable to speak behind their peer's back as long as they maintain amicable fronts. Hence, each situation and person seems to define its or his and her own moral rules.

OVERCOMING THE FINITUDE THROUGH "COURAGE TO BE"

Given the ontological finitudes implied in social participation, individual autonomy, and their dynamic interrelationships, it follows, "Do the three adolescents transcend the binary distinction between sociocentric and individualistic (selves,) or balance conflicting needs and concerns? If so, how do they attempt to do so?"

In Tillich's theological system, finitude cannot be overcome by striving to perfect it to be infinite and unconditional (i.e., to reach the ultimate ends themselves, such as being "perfectly" empathic or individuated). Instead, the "only way of dealing with [the threat of finitude] lies in the courage of taking it [the treat of finitude] upon one's self" (Tillich, 1951, p. 189). Courage in this context means "the ethical act in which man *affirms his own being in spite of those elements of his existence which conflict with his essential self-affirmation*" (Tillich, 1952, p. 3, italics added). Furthermore, the self implied here is not "a thing that may or may not exist; it is an original phenomenon which logically precedes all questions of existence" (Tillich, 1951, p. 169). Unlike its objectified counterparts that are mixed with the threats of finitudes – for example, the finite structures for participation (sociocentrism) and individuation (individualism) – this phenomenally original self is self-transcending because it is uniquely aware of its own finitudes:

> The point is that man is aware of the structures which make cognition possible. He lives in them and acts through them. They are immediately present to him. They are he himself. Any confusion on this point has destructive consequences. The basic structure of being and all its elements and the conditions of existence lose their meaning and their truth if they are seen as objects among objects. (Tillich, 1951, p. 169)

Thus, the finite self transcends its own finitudes through affirming and accepting itself "in spite of that which tends to prevent the self from affirming itself" (Tillich, 1952, p. 32).

That the ontological self overlooks its own finitudes, and in so doing, overcomes the world in which he or she is a finite part-object was demonstrated concretely in the adolescents' life experiences as follows. Takeshi decides to fix the switches in spite of his self-understanding that his prosocial action is not "special," but it is "only to appease his mother" or "to protect the school's image to the outsider" – he knows that he is morally imperfect. Yasuhiko decides to stand up for his bullied friends in spite of the possible threat of social isolation – he knows that he can suffer from his own decision. Yumi decides to remain "two-faced" in spite of the threat of losing her own self-respect – she is willing to face the negative consequences of her personal decision.

Thus, both exclusively individualistic (autonomy) and sociocentric (participation) choices do not eliminate the threat of anxiety (finitudes) in these situations. On the individualistic pole, both calculating instrumentality (e.g., McClelland's need for achievement) and rational moral reasoning (e.g., Kohlberg's postconventional moral reasoning) imply possible social sanctions (such as loneliness or ostracism). On the sociocentric pole, the cultural idea of empathy (*omoiyari*) implies the possible loss of self (through dishonesty, self-denial, etc.). Being aware of these limitations, however, the self transcends them: Instead of striving to find perfect solutions to life's problems, all three adolescents accept the unacceptable (anxiety-producing finitudes) by taking the problems on themselves: living and accepting life's imperfections through courage.

CONCLUSIONS

Being oneself through courage (facing and accepting finitudes) integrates and gives meaning to opposing polarities, each end of which presents finite answers to the person's "ultimate concern" of determining the ultimate goals, or telos, of life's experiences. Viewed from this perspective, the claim that sociocentrism is the "core" aspect of Japanese culture or people has to be addressed conditionally in light of the dynamic and creative tension inherent in the two opposing elements. First, although the three adolescents in Joseph High School are hardly representative of adolescents in Japan, the conflicting theme of social participation and individuation that their life stories demonstrate is one of the enduring themes of Japanese literature (Lindholm, 1997), family and interpersonal relationships (DeVos, 1973), and institutional and political processes (Krauss, Rohlen, & Steinhoff, 1984). Together, both current and past evidence suggest the limitation of applying the "sociocentric" framework of analysis unconditionally, that is, uniformly and exclusively, to individual members of Japanese society, and to their private psychological experiences in particular.

Second, the self that is objectified among other objects in the world, such as the individualistic and sociocentric selves – along with such derivatives as "concepts of self," or "culturally constructed selves" – has to be separated from the ontological self: self-awareness. As the phenomenological anthropologist Irving Hallowell (1955) pointed out long ago,

> Self awareness . . . is a psychological constant, one basic facet of human nature and of human personality. . . . Self-awareness in man cannot be taken as an isolated psychological phenomenon . . . [it] is one of the prerequisite psychological conditions for the functioning of any human social order, no matter what linguistic and culture patterns prevail . . . as one of the consequences of self-awareness, man has reflected upon his own nature as well as the nature of the world perceived as other than self. He has been able, moreover, to articulate and express through symbolic means explicit notions that embrace this polarity. (Hallowell, 1955, p. 75)

The ontological self-awareness transcends culturally constructed selves because the former is the original phenomenon from which the latter are derived. Tillich elaborated this point as follows:

> As long as he is human, that is, as long as he has not "fallen" from humanity (e.g., in intoxication or insanity), man never is bound completely to an environment [i.e., the world of physical or conceptual "objects" that he or she constructs or is constructed by]. He always transcends it by grasping and shaping it [so that even] in the most limited environment man possesses the universe; he has a world. (Tillich, 1951, p. 170)

Finally, the ontological self's capacity to reflect upon its own nature enables human populations elsewhere to *select* cultural-specific means of facing finitudes implied in their livelihood. This participatory process is in turn "guided" (Rogoff, 1990) through cultural and historical variables as well as specific contexts and processes. Thus, a Japanese adolescent, who shares the uniquely human capacity for self-awareness and reflection and courage to transcend life's finitudes, participates in a culturally variable and represented process of self-representation and self-actualization.

REFERENCES

Aida, Y. (1970). *Nihonjin no ishiki kozo* [The structure of Japanese consciousness]. Tokyo: Kodansha.

Azuma, H. (1994). *Nihonjin no shitsuke to kyoiku.* [Japanese child training and education]. Tokyo: University of Tokyo Press.

Benedict, R. (1946). *The chrysanthemum and the sword: Patterns of Japanese culture.* Boston: Houghton Mifflin Co.

Clancy, P. (1986). The acquisition of communicative style in Japanese. In B. B. Schieffelin & E. Ochs (Eds.), *Language socialization across cultures* (pp. 213–50). New York: Cambridge University Press.

Cousins, S. (1989). Culture and self-perception in Japan and the United States. *Journal of Personality and Social Psychology, 56,* 124–31.

Dale, P. (1986). *The myth of Japanese uniqueness.* London and Sydney: Croom Helm and Nissan Institute, Oxford.

DeVos, G. (1973). *Socialization for achievement: Essay of the cultural psychology of the Japanese.* Berkeley: University of California Press.

Doi, T. (1977). *The anatomy of dependence.* Tokyo: Kodansha.

Dumont, L. (1970). *Homo hierarchicus.* Chicago: University of Chicago Press.

Geertz, C. (1983). *Local knowledge.* New York: Basic Books.

Hallowell, A. I. (1955). *Culture and experience.* Philadelphia: University of Pennsylvania Press.

Hamaguchi, E. (1977) *Nihon rashisa no saihakken* [The rediscovery of Japanese-ness]. Tokyo: Nihon Keizai Shinbunsha.

Heidegger, M. (1996). *Being and time.* Albany: State University of New York Press.

Iwasa, N. (1989). *Situational considerations in moral judgment: A Japan-United States comparison.* Unpublished doctoral dissertation, Harvard University, Cambridge, MA.

Kimura, B. (1972). *Hito to hito no aida* [In-between people]. Tokyo: Kobundo.

Kohlberg, L. (1969). Stage and sequence: The cognitive-developmental approach to socialization. In D. A. Goslin (Ed.), *Handbook of socialization theory and research* (pp. 347–480). New York: Rand McNally.

Kohlberg, L. (1981). *Essays in moral development: Vol. 1, The philosophy of moral development.* San Francisco: Harper & Row.

Kondo, D. (1990). *Crafting selves: Power, gender, and discourses of identity in a Japanese workplace.* Chicago: University of Chicago Press.

Krauss, E., Rohlen, T. P., & Steinhoff, P. C. (1984). *Conflict in Japan.* Honolulu: University of Hawaii Press.

Kusserow, A. S. (1999). De-homogenizing American individualism: Socializing hard and soft individualism in Manhattan and Queens. *Ethos, 27,* 210–34.

Lebra, T. S. (1976). *Japanese pattern of behavior.* Honolulu: University Press of Hawaii.

Lewis, C. C. (1995). *Educating hearts and minds: Reflections on Japanese preschool and elementary education.* New York: Cambridge University Press.

Lindholm, C. (1997). Does the sociocentric self exist? Reflections on Markus and Kitayama's "culture and the self." *Journal of Anthropological Research, 53,* 405–22.

Markus, H. R., & Kitayama, S. (1991). Culture and the self: Implications for cognition, emotion, and motivation. *Psychological Review, 98,* 224–53.

Marsella, A. J., DeVos, G., & Hsu, F. L. K. (1985). *Culture and self: Asian and western perspectives.* New York: Tavistock Publications.

Maxwell, J. A. (1996). *Using qualitative research to develop causal explanations.* Unpublished manuscript, Harvard Project on Schooling and Children. Harvard University Graduate School of Education.

McClelland, D. C. (1961). *The achieving society.* Princeton, NJ: Van Nostrand.

Murray, D. W. (1993). What is the Western concept of the self? On forgetting David Hume, *Ethos, 21,* 3–23.

Nakane, C. (1970). *Japanese society.* Berkeley: University of California Press.

Peak, L. (1991). *Learning to go to school in Japan: The transition from home to preschool life.* Berkeley: University of California Press.

Rogoff, B. (1990). *Apprenticeship in thinking: Cognitive development in social context.* New York: Oxford University Press.

Rohlen, T. P., & LeTendre, G. K. (1996). *Teaching and learning in Japan.* New York: Cambridge University Press.

Spiro, M. (1993). Is the Western conception of the self "peculiar" within the context of the world cultures? *Ethos, 21,* 107–53.

Shweder, R. A., & Bourne, E. (1984). Does the concept of the person vary cross-culturally? In R. A. Shweder & R. A. LeVine (Eds.), *Culture theory: Essays on mind, self, and emotion* (pp. 158–99). New York: Cambridge University Press.

Stevenson H., Azuma, H., & Hakuta, K. (1986). *Child development and education in Japan.* New York: W.H. Freeman and Company.

Tillich. P. (1951). *Systematic theology (Vol. 1).* Chicago: University of Chicago Press.

Tillich. P. (1952). *The courage to be.* New Haven: Yale University Press.

Travis, C. (1998). *Omoiyari* as a core Japanese value: Japanese-style empathy? In A.

Athanasiadou & E. Tabakowska (Eds.), *Speaking of emotions: Conceptualization and expression* (pp. 55–81). Berlin: Mouton de Gruyter.

Vygotsky, L. S. (1978). *Mind in society.* Cambridge, MA: Harvard University Press.

Wierzbicka, A. (1996). Japanese cultural scripts: Cultural psychology and "cultural grammar." *Ethos, 24,* 527–55.

Wertsch, J. W. (1985). *Vygotsky and the social formation of mind.* Cambridge, MA: Harvard University Press.

EIGHT

Returnees to Japan

The Impact of Having Lived in the United States

Miya Omori

The word *kikokushijo* ("Returnees") arouses anxiety in Japan, due to the long-standing stigma attached to Japanese children who have lived abroad (Goodman, 1990; Kondo, 1989; Miyachi, 1990; Monbusho Kyoiku Josei Kyoiku, 1991; White, 1988). The stigma stems from being an "outsider" or not belonging to "the group." Japanese teachers, returnee parents, returnee students, and nonreturnee students have a negative image of the "returnee," but for different reasons. The Japanese teacher may draw on previous experiences of *kikokushijo* students, hesitantly admitting that it is difficult to teach a class with a *kikokushijo* in it because of their outspoken behavior. The returnee parents may be anxiety-ridden because they know of this stigma and are afraid that even if their child thinks he is acting and reacting like a Japanese, neighbors will find something strange about his behavior. They also fear that their children will not be accepted in the school environment. Merry White (1988) describes how the returned women in her study were under great pressure to avoid stigma and to observe the strict rules of a Japanese "housewife" and "mother" in order to set an example for the rest of the family to conform to these social norms. This would ultimately reflect on her children and husband's status in the school, community, and job.

The anxieties of the *kikokushijo* resemble those of their parents. They are concerned about being accepted into the peer group. The nonreturnee students, on the other hand, are likely to have preconceived notions of an outspoken "outsider" coming into the school (Sato, 1998). When a child wears or brings something different to school, or talks and behaves in a way they think is strange, that person is subject to teasing and persuaded to conform. Sometimes, the teasing becomes violent and degrading, leading to *ijime* (bullying) problems in the schools (White, 1988).

KIKOKUSHIJO (JAPANESE STUDENTS RETURNING FROM ABROAD)

Kikokushijo are children who were born in Japan, raised in Japan until a certain age, taken overseas with their parents for a few years (being influenced by a foreign culture) and returned to be brought up once again in Japan. Most *kikokushijo* come from highly educated families, where the father/husband has been sent overseas by the company/institution at which he is employed (Goodman, 1990). Parents tend to take children who are younger (sometimes leaving children with relatives, especially if they are older), so as not to jeopardize their educational path to success. Parents are also more likely to take girls overseas and let them stay overseas longer than boys, due to a stronger emphasis placed on male careers. The social category *kikokushijo* was created by the Ministry of Education in the 1960s to label those children who had gone abroad because of their father's occupations for more than one year and had gone to the local schools abroad, but had returned to Japan for further schooling. In 1965, the first school to incorporate a special program for *kikokushijo* was established in Tokyo. Since then, the situation for these returnee students has changed greatly because of the initial movement of the parents of these children back in the 1970s (Minoura, 1998). Back then, the fathers going abroad were those considered to be the "élite" of the company. In other words, they were mostly executives. Thus, they had political power and influence in Japanese society (White, 1988).

In the latter part of the 1960s, these parents let it be known to the government that their children were an issue that must not be ignored. They made it a public issue about the same time the *"kikokushijo* handicap" theory was becoming widespread. The parents of these children insisted that the government treat these children with special care because they were the victims of the families that were sent abroad to support the Japanese economy. In the latter part of the 1970s and earlier part of the 1980s, the number of *kikokushijo* increased to over ten thousand people and became a generally recognized problem. Even with the number of Japanese returning from abroad increasing, however, public opinion and educational institutions took the stance that the returnees should be trained to become "pure" Japanese persons and citizens, and that those who failed to do so were maladjusted (Minoura, 1998). A report issued by the Ministry of Education in 1993 clearly showed an increase in the number of *kikokushijo* sojourning abroad. It reported that the most frequent types of difficulty in school were: (a) inexperience with group activities, (b) different ways of looking at/

thinking about things, and (c) difference in daily customs (Ministry of Education, 1993).

RETURN TO JAPAN AND "REVERSE CULTURE SHOCK"

Japanese children living overseas perceive themselves as different but also take pride in having an "international status" and being able to perceive the world from a broader perspective than those left behind. There is always an element of anxiety that suppresses their enthusiasm, however, when they think about the negative experiences that might accompany their return to Japan (Enloe & Lewin, 1987; Goodman, 1990; Miyachi, 1990). After a long stay in a foreign country whose living conditions and values are quite different from those in Japan, *kikokushijo* face difficulties stemming from Japanese language inadequacy and ways of thinking and behaving that mark them as different (Ministry of Education, 1990). The value of the group and its relevance to personal interactions begin to emerge as a problem for these *kikokushijo*. Returning from overseas, they try to reassimilate, yet some of their newly acquired behavior patterns like speaking up in class may be viewed as a disruption by both teachers and classmates (Goodman, 1990). The problem is compounded by the fact that many children return at a relatively young age when they have not yet fully established their self-identity and are not able to make sense of their overseas experience (Enloe & Lewin, 1987).

Miyachi (1990) and Goodman (1990) have indicated that most children experience "reverse culture shock" on their return to Japan. Trying to blend into a culture that does not regard outside experience valuable and sometimes considers it stigmatizing, is reported to be extremely difficult for *kikokushijo* as they experience constant pressure from peers, teachers, and community members to be "normal." The uncertainty and turmoil encountered by *kikokushijo* and their Japanese peers who have never been abroad has been seen as symptomatic of conservative Japanese institutions in accommodating difference in the classroom and other settings (White, 1988). The *kikokushijo's* inability to blend into the school culture, academically and emotionally, accompanied by a "degree of self-imposed isolation, identity confusion, and depression about the meaning of being Japanese" (Enloe & Lewin, 1987, p. 225) magnifies their adjustment problems as well as making them salient targets for *ijime* (bullying) and ridicule, leading to their acting out or internalizing their frustrations (Goodman, 1990; Kaigaishijo Kyoiku Shinko Zaidan, 1991; White, 1988). It is uncommon for *kikokushijo* to experience *ijime* abroad, but on their return to Japan, they are much more likely to become victims of bullying. It seems that *ijime* of the *kikokushijo* on their return is born out of ignorance, as well as out of jealousy on the part of the other students who have not been abroad.

READJUSTMENT

Efforts have been made to accelerate the assimilation process of the *kikokushijo* by setting up special readjustment classes and schools (along with special university entrance networks) (Goodman, 1990; Kaigaishijo Kyoiku Shinko Zaidan, 1991; Ministry of Education, 1990; Monbusho, 1991; White, 1988). It is important to note the historical context of these programs. Goodman (1990) points to the fact that many of the first *kikokushijo* were children of influential parents in Japanese society with high academic credentials (e.g., diplomats, businessmen from large prestigious companies, academics). Consequently, those parents worried and complained that their children were suffering and being disadvantaged as a result of their being sent overseas to work for their country or company. In addition, the parents believed that their family status was being jeopardized because their children were unable to be academically competitive with their Japanese counterparts, and hence, not being accepted into the top universities (from which they themselves had graduated). Thus, several organizations were established by these parents that subsequently brought the *kikokushijo* problem into the public arena, making it a visible and urgent issue with which the Japanese society had to contend. This public pressure was aimed primarily to motivate the government (i.e., Ministry of Education) to respond by establishing special programs for the *kikokushijo*, which were eventually instituted in light of the problems encountered by them.

The problems of *kikokushijo* stem from their minority status and the judgment that they have somehow lost or never acquired the skills considered necessary to lead a virtuous Japanese life (Goodman, 1990). Hence, the special programs prescribed by the Ministry of Education ease the transition for relearning Japanese skills (academic and social), while relieving the regular school system and the regular students who do not need special instruction, by taking time away from the curriculum. Although these programs are meant to be supportive of *kikokushijo*, however, they also imply by their very existence that they are different. They are later reminded of this fact repeatedly by their peer group (White, 1988). Nevertheless, Kobayashi (1986) sheds light on the situation by claiming it to be not as discouraging as it initially may appear since efforts to "internationalize" Japanese people's minds and manners are slowly but steadily making their way into the educational and cultural arena. This is a process that has continued during the last fifteen years.

Kikokushijo have experienced an alternative lifestyle that may be seen as a threat to the stability of Japanese social structure and ultimately economic growth (as a human resource is considered to be a major "natural" resource). In the efforts to "internationalize" the Japanese educational system (Kobayashi, 1986; Kondo, 1989; Miyachi, 1990), *kikokushijo* are offered as a group exemplifying individualism, creativity, and heterogeneity in Japanese society (Goodman, 1990). Recently, more *kikokushijo* are being accepted to more prestigious university programs and places of employment. This has improved and normalized their reputation, especially in terms of value to business, where internationalization and understanding foreign cultures is critical (Ugaya, 1991).

DANTAI ISHIKI: GROUP ORIENTATION AND COLLECTIVE IDENTITY

Dantai ishiki ("organization consciousness") is an integral aspect of the group-oriented Japanese society. Nakane (1988) has described how this pattern strengthens the foundation of each institution, as each individual becomes emotionally invested in the social group. The cohesive nature of the face-to-face group is augmented by its family-like characteristics permeating the private lives of the individual. This process operates with strong within-group loyalties at structural levels ranging from the family, neighborhood, and factory to the nation as a whole. It also cultivates a sense of "them" versus "us" that can lead to xenophobia. As Japan's economy remains heavily international, many companies are continuing to send their employees overseas on temporary assignments. Accompanying the continuing temporary migration of Japanese families are the difficulties of reintegrating the returning Japanese child back into their native culture. Although the *kikokushijo* are supposed to be problematic in their attitudes and academic adjustment, it is not clear how "different" they are nowadays from their Japanese counterparts who have never lived overseas. The present study was thus conducted as follows.

SUBJECTS

Twenty high school students in their last year of high school were interviewed for this study. Ten were *kikokushijo* students who: (a) had been in the United States, (b) for three or more years with their families, and who

(c) had not been back in Japan for more than three years. Three years was chosen for the length of overseas residence so that the students would have had some time to experience life overseas. Three years was chosen as the limit for having been back in Japan, so that they would still be fresh in their recall of events, as well as the possibility that they may still be in the readjustment stage. The other ten students, non-*kikokushijo*, had never lived outside of Japan.

The subjects attended either a National school in Tokyo or an International school in Kyoto. Ten *kikokushijo* high school seniors (five students from each school) and nine Japanese high school seniors (five students from the Kyoto school and four from the Tokyo school) were each interviewed for ninety minutes. All *kikokushijo* had been in the United States for three or more years and had returned to Japan less than three years prior to the interview date. The non-*kikokushijo* had never lived overseas, and those from the International school were chosen randomly out of a group of willing participants, and those from the National school, through introductions by other students at the school. The number of interviewees was also balanced in gender (i.e., five *kikokushijo* girls, four non-*kikokushijo* girls, five *kikokushijo* boys, and five non-*kikokushijo* boys).

SCHOOLS: PRIVATE CHRISTIAN INTERNATIONAL VERSUS NATIONAL PREPARATORY

The private Christian International high school in the Kansai region was established in 1980 and a junior high school was later attached to the high school in 1988. Two-thirds of the students were *kikokushijo* and one-third non-*kikokushijo*. The entrance examinations given to the two populations were different. The *kikokushijo* were given a choice of either writing a short essay about their overseas experience in the language of the country in which they resided, in addition to submitting their grade reports and interviewing, or they could take a written examination covering three subject areas of Japanese, Math, and English. The non-*kikokushijo* must pass a written examination covering Japanese, Social Studies, Math, Science, and English, followed by an interview in order to be admitted. In 1991, roughly 49% of the *kikokushijo* who applied were accepted, and 20% of the non-*kikokushijo* who applied were admitted.

The National school in Tokyo was originally established in 1954 by the Ministry of Education as a teaching school to train student teachers. It is considered a competitive "prep school" and is usually in the top-five list for successfully sending graduates to the most competitive university in

Japan, Tokyo University. Of the approximately four hundred high school students in a class, approximately twenty are *kikokushijo*.

SELECTION OF PARTICIPANTS

The process for choosing the participants varied with each school, because of the limited enrollment of *kikokushijo* at the National high school in Tokyo. Hence, gathering interviewees in Tokyo was made possible by the cooperation of the teachers who helped identify some *kikokushijo* who had been in the United States, and subsequent selection was a random process. The non-*kikokushijo* who were interviewed were introduced to me by some *kikokushijo* and by some of the non-*kikokushijo* students of the school. Regardless of being a *kikokushijo* or non-*kikokushijo*, the competitive nature of the school made it difficult to first, get permission to interview some students (e.g., parental) and, second, to find students willing to be interviewed, primarily because they were extremely hesitant to give ninety minutes of their day to something not related to their studies.

The school climate in Kyoto was somewhat different, which allowed for a more random selection of the participants for the interview. The first step in choosing the participants was to distribute a background information questionnaire to the students of the high school at which the samples were selected. This questionnaire was distributed to all the students who were in their last year in high school. The main purpose in obtaining this information was to ensure that the *kikokushijo* students' overseas experience had been only in the United States for three years or more and that they had not been back in Japan for more than three years. After the questionnaire was filled out, a list of those who fit the above "criteria" for *kikokushijo* was generated, as well as a list of those who had never lived overseas. A random sample from these two lists was selected for this study.

BACKGROUND INFORMATION QUESTIONNAIRE

Some background information was obtained as a guide for the interview. First, the information about parents' education and occupation (including the company affiliation) offered background information about the status of the family and their lifestyle, especially if the mother was employed. Second, because the students usually had a choice in enrolling in one or more of three types of schools available to them while abroad – (a) the local school (including International Schools), (b) a Japanese language school (teaching Japanese, usually held on Saturday), and (c) a Japanese school (either private or sponsored by the Ministry of Education) – this information offered insight into their schooling experience and peer network. Third, the information about students' siblings offered insight into the educational values of the family, as well as the possible difference in educational experience of children in the same family.

THE INTERVIEW

In-depth interviews were conducted for this study, because much of the past research on *kikokushijo* used quantitative survey data. The qualitative descriptions of students' experience in this study offers more in-depth accounts of personal experience as well as individual variation. Specifically, the thoughts and feelings of students as they had been revealed and elaborated by students themselves were recorded and analyzed according to the nature of students' readjustment process to their native culture. The interviews with *kikokushijo* and non-*kikokushijo* focused on four specific aspects of students' lives: peers, family, school, and self. The last section focused on general opinions regarding internationalization, freedom, individuation, and a conversation on their anxieties.

INTERVIEW PROCESS

Each student was interviewed for ninety minutes. At the beginning of each interview, students were told that they were not obligated to answer any question if they did not wish to, but that cooperation through being honest would be appreciated. They were also informed that any information they offered would remain anonymous so that neither their parents nor their teachers would be informed of their responses. The interviews for the National school in Tokyo and the International school in Kyoto were conducted in two different settings. The students from the National school in Tokyo were interviewed after school in a fast-food type of cafeteria near the train station that was on the way home from school. The students from the International school in Kyoto also were interviewed after school, in a cozy "conference room" at their school.

Each interview was taped with a small portable recorder. Notes were taken on a pad of paper to guide the following questions

1. What are the experiences of the *kikokushijo* students?
2. Do *kikokushijo* students encounter any difficulty on their return to Japan?
3. Are the experiences of the *kikokushijo* students different from their counterparts who have never been overseas?

4. How do these students construct their psychological
    environment – namely through their relationships – to define their
    self-identity?

Particular attention was paid to see if there were differences between the
kikokushijo students and the Japanese students, due to the *kikokushijo*'s exposure to the culture of the United States. The largest differences were expected in the area of students' relationships with teachers, peers, and family, and with thoughts on internationalization, freedom, and individuation,
as some *kikokushijo* might have experienced a more autonomous self while
in the United States (i.e., became more independent). In addition, although
it was anticipated that *kikokushijo* would encounter some difficulties, these
difficulties were not regarded as problematic as the literature has suggested
to maintain the phenomenological and descriptive focuses of this study.

DATA ANALYSIS

All interviews were taped and then transcribed by simultaneous translation. Analyses of the interviews are qualitative and descriptive in nature.
In addition, four students were chosen who seemed most representative of
the two groups. After all the interviews were transcribed, broad themes
were identified (e.g., family, school, peers, group, teachers). This was different from all existing research on *kikokushijo* at the time, which consisted
mainly of questionnaire studies guided by a preconceived idea of these students. All of the studies to date were based on a hypothesis that this population was problematic. This study, on the contrary, attempted to hear the
voices of the students first, namely, about their experiences of being in the
United States and returning to Japan. Consequently, the following themes
emerged from the interview data.

1. SOCIALIZATION: Family, School
2. GROUP ACTIVITIES (*DANTAI ISHIKI*): School, Peers
3. ROLE DEFINITIONS and BOUNDARIES: Family, Peers
4. NATURE OF RELATIONSHIPS: Family, Teachers, Peers
5. INTERNATIONALIZATION
6. FUTURE GOALS: College life, graduate schooling, employment

It became clear that many of the experiences of the *kikokushijo* and non-
kikokushijo were not either a yes or no, or something that could be measured
by a numerical scale. Thus, this interview study allowed the students to
elaborate on their answers and gave them an opportunity to describe their

coping processes and stages of readjustment, which offered a new insight into their experiences.

RESULTS

Differences between *kikokushijo* and non-*kikokushijo* were fewer than expected and were outweighed by similarities between the two groups of students. The assumption that *kikokushijo* experience difficulty in reaccommodating to Japan received some support but did not seem as serious as the literature had suggested. *Kikokushijo*, nevertheless, differed from students who had not left Japan in several key attitudes to Japanese norms and cultural models: They did not like the peer group dynamics in their current school. They were more likely to feel negatively about Japanese social hierarchy, particularly *sempai/kohai* relationships. They felt less comfortable with strict group rules, having experienced a more individualistic lifestyle in the United States.

Many *kikokushijo* had found that, in order to adjust to an American peer group, they had had to express themselves forcefully, declaring their individual opinions and appealing to their American friends to agree. On their return to Japan, however, they discovered that contradictory norms prevailed. Their Japanese cohorts expected them to avoid self-assertion. Instead of expressing their opinions directly, their Japanese peers allowed the flow of the conversation to take its course and listened to others' opinions first before stating one's own. Even after much discussion, things were left undecided. Such behaviors made the *kikokushijo* feel frustrated and uncomfortable. Some even perceived these behaviors to be illogical.

The *kikokushijo*, with first-hand experience of American lifestyles, differed from the others in their opinions about what they considered more "like an American" and about the advice they would give to a friend about to go overseas. Specifically, more *kikokushijo* talked about personality characteristics (e.g., being cheerful, dynamic, open-minded, enthusiastic, assertive, "bubbly," etc.), while more non-*kikokushijo* talked about uniqueness or individuality (e.g., being free, not trying to fit into a "mold," living the way one wishes, etc.) in describing being "American." The "American" characteristics described by the *kikokushijo* seemed to be the personality characteristics or behavior they were trying to assimilate while in the United States, as is seen in Asako's case study. Nevertheless, the key words that stand out when the *kikokushijo* tell their stories in this section are choice, freedom, individuality, and diversity. It is these values they have come to cherish and respect.

The students' responses for the kind of advice they would give to those who had just come back from living overseas differed in an interesting way.

The *kikokushijo* at the National School thought that it was best to follow what others were doing, not letting others label them as a *kikokushijo,* and to focus on the good side of things rather than the negative aspects. They were making an effort to become camouflaged when they reentered Japanese society, putting emphasis on knowing which script to follow under the circumstances. The other students (the non-*kikokushijo* at the National School, and both the *kikokushijo* and the non-*kikokushijo* at the International School) felt that it was best to act naturally and to maintain one's identity, including the part of the self that was acquired abroad. The non-*kikokushijo* at the National School did not even think it was an issue whether or not one was a *kikokushijo*. Although their overall consensus was that the *kikokushijo* should act naturally, they added advice to the *kikokushijo* not to "make waves," or not to be too expressive, which seemed a bit contradictory.

More non-*kikokushijo* said that there was nothing or not much of the Japanese culture that they felt was good to introduce to the United States. By contrast, more *kikokushijo* identified Japanese cultural patterns (e.g., seasonal appreciation, temples, social rules, etc.) when asked what aspect of Japanese culture they would introduce to the United States. The *kikokushijo* have, of course, had the opportunity to reflect on their original culture from a different perspective due to their overseas experience, and, thus, are more aware of the unique aspects of Japan's culture. On the whole, though, there were few differences in attitudes between the two groups.

The *kikokushijo*'s caution of not being labeled a returnee student is also an interesting fact that stands out. Although the non-*kikokushijo* very rarely displayed an attitude stigmatizing the *kikokushijo*, the *kikokushijo* advice to a newly returning student was to be careful not to be labeled a *kikokushijo.* Yet they themselves do not feel stigmatized as *kikokushijo*. Hence, it may be that the term "*kikokushijo*" still carries with it negative connotations, whereas being a *kikokushijo,* or one who has experienced an overseas lifestyle, does not necessarily evoke adverse reactions from others. This difference may be subtle but it is critical to the futures of these bicultural or in some cases multicultural *kikokushijo.*

STORIES OF TWO *KIKOKUSHIJO*

Asako

Asako, now a senior at the International School, lived in Maryland for four years attending the local public school and attending Japanese language school once a week. She had returned to Japan three years prior to the time of the interview. Asako is cheerful and frank and speaks fondly of her experience in the United States. Her mother's education extends through junior college and her father is a physician and his job took the family overseas. Although she has a group of friends in Japan with whom she commutes to school, she has a very deep relationship with another girl who is also a *kikokushijo* and they do many things together and talk about many things including reminiscing about their time in America.

Asako's friendships in the United States revolved around one group of American friends from school and another group who were at the Japanese language school. Asako was closer to her Japanese school friends although she was able to be more her true self in front of her American friends:

> When I was with my American friends, I didn't really think about my vanity or how I appeared and I played around with them screaming and shouting, and I feel as though I was telling them more about my true self, when I think about it now. I also think I was able to be more open and big-hearted. With my Japanese friends, well . . . you know, the type of Japanese people who gather at those places are those who have parents who are distinguished in society, so there were a lot of snobby kids.

For the first three years in the United States, however, Asako could not have a close relationship with her American friends, which was a source of frustration because although they included her in their group and she understood what they were saying, she was unable to respond or to express her problems because of her limited English proficiency. Consequently, she was seen and described by others as always nice and quiet, but she wished that she could be called "promising" or "enthusiastic," too. In the fourth year, Asako was finally able to express her true self as well as have a friendship based more on mutual understanding and sharing. Even then, however, she believes that she was mostly the "listener" especially when it came to "those love problems." With her Japanese friends, Asako discussed more "Japanese-type problems," which included speculating what life would be like after returning to Japan, or exchanging academic information such as which type of schools would accept *kikokushijo*, or wondering what it was like in Japan at that moment, among other more mundane teenage topics of conversations such as, "He's cute, isn't he?"

Asako's was the only family out of all the students interviewed who eat dinner together almost every night. This is probably due to her father's occupation as a practicing physician. She seems to have a slightly closer relationship to her mother at the moment, but has a conscious recollection of switching from being a "daddy's girl" to a "mommy's girl" at around age twelve. It is easier for her to talk to her mother about love relationships and she also exhibits a certain amount of *amae*, especially when she explains when she thinks her mother is a "good mother" which is "when something sad happens at school and when I return home . . . my mother doesn't work so I feel it's nice that she's there for me." She also respects her father, especially from a professional perspective. Therefore, Asako will discuss most of her concerns or have general conversations with her mother. She admits, however, that even when she wishes her father to hear something, and know that he is within hearing distance, she will always start by saying, "Mom. . . ."

Asako seems sensitive to the gender dynamics of a family as was apparent when she explained the switch from being a "daddy's girl" to a "mommy's girl" and describes the difference between American families and Japanese families in these terms also. Asako observed that:

> in Japan, the mother and the father or the mother and the son don't talk much, right? And I think there are a lot of girls who dislike their fathers, and also they don't really go shopping with their fathers and stuff. But in the United States, I feel that everyone is really close, and the father shows that the daughter is really precious. I think the Japanese fathers don't differ in the fact that they like their daughters, but they don't really hug or kiss them at all. The American fathers show their affection. Also, in America, I think the entire family respects the father more, or in other words, I think the father holds a higher position in the family. In Japan, the father's position is ignored and the father is more excluded.

In addition, Asako found one other gender difference, which was that the American boys help out around the house more and that they are assigned chores, whereas Japanese boys are not expected to do chores around the house but Japanese girls are expected to do more. She did notice, however, that American girls also helped with household chores more than Japanese girls.

Asako's school experience in Japan does not seem very satisfying. The aspect of school she enjoys most is the commuting, because she is able to see the boy that she likes, who goes to another school, on the train. Academically, she dislikes tests, because "the test score doesn't always reflect the effort you put in it, and when your score is bad, the teacher will assume you didn't put in too much effort." Socially, she was disillusioned, because when she entered the International school, she thought the large percentage of *kikokushijo* would make it a "fun and energetic school." Upon entering, however, she discovered that "everyone was pretty quiet and aggressive in a negative way. Everyone does fool around together but it's silly." In terms of extracurricular activities, she was initially a member of the tennis club, but because of the *sempai/kohai* relationship where she was obligated to pick up the tennis balls hit by the *sempai*, she quit the club. She quickly compares this with the situation in the United States by mentioning that, "in the U.S., even if you're not very good, they would let you practice and even play matches, so it was fun. That's how everyone got better. They didn't think that you get better by overcoming hardships or effort (referring to Japan) so it was really nice." By contrast, however, when asked directly about *sempai/kohai* relationships, she feels that it is nice to have this relationship, because the *sempai* teach and take care of the *kohai* and admits that it is nice to have a prescribed way of relating to the *sempai* so there is no question of roles. Thus, some conflict is apparent here.

In the United States, Asako enjoyed the teaching style, which was creative and "fun." She also enjoyed the art class, because it gave her an opportunity to show off her artistic talent without having to overcome the language barrier:

> Because I couldn't speak English well, but in this class, I was acknowledged and I was outstanding in this class. And when I would draw, the teacher would ask me if I would be interested in taking another special drawing class. When we drew posters for the PTA, they made me number one, and my teacher entered my drawing in a calendar contest and stuff so, in this class, I felt a real recognition. The friends in that class would take notice, and care about what I was going to draw next and ask me too.

This class seemed to give her the confidence to assert herself through her art, which helped her in her overseas schooling experience. Asako was obviously impressed with her experience in art class, as she describes that she would like to introduce this aspect of thinking about academics to Japan. She feels that Japanese people judge others solely on the basis of academics and "if you don't do well academically, people treat you like a fool," but contrasts this with the United States, where if an individual is talented in one area, he or she is encouraged to build on that talent. She also spoke, however, of understanding teachers who encouraged her by helping her with her homework or by showing some leniency on test scores.

In the future, Asako would like to work as a specialist in her company and would like to "become someone who has a lot of responsibility and to have a job that has to be done by me, not a job that's out there for anyone." She contemplates not working, however, but would like to be a "lively wife" and a concerned mother and wife. She would like to live in a house such as the one she lived in the United States, with a yard (as she also misses mowing the lawn). She would like her children to have an opportunity to live in the United States so that they may "be able to feel and experience the good things about United States as well as the good things about Japan." Thus, it seems that Asako does want to become a professional working woman as long as the family situation permits her and also believes her experience overseas was worthwhile as she would like her children to be able to appreciate both cultures.

It is clear, however, that Asako sees some positive aspects of both the Japanese and American cultures, particularly in terms of personality characteristics or relating to others. For example, she believes being American entails stating an opinion often, but also "someone who doesn't get stuck on detail or trivial things and is broad-minded, like sitting cross-legged when everyone else is sitting formally." Asako describes "being Japanese" as being introverted and someone who "always goes along with other people's opinions and always holding back or reserved (*enryo shiteiru*)." Therefore, Asako believes that it is disadvantageous to be timid when one goes overseas and that it is necessary to try many things "almost to the point of being too assertive." She advises others that might be going to the United States to ask the American people whatever they wish to ask because "they will give you advice . . . if you're timid, you'll miss out because they will take it as you are not really eager either and they'll sort of leave you alone. You have to show them that you're willing."

Similarly, Asako feels that there are both advantages and disadvantages of being a *kikokushijo*. Like many students, Asako feels it is advantageous to know both cultures, because "it broadens your horizons and then little things don't intimidate you." She also has heard that it might help when searching for employment. A long overseas stay may not be too desirable because "there are some people who cannot adapt to the Japanese traditional customs and rules (*shikitari*) and who cannot deal with them." She herself feels, however, that she wished she could have stayed overseas a little longer, because it may have given her more choices as far as planning for the future was concerned (especially if she could speak English better). She also feels that it is a disadvantage to be back in Japan and miss the United States because "it makes you feel sad."

Hiroshi

Hiroshi lived in New Jersey for five years, attending the local public school and Japanese language school once a week. He had returned to Japan two years before the time of the interview. He had gone overseas because of his father's employment, which is at a well-known Japanese electrical corporation. He is currently living in the dormitory at the International School and, thus, has friends from the dormitory (who are all *kikokushijo*) and a group of friends at school. Hiroshi's experience in the dormitory is interesting.

Hiroshi did not like the *sempai/kohai* relationship when he first entered the dormitory, because the *sempai* told the *kohai* what to do and certain greetings were expected. Therefore, because Hiroshi is now the head of the dormitory he decided, "No more of this. I hated it, so to do the same thing, I felt sorry for them and wanted to make it the atmosphere more fun." He admits that there was some opposition at first because the other students thought that because they were treated a certain way as *kohai,* they should do the same thing to the present underclassmen. Hiroshi was able, however, to convince them that, "if we don't stop now, there's no end to the chain."

Hiroshi's group of friends at school are a mixed group of about ten people both male and female. He is closest to two boys from this group with whom he "talks to about everything" and of whom one is a *kikokushijo.* In addition, Hiroshi has a group of club friends with whom he is friendly and "not too deep." He feels that friendships in the United States are "lighter, because in Japan, you feel an obligation to be together all the time, but over there, you are just with your friends when you feel like it."

When Hiroshi went to the United States, he could not understand English. On the first day of school, when he was told to introduce himself and he "didn't know what in the world was going on, but I thought no matter what, the first impression is very important, so I said in a loud voice, 'MY NAME IS, . . .' which I had learned in Japan." It made him very happy when everyone applauded for him when he finished. He "compensated for not being able to speak English by playing sports I was good at." Sports is a large factor in Hiroshi's life, as is apparent throughout the interview. In fact, his role model is Michael Jordan, whom Hiroshi observed and copied and from whom he learned how to play basketball, and an English teacher with whom Hiroshi has a close relationship is also the basketball coach. The importance of basketball in his life is also apparent when he remembers as a significant experience on his return to Japan a very emotional basketball game and the bonding that took place among his teammates. His "dream of dreams" is to be a professional basketball player, although realistically, he thinks he may be a "normal businessman" after studying law in college because "law is highly respected in society."

Hiroshi seems close to his family, although he has been living in the dormitory throughout high school. He returned to Japan before his family for the entrance examination for high school, and although he does not talk to them about "deep things," when asked what kind of parents he thought were "ideal," he pointed to his own because he knows that "they are thinking about me and they scold me when they are concerned. They don't really come out and say it, but I can tell that they are concerned about my academics and college, but ultimately, I decide and they acknowledge that decision and they trust me." He seems to be pointing to a balance between proper guidance and independence. He visits his family once a month:

> When I go home, my mother always fixes me a great meal and my father and siblings jokingly complain that only when I come home do they get to eat such a meal! When I go home, I play ball with my younger brother who is still in elementary school and plays baseball, and that makes him happy and so that makes me happy.

He admits that the bond between his parents and him became stronger in the United States because his mother could not speak English so they "helped each other out." In addition, Hiroshi observed that the parent-child relationship in the United States was closer than in Japan primarily because there is more communication ("the parents talk to their children and I thought it was nice. In Japan, the parents and children don't talk and it seems for the children that the parents are a nuisance"). Although the family lives with the grandmother, he does not feel that he would like to live with his parents in the future. He wishes to live in a house alone in the country, although since he is the oldest, his parents say, "let's live together." He wants "an American house . . . a big house with lots of rooms, a fireplace and an attic."

When asked directly, Hiroshi describes a wife who would be devoted to him and who appears not to be too concerned but in actuality is quite concerned. He would like to live in the United States and also to "take a look at Europe too." He feels that he had such a great experience overseas that he would like his kids to have an opportunity to experience an overseas lifestyle. He misses certain things about the United States, from American pizza to the friendly atmosphere "where everyone said, 'hello,' even if you didn't know them . . . which is unthinkable in Japan." He also thought for a very long time when asked about something he would like to share with the United States from the Japanese culture, but could not think of anything. When he was asked what he would introduce to Japan about the American culture, however, he replied immediately, "If you want to participate in something, there's always a chance for you. They don't force you, but you always have a chance. Like at school, you can take honors classes, or do sports . . . so if you really want to do it, you can."

Hiroshi's advice to someone going to the United States is to take advantage of the fact that one is overseas and experience all the things that is impossible to experience if one is in Japan. Most of all, he suggests that people going to the United States not cluster with just a group of Japanese people but to make friends from the United States. On a more personal level, he recommends that people see the Manhattan nightscape, because it is very pretty, and shop as much as possible, because many things are less expensive in the United States. By contrast, for those people coming back to Japan, Hiroshi would tell them not to become influenced by others and become similar to them, but to treasure the personality one acquired overseas, although he admits that in a regular Japanese school, it may be difficult to do this without encountering *ijime*. In his case, he feels that he was more introverted and passive before he went to the United Sates, but notices now that he is back in Japan that he has become more active and energetic.

Understandably, he feels that being "like an American" means not worrying about what others might think and living the way one wishes and also someone who is surrounded by many friends. When he imagines somebody as "like a Japanese," he says he pictures a serious, quiet person who studies diligently.

Hiroshi realizes that the same aspects of being a *kikokushijo* could be advantageous and disadvantageous at the same time. For example, he feels that it is good that many *kikokushijo* are expressive and active and interested in many things. In addition, he feels that it is good that *kikokushijo* do not always "go along with everybody else" because this is how new ideas are put forth, which is exciting. This same asset can become a loss, however, in his eyes, when one views this from a "Japanese society perspective":

[L]ike, the older person's opinion is always the right one, is a Japanese society perspective, but if someone doesn't think so and makes that clear by saying something, they may be seen as different or rude. Also, the Japanese society expects that everybody be the same way. That may be disadvantageous.

DISCUSSION

The *kikokushijo* understand the contrasts between cultural norms in the United States and Japan, and they differ from their non-*kikokushijo* counterparts in their attitudes to Japanese culture. *Kikokushijo* engage in code-switching between Japanese and American cultural norms, but it is not clear whether this is interpersonal strategy or fundamental psychological transformation. If transformation necessarily involves psychological disturbance with psychosomatic symptoms, academic failure, or inconsistencies in behavior, then there is little sign of its occurrence in the *kikokushijo* interviewed. Although the longest period of overseas stay was ten years, there was no demonstration of a problematic *cognitive* or emotional dissonance between what was expected by their various environments and their behaviors.

In some ways, the Japanese child is socialized at a very early age, to be able to code-switch, not only in terms of language, but also in terms of situation. The Japanese language has situation-appropriate codes embedded, so that the spoken language is different according to the status and degree of acquaintance of the person with which you are conversing (Clancy, 1986; Kelly, this volume; Nakane, 1988). There are the feminine and masculine endings of sentences, the humble speech, and honorific speech. In addition to adjusting one's speech according to the situation, one learns to change behavior also (Lebra, 1976). When these rules of speech or behavior are not followed, there builds an awkward feeling between the parties involved. Even when minor norms are violated, negative emotions occur. In addition, in a *shudan shugi* or collectivist culture, the fear of ostracism can act as a regulator of behavior (Triandis, 1994).

It is evident that many students have coping mechanisms when they are abroad or when they return to Japan. For example, expressing themselves through art, sports, or music when they initially sojourned in the United States is an example of a coping strategy *kikokushijo* used to overcome their language barrier, while abiding by the American cultural norm of "making a statement" as an individual. An instance of a coping strategy on returning to Japan was that of the young girl who wrote her diary in English to express emotions that could not clearly be spoken or even expressed in Japanese. These examples are interspersed throughout this research's findings.

Many *kikokushijo* had a difficult time initially adjusting to the overseas lifestyles of the United States. They especially struggled with the language barrier, and it was difficult for them to form stable peer relations. Some mention that the bond between themselves and their parents grew stronger in the United States because the students who would learn English quicker than their parents could assist the parents, especially the mothers, with their English difficulties. In the meantime, they discover quickly what they must do to get along in their American peer group and school culture. They first seem to find ways of compensating for their English ability by some other talents they may possess, such as art, music, or sports, expressing themselves through these media. These can be considered their coping mechanisms for adjusting to their life overseas. Despite the initial difficulties, they eventually came to reminisce about their experience in the United States privately or with other friends who have returned from overseas. In addition, many of them wish they could revisit the United States in the future and especially offer the same opportunity for their children.

Their stories, thus, portray difficulty and conflict but their ultimate goal is to succeed as Japanese citizens. In addition, contrary to what previous research suggests, they did not seem to suffer from isolation (from their peer or family culture), or for that matter, the stories of these students do not portray any serious maladjustment to their immediate environment. Why do these students, then, seem so well adjusted? Part of the reason may be that these students are reacclimating themselves into their native culture, because they are now focused on a critical stage of their academic career, where the college in which they enroll will determine, to a large extent, the lifestyle they will experience in the future. This is especially true for the students at the National School. These students behave in a manner acceptable to the Japanese society so that problems that keep them from concentrating on their academics may be avoided.

Not only are the *kikokushijo* making an effort to melt into their peer group, but the non-*kikokushijo* also seem to be accepting the different experiences that the *kikokushijo* have had, and, furthermore, are curious and willing to learn from their "first-hand overseas experience." This finding suggests that the younger Japanese population may be becoming more accepting of diversity and individuality, although accepting these concepts intellectually may not be the same as the population actually becoming diverse or individualistic. This new attitude can help *kikokushijo* become part of their peer culture without losing their self-esteem and intercultural dispositions.

The change in behavioral expectations of the *kikokushijo*'s immediate culture can be difficult at this vulnerable stage where many things seem to be critically dependent on their efforts. Who or what is acting as a buffer for these *kikokushijo* to cope during the time of such drastic changes in their lifestyle? It seems that both peers and family act together to help the students reacclimate themselves back into the Japanese cultural norm. Minoura (1992) has suggested that there is a "sensitive period" in which children are affected to different degrees by their cultural environments. She argues that if the children sojourn abroad before the age of nine, they have a fairly easy adjustment into their new cultural climate. She follows by stating that unless a child lives in the same culture through the age of fifteen (the upper limit to the "sensitive period"), behavior learned before the age of nine may not be sustained. She found that spending their "sensitive period" abroad led some students to internalize American cultural values regarding interpersonal relationships to such an extent that they had considerable difficulty upon their return to Japan. Additionally, Minoura found that although her subjects lived with their Japanese parents throughout their overseas stay, they tended to lose their Japanese-like behavior learned before the sensitive period. Thus, she implies that "peers, not parents, are more influential in cultural learning, at least in certain important domains" (Minoura, 1992, p. 331).

In my research sample, some students sojourned to the United States before this "sensitive period." Others spent their "sensitive period" abroad. None of them, however, exhibited signs of such deep internalization of American values. Although they were cognitively aware of the differences between the Japanese and American culture, especially the norms of interpersonal relationships, they were able to switch back and forth with facility between the expectations of their Japanese and American peers and society. Their transition into both cultures seems initially challenging, but is never considered problematic.

Lois Peak's research concerning the transition that Japanese children experience when first attending preschool is also helpful in shedding light on this finding. Peak (1991, this volume) describes the transition from home to preschool for Japanese children as one where the two environments have distinctly different atmospheres and behavioral expectations. Yet Japanese children, at this early age, learn to adjust their behaviors accordingly to each environment. In short, the home remains the domain where the children are allowed to express their *amae* as well as where the mothers are allowed to *amayakasu* (indulge the child) (Kobayashi, this volume), whereas the school becomes the ground for *shudan seikatsu* (literally meaning "group life" or "collective living"), learning to cooperate and restrain oneself (*enryo*), and to think of others (*omoiyari*) (Kelly, this volume).

Thus, starting at a very early age, Japanese children learn to behave differently and to expect different behaviors from the two environments to which they are consistently exposed. This could be a factor facilitating the adjustment of the *kikokushijo*'s transitions into an American cultural environment and subsequently back into Japanese culture. If children at such an early age are socialized to behave differently in different settings, the *kikokushijo*, due to their relatively older age, could have internalized the practice of switching behaviors to the appropriate setting, easing their transition back to their native culture. By Western psychological standards, this inconsistency in behavior may be seen as pathological or dysfunctional. In the Japanese context, however, being able to mold oneself into one's setting implies mental health and is indeed functional.

White (1993) has described the demands of teen culture as similar in the United States and Japan. Peer expectations and standards are so powerful that, contrary to the adult's fear that teenagers cannot wait to rebel, they actively seek to conform to the norms of their peer culture. Whereas in the United States this "peer pressure" may be threatening to the parents, the Japanese parents see friendships as an agent of socialization and support. Thus, even regarding the *sempai/kohai* relationships, the codes of behavior and negotiation are learned in school and not taught by the parents (see Kelly, this volume; White, 1993). White also points out that in the United States the adolescents are encouraged by their parents to become adults through independent behavior. In Japan, by contrast, there is little contradiction between the goals of maturation operating in the culture, family, and school environment, thus causing minor, if any, disruption in the Japanese teenager's life.

As for the students in this research, most of them experienced their first teenage encounters in the United States but returned to Japan during their actual adolescent years. Thus, it is apparent, such as in Asako's case, that these *kikokushijo* were exposed to more mature topics of conversation and activity while in the United States. This can account for the *kikokushijo*'s discovery on their return to Japan that the topics of conversation differed between their Japanese and American peer group. Most *kikokushijo* found the conversations with the Japanese peer group less philosophical. The topics that grasp teenagers' curiosity, however, such as those in magazines targeted for adolescents from both cultures, remained the same. The critical difference, therefore, may be the goals and expectations of the students' local setting. As aforementioned, however, many of the students exhibited *amae* when they spoke of their families, suggesting that exposure to and the influence of the American adolescent culture was not overwhelming enough to launch these *kikokushijos* into an independent and autonomous adolescent world. This ability to appreciate the essence of *amae* may be a critical factor in easing the transition of these students back into the Japanese society.

In contrast to Minoura's argument that peers could be seen as being more influential, Rogoff (1990) uses Piagetian and Vygotskian cognitive theories to point out that, in all cultures, cognitive development is facilitated by interdependence between caregivers and children as well as *interdependence* between children. Moreover, she argues that the construction of meaning cannot be based on the individual but must be placed in the social environment. In other words, children learn the goals and ideals of their local setting through guided participation with either peers or adults. Through these interpersonal activities and engagements, not only do children learn through speech but also through observations and collaboration. This also can be described as an apprenticeship model on which Vygotsky built his theory of the zone of proximal development. Rogoff states that *both* parents and peers act as agents of influence in the cognitive development of the child. She cites Piaget's argument that children reach equilibrium only when cooperating and having discussion with those of equal power, namely their peers, although he does not fail to mention that if the adults are able to interact as an equal with the child, the child is allowed to reach a new level of equilibrium.

It seems then, that at least in their earlier years, Japanese children are able to learn from their teachers who socialize them in an empathic manner, and from their parents who indulge them, as well as from their peers at school. When they are older, they are able to learn from their *sempai* with whom they would have an apprenticeship-like relationship. Thus, in helping to ease the transition of sojourning from culture to culture, the Japanese students are perhaps able to personally find support and guidance in all of their social environments.

If their non-*kikokushijo* counterparts see few problems in the *kikokushijo* population, where does the problem of *kikokushijo* lie? It is true that the *kikokushijo* students have difficulty in accepting and participating in certain aspects of the "traditionally Japanese" society (e.g., groupism, vertical hierarchy). Nevertheless, these students thrive academically and socially. Early socialization practices and subsequent enculturation processes may also account for the *kikokushijo* and their not-so-difficult transitions between two cultures. Furthermore, the non-*kikokushijo*'s knowledge and admiration of foreign cultures may be working in concert with the *kikokushijo*'s effort not to be stigmatized by the word, "*kikokushijo*," thus helping to diminish the psychologically traumatic cultural shocks that have been evidenced in previous generations of *kikokushijo*.

The experience of two cultures valuing differing virtues may initially seem detrimental to the promotion of smooth enculturation. *Kikokushijo* obviously have an extremely rich and powerful set of self-representations that they have acquired in Japan and abroad. Many of the *kikokushijo* in this sample seem to be using these self-representations by testing their boundaries as each occasion will permit (e.g., changing the structure of the vertical hierarchy). In addition, it does not seem too extreme to imply that by changing the cultural milieu of their immediate environment, the *kikokushijo* are also allowing the non-*kikokushijo* to acquire a new set of possible virtues that they will be able to store and, if desired, use to enhance their personal development.

In summary, the three most important findings of this research are as follows. First, the *kikokushijo* and the non-*kikokushijo* differed little in their attitudes, lifestyles, and concept of self, except in their attitudes toward the interpersonal norms of the vertical hierarchy and Japanese peer relationships. Second, the *kikokushijo* did not show as much difficulty in their transition back into their Japanese setting as expected from the existing literature. The findings point to the following hypotheses: (a) The stigma originally attached to the word *"kikokushijo"* itself has been reduced or may be even nonexistent in today's Japanese society; (b) The understanding and knowledge (including the eagerness to learn more) about various cultures has become commonplace among the general Japanese population. The present evidence supports the hypothesis that these two factors interact with each other to help *kikokushijo* have an easier transition on their return to Japan and to become more mainstream; and (c) The Japanese students acquire a tendency in early childhood to behave according to the expectations of each local setting and group of people. On entering preschool, Japanese children are taught to have *"omoiyari"* (trying to find out what other people want or are feeling, or more simply, empathy) and become accustomed to *shudan seikatsu* (group life) at school while they remain able to *amaeru* at home. When this tendency is used in the conditions of immigration, it becomes a metacultural skill facilitating adjustment to the new (and in the case of *kikokushijo*, back to old) conditions.

One can say that the *kikokushijo* in this study literally went "outside" to "grow up." These children already learned how to behave properly in the various situations they would encounter in Japan (e.g., their own transition from home to kindergarten). When they sojourned abroad, they acquired another skill to observe closely the appropriate behaviors of that culture or school. Then, they used these skills to participate actively in this new culture. On their return to Japan, they are once again code-switching and trying to find the situation-appropriate behaviors in this new environment. It seems that the *kikokushijo* in this study did not suffer greatly when they returned because of their code-switching skills (including the observation process), which they had acquired earlier in Japan and later in the United States.

REFERENCES

Clancy, P. (1986). The acquisition of communicative style in Japanese. In B. Schieffelin & E. Ochs (Eds.), *Language socialization across cultures.* New York: Cambridge University Press.

Enloe, W., & Lewin, P. (1987). Issues of integration abroad and readjustment to Japan of Japanese returnees. *International Journal of Intercultural Relations, 11,* 223–48.

Goodman, R. (1990). *Japan's "international youth": The emergence of a new class of schoolchildren.* Oxford: Clarendon Press.

Kaigai Shijo Kyoiku Shinko Zaidan (1991). *Kaigai shijo kyoiku manual* [Manual for overseas education]. Tokyo: Kaigai Shijo Kyoiku Shinko Zaidan.

Kobayashi, T. (1986). The internationalization of Japanese education. *Comparative Education, 22,* 65–71.

Kondo, H. (1989). *Ibunka tekio koza: Global mind no sodate kata* [A lesson on adapting to a strange culture: Cultivating a global attitude].Tokyo: TBS Britannica.

Lebra, T. S. (1976). *Japanese patterns of behavior.* Honolulu: The University of Hawaii Press.

Lebra, T. S., & Lebra, W. P. (Eds.). (1974). *Japanese culture and behavior: Selected readings.* Honolulu: University of Hawaii Press.

Ministry of Education, Science and Culture, Government of Japan. (1990). *Outline of education in Japan 1991.* Tokyo: Ministry of Education, Science and Culture.

Ministry of Education. (1993). *Kikokushijo kyouiku no jyuusitsu housaku ni tsuite: Kaigai shijo kyouiku ni kansuru chousa kenkyuu kai housoku* [A plan for the education of kikokushijo: A report on the survey of Kagaishijo Education]. Manuscript.

Minoura, Y. (1992). A sensitive period for the incorporation of a cultural meaning system: A study of Japanese children growing up in the United States. *Ethos, 20,* 304–39.

Miyachi, S. (1990). *Kikokushijo: Gyaku culture shock no hamon* [Returnee children: Reverse culture shock]. Tokyo: Chuo Koronsha.

Monbusho Kyoiku Josei Kyoiku (Kaigai Shijo Kyoiku Ka). (1991). *Kaigai shijo kyoiku no genjo* [The present state of overseas student education]. Tokyo: Monbusho.

Nakane, C. (1988). Hierarchy in Japanese society. In D. I. Okimoto & T. P. Rohlen (Eds.), *Inside the Japanese system: Readings on contemporary society and political economy* (pp. 8–14). Stanford: Stanford University Press.

Peak, L. (1991). *Learning to go to school in Japan: The transition from home to preschool life.* Berkeley: University of California Press.

Rogoff, B. (1990). *Apprenticeship in thinking.* Oxford: Oxford University Press.

Sato, G. (1998). Ibunkakan ni sodatsu kodomo no kyouiku: Kaigai/kikokushijo kyouiku no kadai [Education for children who are raised cross culturally: The topic of returnee and overseas children]. In K. Iwanami (Ed.), *Kokusaika jidai no kyoiku* [Education in the international age]. Tokyo: Iwanami Shoten.

Triandis, H. (1994). Major cultural syndromes and emotion. In S. Kitayama & H. R. Markus (Eds.), *Emotion and culture: Empirical studies of mutual influence* (pp. 285–306). Washington, D.C.: American Psychological Association.

Ugaya, H. (1991). *Kikokushijo wa mo futsu no kodomotachi* [Returnee children are now the same as nonreturnee children]. *AERA, 11* (March 12), 58–60.

White, M. (1988). *The Japanese overseas: Can they go home again?* New York: The Free Press.

White, M. (1993) *The material child.* New York: The Free Press.

PART V

REFLECTIONS

NINE

Children and Families

Reflections on the "Crisis" in Japanese Childrearing Today

Merry I. White

Ayako, a happy five-year-old, plays with her dolls in a sunny corner of the kitchen-dining area of her family's small apartment. Her mother, in a clean frilled apron, is busy packing a lunch for her in a "Hello Kitty" lunch box, including a set of bright pink chopsticks in a small chopstick case, a freshly ironed napkin, and a small damp *oshibori,* or washcloth, in a special plastic bag. The lunch contains "something from the mountains, something from the sea," a nutritional balance dictated by tradition, school protocol, and the "secret mothers' school" of information passed from mother to mother, consonant with the general high standards for mothering in Japan today (Allison, 1991).

Those high standards for mothering are grounded in both new and old cultural perceptions of the child and changing concepts of family in Japan. It was not always "mother" who was the point person for children's development, the person marked as responsible for the environment and outcomes of childrearing, and in many families mothers cannot fulfill this totalistic responsibility. And, yet, as Yoshie Nishioka Rice describes her (see Rice, this volume), the *kosodatemama* (childrearing mother) is such a strong role designation that it transcends realities of class, opportunity, and personal choice. However entrenched it may seem, the model of the "childrearing mother" cannot always be realized – especially in families where motherhood is not the woman's only defining role. Nor can her family inevitably spare her for the dedication of the "education mother," another epithet describing a woman totally engaged in her child's future success. In

I want to thank Robert LeVine for his thoughtful comments and Hidetada Shimizu for his patience. It has always been a pleasure to work with them.

prewar Japan, most women worked either in family-run businesses or in wage-earning jobs in industry. The "educational imperative" had not yet begun to influence all family decisions. Postwar urban middle-class families have become dependent on educational success in the reproduction of social status in their children (Vogel, 1963). That mothers are seen to be important in this process is a result of the separation of spheres of authority and responsibility in the nuclear urban middle-class family, a formulation that was informally "codified" in the first postwar generation. Fathers were to be dedicated to Japan's reconstruction, a task requiring their devotion to work and workplace; women's virtue resided in maintaining the home as support for the working male. Increasingly more important than the tasks of good-wifery were the demands of good mothering.[1] The notion that all is up to mother is a relatively recent, and class-specific, one that has so thoroughly imbued postwar notions of childrearing that it has guided research and popular common sense, both within Japan and among foreign observers – long outliving, and greatly exaggerating, its relevance to most families.

The centrality of mothers in Japanese childrearing is not, of course, new, only newly emphasized in public rhetoric. That mothers are so exclusively responsible for their children is the result of a combination of factors – social, economic, and political – but the inherent "cultural sense" in the mother-child bond antedates this confluence. Most prewar rural and urban families were extended family households for at least some period of their life course. This meant that most children experienced multiple caregivers and, particularly, grandparental care. Most agrarian families needed the labor of all adults and youths and often small children were cared for by grandparents and older siblings. Members of shopkeeping or tradesmen families, too, were expected to work in the family trade to the extent of their ability, and children rarely received education beyond the minimum compulsory level. There could be no "education mama" if schooling were not valued.

The underlying "cultural sense" making "mama" available to the middle-class postwar construction of family, however, emphasizes nurturant intimacy as a key building block in a child's successful psychological development, and, as in Takeo Doi's formulation, stresses the significance of healthy dependency in key relationships throughout life. This understanding, including the training of children in *omoiyari* (sensitivity to oth-

---

[1] "*Ryosai kembo,*" the phrase epitomizing the "good wife, wise mother," was part of the Meiji Era (1868–1912) imaging of the ideal role of women. See Uno (1993).

ers), and the value placed on a *sunao* or open-hearted, sincere availability to appropriate behavior, appear to be inherent in popular conceptions and practices of childrearing before and beyond the postwar middle class.[2]

The first postwar generation's child- and education-focused middle-class family has retained its power for officials and politicians, who saw this formulation as key to postwar economic reconstruction. These leaders use this evocation to frame family responsibilities in social policies and use this model of the good family, and the good mother, to secure functions of child-rearing and social services in the home where, they would say, they are properly placed. Because the typical (urban) family is now a nuclear family, and because a father's time with the children is often very limited (leading to the coining of a phrase and problem: the "absent father syndrome"), all nurturant care and responsibility has devolved onto mothers. Mothering has taken on such significance in Japan that policymakers can invoke, and indict, mothers in debates over the future of Japan. The sense of crisis now surrounding family has invested women with the power to maintain or destroy Japan's future through what are perceived as their "choices" in reproduction and childrearing.

The happy scene described at the beginning of this chapter is, in fact, an ideological tool in the debate, as managed in media and social commentary in Japan. It is a scene from a recent episode in a "home drama," a television serial playing nationally in Japan every morning.[3] In this series, the lifestyle of a nuclear family including a middle-class, white-collar father and a stay-at-home young mother with her five-year-old daughter is defended, pitted

---

[2] There has been significant discussion of the centrality of such concepts in the literature on Japanese education and childrearing. Postwar observers of Japan have emphasized these qualities and goals of Japanese childrearing as attributes contributing to Japan's postwar economic and social successes or as aspects of an overgeneralized picture of an unchanging uniform culture constructed by "official Japan" for its own ends or "bought" by Western observers in the pockets of the *nihonjinron* (nationalist discourse of Japan's "unique culture") leadership. It is safe to say that the concepts discussed here transcend and antedate explanations for the postwar "miracle," the debates over the uniqueness of Japanese culture, and the trade-war infusions of heat over "apologists" and "revisionists" in American observations of Japan. It is also possible that, in the desire to correct for cultural "mistranslations," some have gone too far either in the direction of the special considerations of Japan's culture and history or toward a convergence model in which we are becoming, or are revealed as being, very like each other. Japanese patterns, or cultural ideals, do underlie family strategies and public policy; what is evident, however, is that socioeconomic and historical change have made it harder for families to engage fully in the particular renderings of those cultural ideals embodied in social policies in the late twentieth century.

[3] "Poka Poka," on TBS Channel 6, first aired in 1999. It occupies a midmorning slot on weekdays, appealing to a (presumably) at-home housewife audience.

against images of nonapproved lives. The most striking contrast in the story is drawn between the mother and a career woman, single and in her thirties (thus in line for "spinsterhood"), whose cutthroat style at the office, hardbitten language, and brusque manners have marked her as hopelessly unfeminine, as well as arrogant and unnurturant as a boss. In another episode, the husband comes home, bringing a workmate to whom he displays his devoted wife; she tells this unmarried male coworker, who has expressed his cynicism about marriage, that there is no one happier than she is. This scene contrasts sharply with the images of women who flee responsibilities as "parasite singles," of marriages that are effectively "in-house divorces," and with the headlines, policy white papers, and social commentary demonizing women who are on a so-called birth strike or who "abandon" elderly relatives.

The future of Japan is said to be at stake. Policies and programs for children have always used a national agenda as rationale: "*kodomotachi no tame ni . . .*" (For the sake of the children . . .) has been a watchword, and the statement that children are Japan's most important natural resource can create support for educational and family-based programs. But there are now fewer children to support, it appears. Headlines and television news chronicle the birthrate decline in Japan. Over the decade from 1990, when the birthrate had fallen to 1.57 per woman of reproductive age, to 2000, when it declined further to 1.3, stories of the future have been bleak. If there is no increase in childbearing, it is said in some projections that there will be only one million Japanese left in 2500, and that, effectively, there will be no Japan. To some, this scaremongering narrative seems to echo wartime injunctions such as *umeyo fuyaseyo* (give birth and multiply), which enjoined women to produce more soldiers in service to the war effort. Japan's survival is said to depend on the reproduction of a Japanese population in self-sufficient isolation. Only a few commentators have noted that Japan might be seen instead as pioneering in effective birth control, or as needing to regularize foreign worker employment instead, but those voices are lost in the concern over economic and social problems soon to surface, it is said, unless "selfish" women have more babies.

The chief of those concerns is not the lack of children (although, as we shall see, their psychosocial development is seen to be at risk); it is the concomitant rise in the rate of elderly in the population. That those over sixty-five will be one-quarter, or one-third (depending on what prediction you use) of the population by 2020 is alarming, as the tax base providing for social services and medical care shrinks concomitantly. What are wanted now are not soldiers for war but workers contributing to social security resources. The life expectancy of men and women in Japan keeps increasing: Men now live on average to seventy-nine and women to eighty-three. Those younger elderly between the ages of sixty-five and seventy-five, retired but healthy and active, outnumber the bedridden and disabled elderly at present but greater numbers of dependent elderly with chronic illness and senility affecting the older group are anticipated and family care cannot at present manage the burden. With a smaller contributing workforce and shrinking social service budgets comes a call for family-based support of those older people. More children also implies a mother at home ready to care for the elderly as well as to prepare the younger generation for productive lives.

It is a real problem, not only the construction of conservatives. The Commission on the Shrinking Birthrate has developed a variety of proposals to increase births. But, unlike the directives of policymakers and conservative politicians, the Commission's focus is not on chastising selfish women but on enabling women to fulfill the many roles they perform and to raise happy, successful children while doing so. Some of the proposals include enhancement of existing policies, such as the Angel Plan, established in the early 1990s but not yet fully enacted by the turn of the twenty-first century. This would increase the amount of available daycare for working mothers (the concept of daycare still evokes "working mothers," rather than families), and, thus, encourage these women to bear more "angels." Encouraging women and men not to delay marriage (the average age at marriage is now twenty-seven for women, thirty-one for men, and rising), providing supports to families and tax and bonus incentives are also incorporated in the long list of proposals (S. Iwao, discussion at Committee on the Shrinking Birthrate, Tokyo, February 17, 2000).

Why are children and women at the core of what are essentially national security debates? It appears true that a shrinking birthrate will drastically affect social services and that increased longevity and good healthcare means a larger population of dependent elderly. But the language and content of discussions of the future of Japan seems to invoke a model of family in which self-sufficiency of the household in service to national priorities dominates. The economics of the problem might indeed be solved by a larger workforce contributing more taxes to public social services and institutional care of the elderly. A more realistic and positive approach to foreign laborers also might be indicated, considering that large numbers are already in the Japanese workforce, and some pay taxes as well. This is not the scene depicted, however: The scenario favored at present involves family members caring for their own elderly relatives and not demanding services beyond the home. Most Japanese families operate in makeshift ways, less in tune with the programs and ideologies of family-making engaged by the conservative establishment.

Whether it will be public or private stratagems that will manage family life in the future, family as the primary locus of childrearing will remain in spite of the perception that women suffer from a failure of faith and duty. Young mothers seem insecure and unconfident in childrearing and commentators decry the loss of grandmotherly influence in an extended family, and the overreliance on "experts" and childrearing manuals and magazines. Schools have not taken over the socializing function of families, although there are calls to provide in classrooms the lessons in cooperation and harmony, the sibling "peer culture" one-child families cannot provide for their "only children," and the functions working mothers cannot serve. *Hitorikko mondai*, or "the single child problem," is part of the fallout of the shrinking birthrate, creating self-absorbed and unhealthy children. Those "only children" are said to be the flip side of the cultural coin whose face depicts the healthy merging of mother and child in an interdependent partnership engaging the child in open-hearted, highly motivated learning. The same culturally approved engagement may lead to less healthy selfishness and lack of Japanese social skills. Lessons in personal virtue and social morality are now seen to be necessary in schooling, overt recognition that the days when families provided these are over.

The constraints on families keeping them from having more children, virtuous and cooperative or not, are most obviously economic. Staying middle class increasingly means having two incomes; women's work is necessary in most families, not only a source of identity or independence. Staying middle class is not only about housing and possessions – it is raising a child to maintain that status, an expensive enterprise. Thomas Rohlen notes that a greater and increasing percentage of the entering classes in the most prestigious universities come from higher-income families, and more of those have taken time out for extra tutoring and examination preparation, all of which cost families significant sums of money (Rohlen, 1977). Earlier meritocratic premises are wearing thin, as most are well aware that raising a successful child is expensive. More children are enrolled in expensive *juku* and *yobiko* (extra classes and cram schools, respectively) more have home tutors and subscribe to correspondence courses, and weekend test practice sessions are heavily attended: Some *juku* themselves have entrance exams (White, 1985).

Not all parents can maintain this kind of support for their children. Some, hoping to protect their children from the pressure, opt for private schools on an "escalator" system, in which entrance into a kindergarten offers a relatively easy track up through affiliated elementary, secondary schools, and an attached college – but this, of course, is expensive. Some encourage their children to study overseas, forgoing the social capital assured by a Japanese college education. Those who don't have the resources these alternatives imply must either rely on an at-home mother (herself less likely to be available in a family whose financial resources are tight, as she would usually be working outside the home) to coach the child(ren) or must consider different (less securely middle-class) futures for the child unsupported by mother's coaching or professional services.

Recently, there has been evidence that families from lower-middle-class or working-class families (or from the "old" middle-class urban sector, traditional shopkeepers, and craftspeople) have trouble modeling themselves after the late-twentieth-century middle-class family. Working mothers in these groups are said to believe more in innate attributes of children, more in given ceilings of achievement, and less in their own efficacy in creating successful children in academic terms than do women who have the luxury of staying home with their children to act as "home coaches" – who believe what is thought to be the mainstream view: That all children are born without limits on their abilities – in fact, without abilities or attributes of any kind. This conventional view places all the responsibility for children's development on mothers providing the environment and motivation for children's success. How frustrating this perspective would be for a mother who must work to support her family, whether she works alongside her husband in a small family-run business, or in a factory or other outside employment, whether or not there is a father or other relative at home. It is clear that all parents want their children to succeed, and most hope for a mainstream career or status for their children, whether the family of origin has that status or not and more research is needed on social class distinctions in beliefs and outcomes (Stevenson, 1998). These as yet unproven conjectures about class differences in beliefs about childrearing do not imply that cultural ideals of interpersonal relationships strongly diverge by class. Indeed, Japanese relational models are strikingly similar across society, at least as far as childrearing is concerned. Where parental goals for children may diverge, however, is where the demands of schooling and certain types of occupational institutions are invoked.

Sources of variation and diversity in the patterns of family culture and reality lie in the relationships between families and social institutions. Values of these kinds have never been homogeneous and unitary in Japan, in spite of observations to the contrary. Different views of success do exist in spite of the monopoly said to be held by the middle class. One family, whose restaurant and catering business had been the occupation of its members for over four generations, openly encouraged its children to take over the shop but, realizing this would not happen naturally, the family supported the eldest son's culinary studies in France. They then gave him the chance to revise the purely Japanese cuisine of the traditional enterprise and to create either a French restaurant or a "fusion" style of cooking. They are prepared for him to bolt altogether, to leave the food business, and go out on his own. A niece might provide continuity if he doesn't, or the family can just sell out. In any case, no child in this extended family, even the daughter with an élite university education, has entered the "new middle-class" bureaucratic and corporate world. This family, located in the "old middle class" of urban shopkeepers and tradespeople, does not see itself as marginal to the "new middle class," not unachieving: They demonstrate one of many diverse strategies and family cultures that exist in Japan's supposedly homogeneous society. In any case, their children were raised by mothers whose singular devotion to them is recognized as a core "family value" and the centrality of children in their households reflects the same set of virtues and psychocultural models for the good family reflected in middle-class and conservative political ideologies: All that is different, in fact, is that they will not employ these in service to national educational agenda.

Middle-class parents increasingly wonder why the struggle to stay middle class must put so much pressure on their children, and many are disengaging from the norms that drive educational credentialing. The sheer cost of raising a successful child, in the terms of the "examination-driven" system, is what is driving more families to shift the mother's role from housewife and home-coach to working woman. And this cost – and the time work takes from family concerns – also reduces the possibility that couples will choose to have several children. In spite of the accusatory rhetoric of politicians, it is not the selfishness of women that drives them out of the home and into the workplace – it is quite the opposite: the increasing cost of keeping their families middle class. Women's salaries are often dedicated to educational extras for their children, an indirect version of the devotion of the "*kyoiku mama.*"

The "good child" everyone wants has not changed: A child open and resilient, self-reliant and motivated to work hard, compliant without being passive, healthfully dependent but bright, alert, and proactive is what all parents want (White & LeVine, 1986). What families expect, like the institutions with which families interact, is that every child, those sad "only" children as well as those blessed with siblings, will have these qualities and that these qualities will serve him or her well in the effort it takes to acquire the credentials success demands. One interesting finding among the smaller families is that the shrinking family can be satisfactory with a girl as much as with a boy, or even more so. Of those saying that they will keep to one child, 70% of men and women say that they would prefer a girl. The older preference for boys has given way to the recognition that a girl can complete a household, and supporting her educational progress can absorb a mother as much as raising a successful son.

Japanese families have often in the past been contrasted to those of the West, such as those comparisons drawn by Caudill, Doi, and others (see LeVine, Preface, this volume). These evocations and contrasts have been useful in decentering Western understandings by introducing cultural variations in our consideration of the role of culture in childrearing. The critical discussions in Japan today now demonstrate that within Japan itself there are debates and divisions, most of which are not new, surrounding what Westerners had come to consider as a monolithic, homogeneous view of childrearing. Official efforts to buttress the "middle-class family" model in Japan have shown that it is, at least to them, at risk. When we see what lengths are gone to in defining a contemporary and novel "crisis" in Japan, we also see that the conditions decried represent older verities of diversity and change, unrecognized officially in Japan in pursuit of a normative model of family, and rarely treated in the Western literature. Scholars in the social and behavioral sciences have undertaken to confront Western ethnocentrism as they observe Japan. In this, they must both recognize distinctive and enduring features of Japanese cultural models and practices and see them as fully viable in a large-scale modern society, as well as recognizing within that society diversity and dynamism. We recognize that Japan may be modern and not Western; now we might look for sources of change and plurality there as well.

REFERENCES

Rolhen, T. (1977). Is Japanese education becoming less egalitarian? *Journal of Japanese Studies, 3*, 37–70.

Stevenson, H. (1998, October). Presentation at E. O. Reischaer Institute of Japanese Studies, Harvard University, Cambridge, MA.

Uno, H. (1993). The death of "good wife, wise mother." In A. Gordon (Ed.), *Postwar Japan as history* (pp. 298–322). Berkeley: University of California Press.

Vogel, E. F. (1963). *Japan's new middle class.* Berkeley: University of California Press.

White, M. I., & LeVine, R. A. (1986). What is an *ii ko?* In H. Stevenson, H. Azuma, & K. Hakuta (Eds.), *Childhood development and education in Japan* (pp. 55–62). New York: W. H. Freeman.

White, M. I. (1985). *The Japanese educational challenge: A commitment to children.* New York: Free Press.

Index

achievement: and McClelland's theory of motivation, 206–7; and moral judgments of American university students, 47–8; and personal experiences of Japanese adolescents, 210, 214–15, 217–18

adjustment: of Japanese adolescents as returnees, 231–2, 246–7; of Japanese preschool children to group behavior in preschools, 149–67

adolescents: individualism and sociocentrism in personal experiences of Japanese, 205–25; and *omoiyari,* 4–7, 11–14, 20; and returnees to Japan, 228–52

aggression, and moral judgments, 43

Ainsworth, M. D. S., xiii–xiv

altruism, and concept of *omoiyari,* 9

amae: and adaptation of Japanese preschool children to group behavior, 160, 248; and characteristics of Japanese culture, 54; and concept of *omoiyari,* 9; and Japanese adolescents as returnees, 250; and Japanese ethnopsychology, xv; and Japanese family, 147–8, 149, 169; and maternal role in Japan, 86–7, 88, 93, 97, 106, 107n8, 108; and mother-preschool child relationships in Japan, 112, 121, 123, 133–4, 137; and peer interactions in Japanese kindergarten, 198

amayakasu, and mother-child relationships in Japan, 133–4

ambivalence, and *omoiyari* as Japanese cultural norm, 11–14

anthropology: and psychological universalism, xi; and role of mother in Japan, 86; and studies of socialization and cultural behavior, 143

anxiety, and attitudes toward returnees in Japan, 228. *See also* separation anxiety

apology: Japanese and American concepts of compared, 18; and Japanese ethnopsychology, xvi, xviii

assurance, trust and concept of, 33–4

authority: and approach of Japanese preschool teachers to discipline, 166–7; and comparison of American and Japanese attitudes, 168

autonomy, and Kohlberg's theory of moral development, 58n2, 79

Azuma, H., xiii, xiv, 31, 32, 36, 87, 181, 187, 206, 220

Baldwin, J., 58n2

Baumrind, D., 138

Beardsley, R., 172

267